THE GOOD, THE BAD, AND THE UGLY
DETROIT RED WINGS

THE GOOD, THE BAD, AND THE UGLY
DETROIT RED WINGS

HEART-POUNDING, JAW-DROPPING, AND GUT-WRENCHING
MOMENTS FROM DETROIT RED WINGS HISTORY

Ted Kulfan

TRIUMPH
BOOKS

Library of Congress Cataloging-in-Publication Data

Kulfan, Ted, 1966–
The good, the bad, and the ugly Detroit Red Wings: heart-pounding, jaw-dropping, and gut-wrenching moments from Detroit Red Wings history / Ted Kulfan.
    p. cm.
ISBN 978-1-60078-240-4
    1. Detroit Red Wings (Hockey team)—History. 2. Hockey—Michigan—Detroit—History. I. Title.
GV848.D47K85 2009
796.962'6409774'34—dc22   2009010257

This book is available in quantity at special discounts for your group or organization. For further information, contact:

Triumph Books
814 North Franklin Street
Chicago, Illinois 60610
(800) 888–4741 | Fax (312)337–1807
www.triumphbooks.com

Printed in U.S.A.
ISBN: 978-1-60078-240-4
Design by Patricia Frey
Editorial production by Prologue Publishing Services, LLC
All photos courtesy of AP Images unless otherwise noted

This book is dedicated to the legions of Red Wings fans everywhere, who've made reporting about this team such an exciting and memorable experience.

CONTENTS

FOREWORD

There are a lot of great hockey towns out there, cities that really appreciate and love the sport, but Detroit is unique. Regarding the city of Detroit and the Detroit Red Wings organization—and Detroit being called "Hockeytown"—that's an earned label.

The city of Detroit has gone through, and is going through, drastic times. Economically, times are tough. They will get better, but right now, it's difficult. For now, the Red Wings enable the hockey fans in the Detroit area to forget about their problems for a while. The organization has been consistently successful for so long.

When you look at the records, the Stanley Cups, it's amazing what this organization has accomplished over the years. Just recently the Red Wings passed the 100-point mark for a ninth consecutive season, a new NHL record. That's a credit to the ownership of Mike and Marian Ilitch, the front office, with people like senior vice president Jimmy Devellano, general manager Ken Holland, and assistant GM Jim Nill, and the coaching staffs that have been here. And the ability to find talent in Europe, get players such as Pavel Datsyuk and Henrik Zetterberg in the draft when other teams passed them up, has kept this organization among the elite in the league.

I had the good fortune of winning two Stanley Cups with the Red Wings (in 1997 and 1998). I was traded to the Red Wings

Larry Murphy was inducted into the Hockey Hall of Fame in 2004. *Photo courtesy of Getty Images*

from Toronto at the trade deadline in 1997. At the time, everyone around the league knew the Red Wings had the talent and were a team capable of winning. Although leaving Toronto was difficult, I was excited about the opportunity of playing with the Wings.

When we finally did win the Stanley Cup that spring, it was great to see a player of Steve Yzerman's stature finally be able to lift the Stanley Cup. But I have to tell you, I couldn't wait to get my chance to lift the Cup, also. I had won the Stanley Cup twice in Pittsburgh, and that's a feeling that never gets old. And to win it in an Original Six city, with all the tradition of the Wings organization, the excitement in the arena that night, it was a moment I'll never forget.

Unfortunately, that emotion was short-lived. I heard about the automobile accident involving teammates Vladimir Konstantinov and Slava Fetisov and team masseur Sergei Mnatsakanov while I was heading back to Toronto, just days after we had won the Stanley Cup. I couldn't believe it. I immediately turned around and headed back to Detroit. It was a shock. You never expect something like that, and so close, just days after we had won the Cup.

Vlade, of course, had his playing career ended. It's difficult to say how much of a motivation he was for our team that season, you can't measure those things, but I'm sure it had an effect. We were a determined team that season.

Since then, the Wings have won more Stanley Cups and, like I said, the city has earned the label of "Hockeytown." There may not be a better one around.

Here now, are some of the more memorable moments and players in Red Wings history.

—Larry Murphy

ACKNOWLEDGMENTS

I'm glad I saved all the notes. In the makeshift office in our house, in a narrow spot between a filing cabinet and a bookcase, I've been accumulating all my filled notebooks while covering the Red Wings for the *Detroit News*.

Every so often I thought about throwing them out. Some of them are stained with coffee or soda pop, a few pages are ripped. In some of the pages, I can't even understand what I've written.

Handwriting has never been a strong suit of mine.

But then I would hear the voice of my wife, Angela, somewhere deep in my mind, saying what a good book could be developed from all those notes. She was right, there was a book. And hopefully you'll find it a good one.

I owe a lot of thanks to Michael Emmerich at Triumph for giving me this opportunity. I'll forever be grateful. And to Adam Motin, thank you for guiding me through this project.

I've been fortunate for over a decade to report on one of the most successful organizations in professional sports: the Detroit Red Wings.

Winning isn't easy. But the people who make up the Red Wings put in the time, on and off the ice, from those in the owner's box to the coaches and players on the bench, to give themselves an opportunity to win.

Hockey people are said to be the most approachable and down-to-earth of any of the professional athletes. After so much time on the beat, I can agree with that statement.

I'm not going to list everyone who has helped me do my job over the years at the *News* and for this book because the list would be too long and I would probably forget someone.

But, as a whole, I can't say enough about the people in the Wings organization. They've been first-class all the way.

A huge amount of resource materials were used to complete this book, but I'd like to single out these specifically: Jimmy Devellano and Roger Lajoie's *The Road to Hockeytown*, Gordie Howe's *My Hockey Memories*, Nicholas J. Cotsonika's *Red Wings Essential*, and *Heroes of Hockeytown* by Paul Harri. All are wonderful, informative, and entertaining books that helped with details and facts.

My colleagues at the *Detroit News*, John Niyo, Bob Wojonowski, and Dave Dye, all of whom I've spent time with on the hockey beat, you all are friends and professionals. As are Ruben Luna, Phil Laciura, Brian Handley, Jim Russ, and Craig Yuhas. It's been an honor to work with all of you.

To fellow beat writers George Sipple, Helene St. James, Ansar Khan, and Bruce McLeod, along with Cotsonika, Jason LaConfora, and Chuck Carlton, I've enjoyed all the time in the airports, restaurants, and waiting around in the locker rooms. You all made the time go that much quicker.

And, of course, I'd like to thank my family. Angela, my wife, who has been an inspiration from the second I met her. Thanks for telling me to save the notes. I thank my son, T.J., for just being himself. It's been a joy watching you grow up.

My mother, Helena, for inspiring me to read. As a youngster, watching her read a newspaper every day made me want to write for one. I've loved every single day.

And, finally, you the reader. Without you, none of this would work. You provide the outlet for someone like me. Thank you.

It's time to cobble those notes together.

THE GOOD, THE BAD, AND THE UGLY
DETROIT RED WINGS

THE GOOD

DETROIT IS HOCKEYTOWN

If there was any doubt about Hockeytown's existence, on this warm summer day in June, those questions were answered emphatically and clearly.

The city of Detroit had its problems, probably more than other big cities. Unemployment was rampant because of the continuing collapse of the auto industry. The mayor was on his way to being booted out of office. The future looked grim.

But Detroit still had its hockey, specifically the Red Wings.

And as nearly a million metropolitan Detroit residents came downtown to celebrate winning the 2008 Stanley Cup championship, they also could have been celebrating Detroit reaffirming itself as the true Hockeytown simultaneously.

"There were times I had to wipe away some tears," said Chris Osgood, after arriving at Hart Plaza, the site of the rally. Osgood, the rest of the team, members of the coaching staff and front office, and some former Wings stars had just been driven in parade-like fashion down Woodward Avenue, and fans lined up five or six deep in some spots, cheering on their hockey heroes.

"Some of the guys who've done it before, like after they won in 2002, were trying to explain to the other guys what it would be like," said Niklas Kronwall, who wasn't part of the 2002 championship team. "But words can't describe it. It was something you'll never forget, all the people."

ROUGH START

How did professional hockey in Detroit actually begin?

Charles Hughes, a one-time sportswriter who also served as a public relations man for Theodore Roosevelt, attracted 73 local investors in 1926, including the likes of industrialist Edsel Ford, department store giant S.S. Kresge, and newspaper publisher William Scripps.

The group paid $100,000 to the NHL and another $100,000 for 15 players on the Victoria Cougars of the Western Hockey League.

The Cougars, incidentally, won the 1925 Stanley Cup.

Hughes kept the name Cougars, but the success of the previous season didn't carry to the Motor City.

With Olympia Stadium still in the process of being built, the team essentially played all road games.

The Cougars finished last in the league with a 12–28–4 record.

The term "Hockeytown" was born in 1996 just before the Wings would go on to win two consecutive Stanley Cups. From the long, storied tradition of the Wings organization, to the numerous junior hockey leagues in the area, to the close proximity to Canada, to the numerous hockey players who've become part of the fabric in the community, all these factors made Hockeytown a truth, not just something an advertising agency (Bozell Worldwide, in this case) accurately created.

Detroit was, and is, Hockeytown.

From the thousands of Wings jerseys at Joe Louis Arena, with the names of Yzerman, Fedorov, Lidstrom, Datsyuk, Zetterberg, and Howe on the back, to thousands of school-age kids heading to the rink weeknights and weekend mornings—often with their parents chugging along, dragging equipment—wearing their city's hockey colors on a jacket with the American and Canadian flags intertwined on the sleeve, Hockeytown is a way of life in Detroit.

"A lifestyle or philosophy" is how Steve Violetta, the Wings' senior vice president of business affairs, describes it. "Not necessarily a location."

There aren't many U.S. cities where a free-agent signing or trade in June, July, or August by the local hockey team is hotly debated in newspaper forums and talk radio. In Detroit, it is.

In Detroit, the town's quarterback is actually the No. 2 toughest position. You don't want to be the Wings' goaltender, especially during playoff time. Every goal against is analyzed and scrutinized.

Legends like Steve Yzerman, Gordie Howe, and Nicklas Lidstrom are revered in a rich sports town such as Detroit, more than any football-playing Lion or basketball-playing Piston.

"It's something that's been built up over the years," general manager Ken Holland said.

Hockeytown North

How popular are the Wings, and how strong is the Hockeytown hold in the state of Michigan?

Consider this. The team has taken its training camp to Traverse City, a gorgeous resort-style town in northwestern Michigan every early September for the last 10 years.

The Wings hold a weeklong (or slightly less) series of scrimmages and practices, along with the minor leaguers and junior players who've been drafted.

Traverse City residents more than open their arms for the Wings. Many residents will take a week off from work to volunteer

MILLION FAN MARCH

It's always difficult to actually count each and every fan at one of these things.

But, anyway, it was estimated by various sources and departments in the city of Detroit that approximately a million fans attended the victory parades of the 1997, 1998, and 2002 Red Wings.

The team went down Woodward Avenue and ended up at Hart Plaza, where the party was in full bloom.

The route was the same in 2008, when the Wings celebrated that championship. But on a hot, humid day, even though hundreds of thousands attended, nobody said a million fans showed up to that one.

to shuttle players from Centre ICE Arena back to the resort the organization occupies. Fans from all over the state, and everywhere else, flock to see the Wings in this little hamlet.

"We've had people travel here from nearly 40 states and Canada," said Pete Correia, the training camp coordinator who was pivotal in bringing the training camp north from Joe Louis Arena. "People will plan their vacations, take a few days off, but it continues to grow in popularity."

All the sessions are usually sold out. Further, before the Wings arrive, the team's top prospects play in an eight-team tournament against other organizations' top young players in a weeklong tournament that whets the appetites of hockey fans in the region.

"Those are the future NHL players right there," Correia said.

Those games, too, are usually sold out. But in the end it's the Wings the fans want to see.

"It really shows you how deep the passion is all over the state of Michigan," coach Mike Babcock said. "It's really something to see."

Hockeytown's Rebirth

The last few years before the 2008 Stanley Cup victory, just how much of a Hockeytown Detroit was, or had become, was free to debate.

An organization that had more than 10,000 on a waiting list for season tickets suddenly didn't have a list at all. Sellouts had stopped. Ratings for the games had fallen as the town grew to love the baseball Tigers, who had unexpectedly gotten to the 2006 World Series.

POSTSEASON REGULARS

The Red Wings have appeared in more than 200 playoff games since 1991, the most of any team in the four major professional sports leagues heading into the summer of 2009.

The San Antonio Spurs (NBA, 189 games), New Jersey Devils (NHL, 185), Los Angeles Lakers (NBA, 176), and Colorado Avalanche (NHL, 165) followed the Wings.

The New York Yankees led major league baseball with 128.

4

Directly after the 2004–2005 lockout, hockey suddenly wasn't as popular in Detroit.

"There were probably a few reasons for it," said Lidstrom, one of the most popular Wings and a longtime fan favorite. "The lockout probably didn't help, and the economy is another reason."

Few American cities are as dependent on a sole business as Detroit is on the auto business. And when General Motors, Ford, and Chrysler began gradually sinking in 2005, so did ticket sales for all local sports teams, especially the slightly higher-priced Wings.

Add the retirement of Steve Yzerman after the 2005–2006 season, a young, talented roster that hadn't won a Stanley Cup nor truly connected yet to the local fan base, plus residual bitterness over the lockout, and you had a perfect storm of issues.

Hockeytown? Sure, but maybe not as passionate as before.

The economy was still a problem in 2008, even more so than ever. Foreclosures were rampant in metro Detroit, with former automakers losing their homes while watching their savings vanish.

But on a hot, humid day in June 2008, after the organization's 11th Stanley Cup was won, Hockeytown was on top of the world again.

"When you see all the fans out there celebrating, wearing their jerseys and raising their arms shouting, you know this is Hockeytown," Wings forward Jiri Hudler said.

ORIGINAL SIX

There really is something about those brilliant red-and-white sweaters, the winged wheel, the history in those jerseys that makes the Red Wings' brand so special, especially among hockey fans in North America, even the world.

Same goes for the New York Rangers. Or the Boston Bruins. Or the Chicago Blackhawks. And for sure the Toronto Maple Leafs and Montreal Canadiens.

They, the Original Six, the six franchises from which the National Hockey League exploded to what it is today. They are the bedrock of the league. The base.

And in Detroit, just like in those other Original Six cities, there's a certain pride in being the first ones there to the party. The rivalries, dynasties, and legendary players that skated during the Original Six days—1942 to 1967 is generally regarded as the heyday in the minds of many hockey historians—are special to fans even now. That's not always the case in other sports.

It seems the past is treasured a little more among hockey fans—in Detroit just as much as in other places.

"Being in an Original Six city, the feeling is a little different when you go to play," said Wings defenseman Brett Lebda, who also happened to grow up in Chicago and followed the Blackhawks. "The history in these places is amazing. Hockey means a little more."

For as illustrious career as Brett Hull had in the NHL, one of his most treasured experiences was playing for the Red Wings, an Original Six team.

"There is something to that," said Hull of the entire Original Six mystique and aura.

Wings Fans All Over

As many Wings fans as there are in the state of Michigan, there's nearly as many, it seems, in other arenas across North America— places like Tampa Bay and Phoenix, where Coyotes management rose ticket prices to Wings games to curtail the amount of Wings fans in the rink, and cities like Washington and Atlanta, both arenas where Wings jerseys outnumber the home team's colors. And don't forget South Florida and Raleigh.

The Wings are often referred to as the New York Yankees of the NHL because of the tradition, history, and success of the organization and the cavalcade of stars on the present-day rosters.

"It really is amazing when you go to these different rinks and see all the Wings fans in the seats," Wings defenseman Chris Chelios said. "A lot of them are transplants from the Detroit area in these other cities. But being an Original Six team, the success of the Wings over the years, it's a team a lot of fans follow."

Fans in opposing rinks, wearing their Red Wings sweaters, will throw octopi onto the ice, symbolizing another Wings

ROAD ICE ADVANTAGE

The Red Wings may be the only team in the NHL that doesn't mind going on the road. The reason? It's just like a home game.

Sun Belt cities like Phoenix, Tampa Bay, Raleigh, Atlanta, and Nashville have many Detroit transplants. When the Wings play games in those rinks, the crowd is actually more supportive of Detroit.

"It just shows how popular the Wings are across the country," Chris Chelios said. "It's almost like the New York Yankees."

One place where the Wings aren't all that popular? Any of the Canadian cities. They much prefer the home team, whichever one it is, rather than the Wings.

victory. They'll cheer Wings goals and be indifferent when their home team does anything positive. Chants of "Let's Go Red Wings!" thunder from the upper bowl of these supposed enemy arenas.

More than a few players opposing the Red Wings in these situations have complained to reporters about how conditions are similar to playing yet another road game, in actuality. "I'm sure it could be a little frustrating," forward Henrik Zetterberg said.

But not nearly as frustrated as Wings fans were after the lockout when the NHL went to a division-heavy schedule, with few games against the rival Eastern Conference. For three consecutive summers, when the actual schedule was unveiled, Wings fans railed against the idea of Columbus Blue Jackets, Nashville Predators and St. Louis Blues (the only good thing was the Blackhawks, too) playing four times each at Joe Louis Arena. On the other hand, the Eastern Conference Rangers, Bruins, Maple Leafs, and Canadiens played at Joe Louis Arena only once in three seasons (the Wings would go to those rinks once, also). Some years, depending on the division from the East the Wings were scheduled to face, the Wings wouldn't play those teams at all.

Wings fans felt commissioner Gary Bettman and the powers that be in the NHL were trying to abolish the Original Six tradition totally.

TEAM OF THE 1990S

The Red Wings are generally considered to be the premier organization in hockey, particularly in the decade of the 1990s.

Numbers bear that out.

The Wings had a .614 winning percentage during the decade, best in the league, with a record of 431–252–100.

The New Jersey Devils were next at .578 (396–275–110), and the Pittsburgh Penguins were third at .577 (406–286–90).

"We're seeing the same teams all the time, and not the teams everyone around here wants to see, the teams many fans grew up with," said Margy Bishop, of Dearborn Heights, a longtime Wings fans who enjoyed the Original Six days.

Fans and front-office personnel also were disappointed with the schedule matrix.

Owner Mike Ilitch, general manager Ken Holland, and senior vice president Jimmy Devellano all felt the schedule was a major reason attendance declined after the lockout, with Wings fans tiring of seeing the same Western Conference teams over and over.

"One week, a few of the Eastern teams were on the schedule, and there was a buzz throughout the city, the rink, in the locker room," Holland said. "You could really sense it."

Players do indeed sense a buzz when facing an Original Six rival. "There's a different kind of spark in the arena, and it carries onto what's happening on the ice," Wings forward Kirk Maltby said.

Long Live Tradition

You want to get an idea of what the Original Six means? The atmosphere when the Wings travel to Chicago or Toronto can pretty much sum it up.

When the Wings play a game in Toronto, you'll see many fans take the train in Windsor, just across the Detroit River, and make the four-hour trek to Maple Leaf country. They'll do so with their

Wings jackets, hooded sweatshirts, Wings duffel bags, and of course Stanley Cup championship caps.

They'll walk around the city streets of Toronto easily recognizable. And on game night, they're not afraid to be vocal in a hostile hockey environment as in Toronto.

Same goes with Chicago. No example could be as perfect as January 1, 2009, the date of the Winter Classic at Wrigley Field, with Wings and Blackhawks fans milling around before the game, soaking up the atmosphere (and beer in Wrigleyville corner bars), and pretty much embodying what was right about the NHL...and the Original Six in particular.

These franchises have been in existence for more than 75 years. Grandparents and great-grandparents could talk about players they'd marveled at. Fans didn't care much for the opposing team, but there was a grudging respect.

Two Original Six teams in the spotlight.

"The way it should be," Chelios said.

RUSSIAN FIVE

Simply put, they had a hand in revolutionizing the way the game is played in the NHL. The puck-possession style these five players adhered to transformed the way the game was played, particularly for the Wings, who had a heavy Russian influence on their roster in the late 1990s and would continue to be dominated with that influence as late as the 2008 Stanley Cup championship season.

When coach Scotty Bowman put together forwards Igor Larionov, Sergei Fedorov, and Slava Kozlov, along with defensemen Slava Fetisov and Vladimir Konstantinov, it was the start of something much bigger than anyone could have imagined.

"Nobody had ever played that way in the league before," said former Wings coach Dave Lewis, an assistant on three Stanley Cup teams that were influenced by at least a few of the Russian players.

Bowman put the five together on the ice on October 27, 1995, in Calgary, and the Wings won 3–0. Fittingly, the Russian unit contributed a goal: Kozlov scored after no-look passes from Fedorov and Konstantinov.

Bowman lived, breathed, and studied hockey as much as anyone during his days as an NHL coach. He was intrigued by the Russian system of possessing the puck, keeping it away from the defense, and felt it was a style that could work in the NHL, particularly with the group of Russians the Wings had.

But to bring it all together, the Wings needed one more playmaker, a conductor. And when Bowman acquired Larionov from the San Jose Sharks in 1995 (for Ray Sheppard), no player could have been a better fit. Larionov was the last piece in a puzzle that culminated with consecutive Stanley Cup victories. "He was one of the most intelligent players I've ever played with," Nicklas Lidstrom said. "He wasn't a big player, but his smarts helped him get so much success."

Bowman learned the Soviet hockey system would keep groups of five together to maintain and build chemistry. He would do the same with this group of five Russians on the Wings.

"We've had great success, and Europeans have been a big part of that," general manager Ken Holland said. "When Scotty put together the Russian Five, that was really the start of the Red Wings we see today. It even had an impact on how we developed our drafting philosophy and scouting philosophy."

From the start, when Larionov, Fedorov, Kozlov, Fetisov, and Konstantinov would hold on to pucks for seconds on end during practice, then the game, the rest of the Wings players were as dazzled as anyone else. "When they first started playing together, everybody on the bench would just watch them and couldn't believe what we were seeing," forward Kris Draper said. "Igor had a way of slowing everything down. It all goes back to the way he saw the game, the vision he had on the ice, and his ability to slow things down."

How dominant was the unit that first season?

One need only look at the plus-minus statistics of each. Konstantinov led the league with plus-60 (on the ice for 60 more goals scored than goals against at even strength). Fedorov (who won the Selke Trophy that season as the league's best defensive forward) was plus-49. Larionov and Fetisov were both plus-37. Kozlov was plus-33.

With 644 points in 14 NHL seasons, Larionov was a fine player in the NHL. But he earned much of his acclaim in Russia as part of the greatest national teams ever assembled. By the time Larionov arrived in Vancouver, he was slowly trending toward the downside of his career. Although a fine, unique player, hockey fans could only imagine what the Russian KLM Line with Larionov, Sergei Makarov, and Vladimir Krutov could have accomplished in the NHL.

"To me, there was no disappointment," Larionov said.

"Igor has had a tremendous impact on hockey at both the international and NHL levels," Holland said. "He was one of the most intelligent players to ever play the game."

Larionov excelled on those teams, along with defenseman Fetisov. The two were pioneers for other Russian players to enter the NHL.

"For so many years he [Larionov] was a great player in Russia, then he came over here and was a great player, too," said Pavel Datsyuk, who regards Larionov as a mentor.

In Datsyuk's rookie season in 2002, Larionov took Datsyuk under his wing, having Datsyuk live in his house. Larionov taught him how to open a checking account in the United States, got Datsyuk to begin speaking the language, and helped get him a driver's license.

Simply put, Larionov taught Datsyuk about NHL life on and off the ice. "Very much so," said Datsyuk, who admires Larionov to this day. "He helped me so much. Not just a great hockey player, Igor is a great man, too. He helped so many young players.

"He's just a classy guy."

Larionov joined the Vancouver Canucks in 1989 at the age of 29 and also played with the San Jose Sharks before joining the Wings. He looks back fondly on his days with the Red Wings and being coached by Bowman. In terms of his authoritative style, love of puck possession, and wanting discipline on and off the ice, Bowman was as close to an old-school Russian coach as you could get in North America.

Larionov said Bowman called him at 7:00 AM Pacific Time the morning Larionov was acquired by the Wings. "I was excited immediately," said Larionov, who drinks two glasses of wine every day, which he says has helped his amazing physical condition. "I was looking forward to it because I knew they had the Russian players, but they had so many great players it would be a pleasure to play with.

"Detroit is such an unbelievable sports town, and the organization was tremendous from top to bottom. Those were unbelievable years."

The puck-possession style and the winning atmosphere in the organization was quickly embraced by Larionov. "Unbelievable support from the fans and the team," Larionov said.

Nicknamed "Professor," Larionov looked the part of a literary academic, but one who also dissected opponents with his patience and savvy passing skills. But he used that guile on the defensive end, too, and was extremely underrated at that end of the rink. "Until we got him from San Jose, we had no idea he was such a good two-way player," Bowman said. "He was so smart on the defensive end."

"Smart" was also an adjective former teammate Lidstrom used to describe Larionov. "I played with those great Russian teams, they never gave up the puck. Playing with him [on the Wings], he was like that, too," Lidstrom said.

Bringing the puck-control and offensive style to North America and integrating it with the NHL's way was one of Larionov's proudest achievements. "It's nice to see European players give the game more finesse," Larionov said.

Larionov was inducted into the Hockey Hall of Fame in 2008.

Character Is Added
Having Larionov and Fetisov on the roster certainly added to the character and leadership of the Wings teams in the late 1990s.

The two legends fought against the Soviet hockey system to win their freedom and play in the NHL. Larionov was openly critical of the Russian Hockey Federation; its total control over players; the vast amount of time spent training, preparing, and practicing; and the time away from home because of it.

Larionov's courage and perseverance have allowed players such as Datsyuk, Alex Ovechkin, and Ilya Kovalchuk the opportunity to come to North America, test their talents against the very best of the NHL, and escape the claws of Russian hockey.

"I'm so happy for the young Russian players, who have the freedom to come and choose their own path," Larionov once told Canada's *National Post*. Larionov has often said his career would have been unfulfilled had he not played in the NHL. "I'm just grateful I was fortunate enough just to be able to make it, because how many fantastic hockey players just didn't make it from my home country?"

Fetisov, as a Russian army member, risked being sent to Siberia but eventually won his release before the 1989–1990 season and joined the New Jersey Devils. The Wings acquired Fetisov in 1995 for a third-round draft choice, and the rugged defenseman—"Papa Bear" he was called by teammates—made a huge impression in a short period of time.

Like Larionov, Fetisov was elected into the Hockey Hall of Fame in 2001.

Fetisov is currently the minister of sport in Russia.

Slava Kozlov
Kozlov was drafted by the Wings in 1990 but didn't arrive from Russia until a year later.

Always a clutch player, Kozlov made a memorable impact with the Wings from 1994 to 1998 in the playoffs. His 30 playoff goals in that span (11 were game-winners) trailed only Jaromir Jagr, Claude Lemieux, and Joe Sakic.

A crafty player who could find successful spots on the ice, Kozlov was traded to the Buffalo Sabres in the summer of 2001 for goalie Dominik Hasek. While Hasek helped the Wings to a Stanley Cup, Kozlov suffered through an injury-plagued season, frustrated the Sabres' management and coaching staff, and was traded to Atlanta.

With the Thrashers, Kozlov instantly found chemistry with young Russian star Ilya Kovalchuk and became a leader on an expansion franchise.

Sergei Fedorov

Fedorov starred with the Wings for over a decade but left as a free agent to the Anaheim Ducks.

The popular belief was Fedorov wanted to be the leader/star of his own team, and was never going to get that opportunity as a member of the Wings with Steve Yzerman on the roster.

Life quickly soured in Anaheim, though, on a roster bereft of talent. Fedorov never made the playoffs and was traded after the lockout (in his second season with Anaheim) to the Columbus Blue Jackets. He couldn't get comfortable in Columbus, either, with a roster significantly younger and, again, low on talent.

Approaching unrestricted free agency again, Fedorov was shipped at the 2008 trade deadline by Columbus to the Washington Capitals.

Fedorov, now in the twilight of his career, found a comfortable situation with the Capitals, a rapidly improving team led by Russian forwards Ovechkin and Alexander Semin.

Vladimir Konstantinov

A tragic limousine accident less than a week after the Wings won the Stanley Cup in 1997 crippled Konstantinov and cut short what was shaping up to be a brilliant career. Many scouts, including most members of the Wings organization, felt Konstantinov was on his way to being a Norris Trophy–caliber defenseman.

Konstantinov established himself as one of the best open-ice hitters in the game during his too-short six-year career. A physical, rugged player, Konstantinov had epic battles with Philadelphia's Eric Lindros and the New York Rangers' Mark Messier, both of whom accused Konstantinov of borderline dirty play but respected his all-out, aggressive style, as well.

The tragic accident, only six days after the Wings had won the Cup, cast a pall throughout the city of Detroit and the NHL. Konstantinov was just coming into his own in the league and was gaining notoriety in the game.

Today, through aggressive therapy, Konstantinov is able to walk with the aid of a walker and personal assistant, but can't communicate clearly.

2008 STANLEY CUP CHAMPS

Really, not many thought the Red Wings were going to raise high another Stanley Cup, as they did in Pittsburgh on June 4, 2008, their fourth Stanley Cup in 11 years.

Most folks who follow the NHL felt the Wings were cooked after the lockout ended in the summer of 2005 and the league was able to institute a salary cap. The Wings had spent as much as $78 million per season on player salaries. Now, it was going to get cut in half. How would the Wings react to such a development? They searched for players who fit their style of play even harder.

"I'm so proud of our organization," said general manager Ken Holland after the Wings had defeated Pittsburgh 3–2 to win the Finals in six games. "We won three Stanley Cups [before the lockout], and there's no doubt we had a higher payroll. We thought we did a good job in building a team. But you come into a new world [post-lockout, with a salary cap], and everybody thought we were going to go down.

"It's a level playing field, it's a cap world, and we're the champs. It doesn't get any better."

The Wings won it with two of the best forwards in the world, Pavel Datsyuk and playoff Most Valuable Player Henrik Zetterberg; the planet's best defenseman, six-time Norris Trophy winner Nicklas Lidstrom; several promising young players; and some role players who couldn't land permanent jobs elsewhere around the NHL.

"We also found players who were looking for a home," said Holland of players such as Mikael Samuelsson, Dan Cleary, Brad

MUST-SEE TV

NBC got its wish with the Red Wings and Pittsburgh Penguins, with prime-time players such as Sidney Crosby and Evgeni Malkin for Pittsburgh and Nicklas Lidstrom, Henrik Zetterberg, and Pavel Datsyuk from the Wings, in the 2008 Stanley Cup Finals.

The star quality worked, as the series was the highest-rated hockey series NBC has ever televised.

The Wings won their 11th Stanley Cup championship in 2007–2008.

COMING HOME

Defenseman Brian Rafalski grew up in the Metro Detroit area, was a fan of the Red Wings, and always thought of what it would be like to play for his hometown team.

After a career in Europe, Rafalski came into the NHL as an undrafted free agent with the New Jersey Devils.

When he became an unrestricted free agent in 2007, Rafalski jumped at the chance to play for the Red Wings. A five-year contract worth $30 million helped, but Rafalski said the chance to play in front of his parents, other family members, and friends was a driving force.

Stuart, Andreas Lilja, and Dallas Drake, all of whom made significant impacts during the playoffs.

Euro Captain

Finally commissioner Gary Bettman bellowed the words all Red Wings fans wanted to hear. "Nicklas Lidstrom, come get the Stanley Cup," said Bettman, as the Mellon Arena crowd in Pittsburgh continued to file out, leaving the place to hundreds of Wings fans. "It's yours to take back to Hockeytown."

Lidstrom raised it high for all to see. It was a special moment for Lidstrom, the first European captain to ever hoist the Cup skyward. He admitted the honor of being the first Euro to do so was special. But right now, he was just proud of his Red Wings team, the one that had defeated the Penguins.

"People didn't think we could do it after the lockout with the salary cap," Lidstrom said. "But the organization found players that were sleepers. Other may have thought we were going to slip more than we did."

Lidstrom was superb throughout the series. He and partner Brian Rafalski shut down the likes of Pittsburgh star young forwards Sidney Crosby and Evgeni Malkin.

This series was another great opportunity for the hockey world to see the brilliance of Lidstrom, as subtle and wondrous as he is on the ice.

"There isn't any one better in the world," coach Mike Babcock said. "There just isn't."

After years of watching Steve Yzerman raise the Cup whenever the Wings were fortunate enough to win, this was Lidstrom's first opportunity as the Wings' captain.

Teammates came around to congratulate him. Friends and family, too. He actually seemed a touch more animated than usual, excited. "You can't describe it. It's a great feeling," Lidstrom said.

Finally, a Winner

The smile never left Dallas Drake's face.

After so many years, Drake, 39, was finally a Stanley Cup champion with the team that originally drafted him. "I've dreamed of this moment," Drake said. "I wasn't sure it was ever going to come. I'm just so excited right now."

Drake signed with the Red Wings in the summer of 2007. He wanted to play one more season, leaving his family back in Traverse City, in northern Michigan.

Drake felt the Wings presented him with the best, and final, chance for that elusive Cup.

"What a team, what an organization," Drake said. "Everything about this team is first-class, from the ownership, to the front office, to the coaching staff, and the players.

"This season is something I will never, ever forget."

FAMILIAR NAMES

There are five players who've been with the Wings for all four of the most recent Stanley Cup runs (1997, 1998, 2002, 2008): Kris Draper, Tomas Holmstrom, Nicklas Lidstrom, Kirk Maltby, and Darren McCarty.

McCarty left Detroit after the lockout, because of salary cap difficulties, but returned to Detroit during the 2007–2008 season.

"I feel very fortunate," McCarty said. "This is home. To be part of this, I can't say how great it feels."

DOWN, BUT NOT OUT

Red Wings radio announcer Ken Kal wasn't able to broadcast the deciding Game 6 of the Red Wings 2008 Stanley Cup Finals series against Pittsburgh because of laryngitis.

Television play-by-play man Ken Daniels took Kal's place.

"It's disappointing," Kal said. "You work all season to get to this point, and now this happens."

"I'm excited, but obviously you hate to see this happen at Kenny's expense," Daniels said.

Daniels worked the game with Paul Woods, but in the waning minutes, gave Kal the opportunity to make the final call.

From Last to First

Nor will Brad Stuart, who was with the last-place Los Angeles Kings at the trade deadline in March, then found himself landing with the eventual Stanley Cup champions.

"Knowing what it takes to win and what you need to do to prepare to win," said Stuart, of what made this Wings team different from other teams that Stuart had been on. "It's pretty calm in here. That comes from experience."

Never Easy

The Wings lost a triple-overtime contest in Game 5 to bring the series back to Pittsburgh for Game 6.

Malkin, the Penguins' young star, was ridden with the flu early in the series but was getting healthy and was playing better.

Even in the final seconds of Game 6, the Penguins pressed and nearly scored, with forward Marian Hossa (who would sign with the Red Wings in the off-season) and Crosby both coming up with good scoring chances.

"We fought to the bitter end, but that's what this team is all about," goalie Chris Osgood said.

They got that determination and fortitude from Babcock, a perfect coach for this bunch of players. Passionate, determined, focused, Babcock is able to drive an already driven team.

"That's what he kept reminding us the whole playoffs, that we were going to be successful," Kris Draper said. "If we played a certain way, we were going to win."

THE OLYMPICS

When the NHL decided to let its players participate in the Winter Olympics, no one really knew how the experiment would work.

These are professionals in the NHL, they earn salaries the average person can only dream about, and true emotion has sometimes escaped them after the endless games, practices, and wear and tear on the body.

The Olympics had always been for young players on the way up, who still had dreams and ambitions, and played for the pure fun of it. Quickly, though, myths and concerns about the pros not playing for the right reasons at the Olympics went away.

All that was needed was one look at Steve Yzerman rolling around the ice after a key goal for Canada.

The pros cared, too.

"It's hard to contain your emotions," said Yzerman after helping lead Canada to a gold-medal victory over the U.S. in 2002 in Salt Lake City. "Guys were trying to be all calm and stoic, but you can't. You let it loose. You become a kid again, and the boyishness just comes out."

Yzerman was one of the best players in the tournament, despite the fact he was just returning from arthroscopic knee surgery. He would need more of it later that summer, and competed in the NHL playoffs with lingering pain in his knee.

But he wasn't going to miss the Olympics.

Few teams have had as many memorable moments in the Olympics as the Red Wings have. It makes sense. The Wings' star-laden roster is filled with players from the top hockey-playing countries. Every four years, when the Olympic rosters are announced by the different countries' federations, the Wings' locker room is as interested as anyone's to see who has been picked.

"I have to say, it's such an honor," said Mikael Samuelsson, part of the 2006 Swedish gold medal–winning team. "You grow up thinking about it, of playing for your country. When you get the chance to actually do it, it's hard to believe."

"The Olympics, that's something else, that's the whole world watching," said goalie Dominik Hasek, who, as a member of the Buffalo Sabres, was instrumental in the Czech's 1998 gold-medal victory.

The Wings had an interesting dilemma in 2006 because of Sweden's victory, a victory in which Red Wings Henrik Zetterberg, Niklas Kronwall, and Nicklas Lidstrom (a third-period game-winner) all scored in the 3–2 win over Finland.

"It could be the biggest goal I've ever scored," said Lidstrom afterward.

The Wings had a large contingent of players on the Swedish roster (Samuelsson, Lidstrom, Zetterberg, Tomas Holmstrom, and Kronwall), and the national team was scheduled to have a rally in Stockholm to celebrate the gold medal.

The Wings were opening up a West Coast trip in San Jose as the Olympics ended. Logistically, there was no way the Swedes were going to get back in time. And general manager Ken Holland wasn't going to push the matter, even though Kronwall was expected to return early because he was a substitute on the Swedish roster.

A million Swedish fans were expected to attend a victory celebration at a square in Stockholm. Holland wasn't going to cut short the party for his players. "They just played eight games in 12 nights," said Holland of the Olympic tournament. "To expect all those guys to travel all day on Monday and play here in San Jose on Tuesday and Wednesday [in Anaheim], that's asking a lot. And how do you not let Niklas Kronwall go [to the celebration in Stockholm], when the other four are going to celebrate?

"You don't win a gold medal every day."

The Swedes returned in time to play against Anaheim—and spurred a Wings victory.

"It's been a whirlwind," Holmstrom said.

In 2002 Yzerman and Brendan Shanahan were part of the Canadian roster that defeated teammates Chris Chelios and Brett Hull, who represented the U.S.

Shanahan injured his right thumb during the tournament, but didn't think of sitting out. "Painkillers mixed with adrenaline," Shanahan said. "The doctor said he didn't think there was a risk of injuring it further. It was just a matter of playing with the pain."

Canada hadn't won an Olympic gold medal in 50 years. The pressure on the 2002 team, with such stars as Yzerman, Mario Lemieux, and Joe Sakic, was enormous.

"You're secluded in the Athlete's Village so you don't realize the pressure back home," Yzerman said. "Canadians are like everybody else. They love to win. But if we had lost, it's not like they wouldn't let us back in the country. They let us come home in '98 [after a medal-less Olympics].

"Hey, the Americans played great. We won one game, and we won the right game, but it doesn't really prove dominance."

Chelios, possibly playing in his last Olympics, was hurt by the defeat on American soil.

"I'm not sad, I'm not upset, I'm just disappointed," said Chelios, who relished the opportunity to play for legendary American coach Herb Brooks, who coached the 1980 U.S. gold-medal team. Brooks would die the following year in an auto crash. "But I've got no complaints. We got beat by the better team. I'm proud of the way we represented the United States. And I'm happy for Yzerman and Shanny. I've been growing up with those guys and been through the wars with them. I'm proud of them, too."

Yzerman pulled Chelios, Hull, and Shanahan aside after the gold-medal game and got a photograph with the four players. The photo was a nice ending to a special week. It's certainly not easy competing against teammates on such a world stage. "It was wild, just the looks we'd give each other in the cafeteria," Chelios said. "Unfortunately with so many of us [Red Wings competing], someone had to win, and someone had to lose."

Already, the Wings are looking forward to the 2010 Olympics in Vancouver. Yzerman, now retired, will be Canada's executive director. Sweden will defend its gold medal with the nucleus of Red Wings. And Russia, with Pavel Datsyuk serving as a leader on a promising young roster, could pose a serious threat for gold.

2002 HALL OF FAME TEAM

The Red Wings often get compared to the New York Yankees because of the success, the world championships, and the ability and desire of Red Wings management to spend money on top talent before the salary cap in the NHL leveled the playing field.

The Yankees have that aura in baseball, a team with a bunch of stars that every fan needs to see when it arrives in the fan's home town. The Boston Celtics and Los Angeles Lakers have had that quality in the NBA.

Never did star quality reach its zenith with the Red Wings as it did during the 2001–2002 season. Every town they played in, with a roster of nine potential Hall of Famers, media and fans came to watch. Many players joked it must have felt like touring with the Beatles—cameras and autograph seekers everywhere, and more Wings fans in the arena, usually, than the home team.

The season before, the Wings were upset in the first round, in six games, by the Los Angeles Kings. Fans and media ached for changes. The team was getting old, the goaltending became suspect, and an era of success seemed to be ending. But owner Mike Ilitch and the front office weren't about to pull the plug on an unequalled run of success. "The city gets used to it," said Ilitch of the Wings' winning ways. "The Red Wings are so much a part of the city now, you just want to keep it that way."

In the summer of 2001 general manager Ken Holland acquired goalie Dominik Hasek for forward Slava Kozlov and future draft picks. Hasek was one of the elite goalies of the time, on the verge

MEMORABLE GOAL

Igor Larionov scored at 14:47 of the third overtime to give the Red Wings a 3–2 victory over Carolina in Game 3 of the 2002 Stanley Cup Finals.

The victory gave the Wings a 2–1 series lead over the Hurricanes.

"One of the biggest goals of my career," said Larionov, 41 at the time, and looking as spry and fresh as any player the next day at practice.

GUITAR BOYD

The Red Wings' former center Boyd Devereaux was one of the more musically inclined players the team has had in recent years. Devereaux played the guitar and was featured on several NHL programs for his ability to strum.

He played on a line with Pavel Datsyuk and Brett Hull during the 2002 Stanley Cup run—nicknamed "The Two Kids and a Goat" line.

of leaving the Buffalo Sabres, and was aching to win a Stanley Cup. He signed a one-year deal worth $8 million with the Red Wings.

Goaltender Chris Osgood would become expendable. But after a disappointing series against Los Angeles, a change of scenery was probably best.

"Going into the playoffs next year, everybody's going to say they don't want to play the Red Wings in the first round, and the sole reason will be because of Hasek," Steve Yzerman said. "We've got a goalie who can win any game any time, and win a playoff series by himself. He's an impact guy, an impact on a team, an impact on the league. It's a real coup for our organization."

"We felt good about our goaltending," Holland said. "But when a goalie of Dominik Hasek's stature becomes available to you, you have to react."

Next, after having come close but not being able to secure free agent-to-be Jeremy Roenick (who decided to sign with the Philadelphia Flyers, instead), Holland signed Luc Robitaille, the former L.A. Kings star, to a two-year contract worth $9 million.

"I came here because I want to win the Cup, no question," Robitaille said. "Nothing else, nothing less."

Robitaille watched defenseman Ray Bourque raise the Stanley Cup for the first time just months before with the Colorado Avalanche. Robitaille had never won the Stanley Cup. His Kings battled Colorado to a seventh and deciding game in the conference semifinals before losing to Bourque and the Avalanche. Robitaille wasn't sure how many opportunities he would get to raise the Stanley Cup. "I watched Ray Bourque win it," Robitaille said. "I watched the game all by myself and I selfishly thought, *I wish that was me.* I was very happy for him. I want to feel the same way—lift the Cup over my head before I retire."

Robitaille decided to leave his wife and two kids in Los Angeles while living in Detroit himself.

Everyone was willing to sacrifice, it appeared, for this grand collection of talent to come together. But general manager Ken Holland did have concerns about how the chemistry was going to work. "You're always worried about chemistry," Holland said. "I would say that's one thing that will need to come together as we look ahead. It will be a challenge. Things such as ice time, who'll see the time on the power play. But as I sit here now, I feel we have a group of players [for whom] things like that will not be an issue."

Scotty Bowman led the 2001–2002 Wings to another Stanley Cup title.

MOTOR MOUTH

Sean Avery, one of the premier antagonists in the NHL, actually began his NHL career with the Red Wings during the 2002 season.

Avery was an undrafted free agent who worked his way through the minor league system. The Wings felt he could be a useful NHL player, but simply couldn't tolerate his antics.

They traded Avery and Maxim Kuznetsov to the Los Angeles Kings in 2003 for Mathieu Schneider.

TWICE AS NICE

Two old friends who thoroughly enjoyed winning the 2002 Stanley Cup with the Wings were Luc Robitaille and Steve Duchesne.

Robitaille had never come close to a Stanley Cup while playing 15 years, mostly with the Los Angeles Kings. He came to Detroit as a free agent looking for an opportunity to finally hoist the Cup.

His wife and two sons remained in Los Angeles during the season.

"There was a lot of sacrifice," Robitaille said. "This [winning the Cup] makes it all worthwhile."

As for Duchesne, he couldn't keep his emotions in check after the Stanley Cup was finally won.

"I've waited 16 long years for this," said Duchesne, who arguably played the best hockey of his career during the 2002 playoffs.

Hull, 37 at the time, was one of the outspoken players in the game. He was said to have been a distraction in Dallas, his opinions clashing with Stars coach Ken Hitchcock. But the Wings' players felt Hull would be fine in an environment such as their locker room, with a stable and strong group of veterans. Hull was the final piece, a player for whom several players such as Chris Chelios, Brendan Shanahan, Nicklas Lidstrom, and Steve Yzerman deferred salary so the Wings could bring him aboard to a payroll that approached $70 million.

FIREMAN IGOR

Igor Larionov dished out many assists during his illustrious career, but never one like this. On January 20, 2002, a season in which the Red Wings would go on to win a Stanley Cup, Larionov set up the game-winning goal in a 3–2 victory over Ottawa.

Later that evening, already at home, Larionov smelled smoke. The house next door was on fire. He ran outside and managed to wake up Bob Ray and the rest of his family. The fire began in the Rays' garage and spread.

Ray credited Larionov with saving the house, and possibly, lives. Larionov deflected praise, saying anyone would have done the same thing.

Still, teammates had a little fun at Larionov's expense the next day in the locker room. A red, plastic fireman's helmet was situated above Larionov's locker.

"Do you believe that?" Larionov smiled.

Everyone was willing to sacrifice.

"We've got a strong group of veteran leaders in that locker room led by Steve Yzerman," Holland said. "We have a strong-willed, veteran coach who has been extremely successful. I don't think any of that will be an issue."

It wasn't. The group seemed to genuinely enjoy playing for each other, for the team. Personalities seemed to meld and never conflicted. No one player had to handle all the pressure, which also helped.

"With this veteran team, there are so many guys, you're not always the one counted on, or the go-to guy," said Hull after scoring three goals in a 6–4 series-clinching first-round win over Vancouver. "It's tough sometimes, but we've got enough guys that when someone is struggling, there's another guy to pick it up."

In the end, after an exciting, emotional seven-game Western Conference Finals victory over bitter rival Colorado, then winning the Stanley Cup Finals in five games over Carolina, the grand experiment worked.

The Hall of Fame roster, under supreme pressure from the previous summer, succeeded.

HALL OF FAME TEAM

How talented was the Red Wings team in 2002 that won the Stanley Cup?
It's generally considered there are nine future Hall of Famers from that
team, and that doesn't count coach Scotty Bowman, who already is
enshrined.

The players who are considered to be Hall of Fame material include Steve
Yzerman, Chris Chelios, Sergei Fedorov, Brett Hull, Nicklas Lidstrom, Dominik
Hasek, Luc Robitaille, and Brendan Shanahan. Already in is Igor Larionov.

"What's the word for being really happy and really tired?"
asked Yzerman, on the ice after the Stanley Cup had been won.
"Exultation? Is that it? That's the way I feel right now. I never
really felt uptight during the playoffs because I always felt we were
going to win. This is the most rewarding of the Cups, maybe
because I've been through it and could enjoy it."

THE OLYMPIA

For the younger fans, the ones who hopped aboard during the
Yzerman, Fedorov, Lidstrom years, it'll be Joe Louis Arena. That's
the place where Stanley Cups were won, the Colorado Avalanche
were hated and booed out of Detroit, and Datsyuk and Zetterberg
will take the Wings into a new era.

But for the older fans, the ones whose favorites had names like
Howe, Delvecchio, Sawchuk, it'll always be the Olympia, or the
"Old Red Barn."

It was big, sturdy, didn't have any of the luxuries that the
modern-day palaces have, and if you ask any of the older Wings
fans, they'll call it one of the most wonderful places ever to watch
a hockey game.

The smell of popcorn wound through every corridor. There
was hustle and bustle through the too-tight concourses, as
vendors sold cheap programs, cold beer, and tasty peanuts.

For the fans who grew up with Olympia, there was no better
place to watch a hockey game. Ask Greg Innis, the Wings' minister of statistics and research, a team historian who saw his first

game there when he was in the first grade, during the 1956–1957 season, over 50 years ago:

> The biggest memory I have about that day was after the game, I still remember the fact we went back downstairs and they brought a lot of Red Wings out into the hallway and sat them down at this long, long table to sign autographs.
>
> It was almost like a buffet line of Wings players, and I got about 10 or 12 autographs, from what I remember, on my program. My only wish is I still had that program.
>
> So many memories about the Olympia. It's dear to my heart. I got season tickets in 1963–1964, and they were incredible seats. They were in the front row of the balcony, just above the blue line. It was section 10, row A, and seats 6 and 7. They were at the end of the row. Let me tell you, you were so close to the ice, right above the action, you could lean over and hear the players talk.
>
> The way the place was built, the fact you were so close to the ice wherever you sat, that's what really made the Olympia special in my mind. There simply weren't many bad seats, if any, in the place. I can't think of any obstructed-view seats.
>
> Another thing that made the Olympia special was the fact that after the game, you could hang around downstairs and wait to get autographs of players when they left the locker room and were headed outside to the parking lot. I can remember the scene so often of kids just waiting around and getting autographs from Howe, Lindsay, and that bunch. It was special. You just don't see that anymore, obviously. The bus takes them into the arena in back, and you never even see the guys.
>
> I remember I saw my first game from the press box at the Olympia in 1975. Again, you were so close, I could hardly believe it. The press box actually hung over the ice.
>
> And they had this great escalator in the back of the arena that took you to the upper level. There was a tradition there of placing a penny on top of the escalator, and having it go

CAN I PARK YOUR CAR?

If you ever parked in a certain lot near Olympia Stadium, you may have run into a former NHL player.

Jimmy Carson enjoyed a fine NHL career, but in his younger days, he helped out his dad, Chuck Carson, who ran several of the parking lots near Olympia.

Carson did wind up playing for the Wings, but at Joe Louis Arena, not Olympia. Carson was with the Wings from 1989 to 1993.

all the way back down. I don't know why, a traditional thing, but everybody did it.

My greatest regret is I never saw a Stanley Cup won there. I remember in 1978, the Red Wings got into the playoffs for the first time in eight years and defeated the Atlanta Flames in a best-of-three series. Bill Lochead scored the game-winning goal in the deciding game for the Wings.

Outside, the fans went nuts. It was Mardi Gras, New Year's Eve, and Fourth of July all rolled into one. People were honking horns, slapping hands, and making so much noise, and I'm thinking to myself, *This was the first round.*

But the fans were so desperate for a winner, it had been so long, and just winning that one round in the playoffs meant so much. I only wonder what it would have been like to have won a Stanley Cup around the Olympia.

I can still envision parking my car in one of the lots around there and making that walk to the arena. I can still see myself doing it.

The Olympia opened on October 15, 1927, for the Detroit Cougars, who were forced to play in Windsor the season before while the Olympia was being built.

Olympia's prime was during the Red Wings' glory years in the 1940s and '50s, with players such as Gordie Howe, Ted Lindsay, Sid Abel, Red Kelly, and Terry Sawchuk. The Wings won four Stanley Cups and finished first atop the league regular-season standings eight times in nine years during one incredible stretch.

Crowds of over 16,000 attended regularly, the noise reverberating in the din that Olympia could create.

Olympia was structurally superior, and because it was built in tiers, nearly every one of the 16,000 fans was able to get a tremendous sightline onto the ice.

"This is a tremendous building," said Lincoln Cavalieri, the general manager at Olympia. "If an atom bomb landed, I'd want to be in Olympia."

Paul Woods was a Red Wings player from 1977 to 1984 before becoming a radio analyst for the team. Woods played nearly three seasons at Olympia and doesn't think it received the credit it deserved for its home-ice advantage:

> The thing I remember most clearly was the fact the fans were right on top of you. You don't get that nowadays in a lot of these newer rinks. Olympia was special. The fans would be right there, every game, and make as much noise as any of the other places.

THE LINK

That's the nickname given to Wally Crossman, who spent 61 seasons as the dressing room assistant to the Red Wings.

Crossman lived near Olympia Stadium, worked at the drug store down the street, went to practice, and paid the 25¢ to watch games in the balcony.

In 1940 general manager/coach Jack Adams asked Crossman if he'd replace the regular locker room man who was called away for war duty. Crossman never received a paycheck, only two tickets to each game and a tip at the end of the season from the players. He finally retired in October 2002 to care for his sick wife, Peg.

"I've smelled enough sweat," Crossman said in *Red Wings Essential.* "I don't want to stay here 'til I'm 100. That's too long."

The ice was fantastic. Some of the best ice in the league at that time.

When you look at the rinks at that time, Olympia, the [Montreal] Forum, Maple Leaf Gardens, Chicago Stadium, you just never thought any of those places would go away. But time moves on. I never thought the Forum would not be there. But it moved on, too.

Olympia is the same way. But for the players who played there, the fans who watched so many games there, that's a special memory, let me tell you.

Even when the Wings faltered in the 1960s and 1970s, Detroit was consistently near the top of the league in attendance, as die-hard fans made their way to the aging arena.

Serious discussions of moving the Wings began after the 1967 riots in the city of Detroit. Two killings had occurred close to the arena, and the neighborhoods around the Olympia began deteriorating.

The team was offered a new arena by the city of Pontiac, in wealthy Oakland County, about 40 minutes from downtown Detroit. The Lions moved to the newly built Pontiac Silverdome in 1975. Wings owner Bruce Norris was offered an arena next door to the Silverdome. That caught the attention of the city of Detroit, which offered Norris a riverfront arena at minimal rent, control of the Cobo Arena next door, and a newly built parking structure.

That was enough for Norris, and the Wings moved to what would become Joe Louis Arena midway through the 1979–1980

HOME AWAY FROM HOME

While awaiting the completion of Olympia Stadium, the Detroit Cougars never really did play any home games in their inaugural 1926 season.

The Cougars would cross the bridge into Windsor, Canada, and play at the Border Cities Arena.

In the Cougars' debut they lost 2–0 on November 18 to the Boston Bruins, in Windsor.

season. The last game played at Olympia was a Wings alumni game in 1980.

Olympia was demolished in 1986.

"I was able to get a few bricks and got still photographs of it being torn down," Innis said. "It was a sad time for a lot of us who basically grew up in the place, watching so many games."

Hockey was king at Olympia, but boxing was a close second. According to newspaper accounts, more than 16,000 fans attended a big bout between heavyweights Tom Heeney and Johnny Risko, the first big crowd in 1927. Hometown favorite Joe Louis was a fixture at the Olympia with his bouts, and Olympia also hosted memorable matches between Jake LaMotta and Sugar Ray Robinson. Thomas Hearns also began his illustrious career at the Olympia, rising from the streets of Detroit to win several world championships.

Elvis Presley, The Beatles, The Rolling Stones, and The Who had legendary concerts there, and artists and fans raved about the acoustics.

But hockey was king.

"A special place," Innis said.

HENRIK ZETTERBERG

He could have gone anywhere during the summer of 2008, likely being the most sought-after unrestricted free agent available, but on a cold, snowy day in January 2009, a day only native Detroiters could appreciate, Henrik Zetterberg was agreeing to a 12-year contract worth $73 million with the Red Wings.

To a small extent, it didn't make sense. Some outsiders probably felt like Zetterberg's prison term was expiring. He could leave Detroit. He could go to the bright lights of New York or the sunshine of Phoenix or a hockey hotbed like Toronto.

Why would Zetterberg, in the prime of his career at age 28, stay in economically depressed (although hockey-loving) Detroit? "Just like Sweden," said Zetterberg of the weather outside, and one reason Zetterberg had become so comfortable with metro Detroit.

There was a little more to it than that. It's the same reason many other Red Wings have taken a little less economically to stay with the Wings organization and allow for owner Mike Ilitch to retain other key players as well. Players buy into the system in Detroit, a team system where loyalty is rewarded by playing with other great players and the team is in contention for a Stanley Cup seemingly every season.

"I've never seen any reason to go anywhere else," Zetterberg said. "I really like it on and off the ice. I have great teammates and a great coaching staff. Owners who we know will do whatever it takes to have a good team every year. I don't see any reason why I shouldn't stay. I love it here. I want to be here forever."

"We watched him grow from a prospect to one of the best two-way players in the game," general manager Ken Holland said. "Henrik wanted to be a Red Wing for life, and we wanted to keep him a Red Wing."

Red Wings fans are extremely happy the relationship between player/organization/town has taken off so well. In a short period of time, Zetterberg had rocketed himself to being one of the best players in the NHL. The Conn Smythe Trophy (playoff Most Valuable Player) winner during the 2008 Red Wings Stanley Cup playoff run (with 13 goals in 22 playoff games), Zetterberg has shown all the ingredients necessary to possibly become one of the organization's all-time greats when his contract finally runs out.

"He's the best," Wings coach Mike Babcock said. "He's beyond smart. He's a great penalty killer. Really strong in the faceoff circle. Real good defensively, and real good offensively. He's just a good player.

"Hank has the skills of the good players in this league, but he works harder. So you add all of that together, and that's why you're successful. He brings it every night. He has the work ethic, and you have a lot of will there."

Zetterberg gained a little more attention nationally in that 2008 playoff run. Matched up against NHL marquee cover boy Sidney Crosby in the Finals, Zetterberg outplayed the Pittsburgh Penguins star, particularly on the defensive end.

"I was so proud in the Stanley Cup Finals, how he went toe-to-toe with Sidney Crosby and showed the grit and toughness of European players," owner Mike Ilitch said.

SWEDISH STAR

Henrik Zetterberg can mill around metro Detroit with his girlfriend, Emma, in relative ease. Things have changed over the years, and especially after winning the Stanley Cup, but Zetterberg is still able to keep a relatively low profile.

Not so in Sweden. Emma is a Swedish winner of a *Survivor*-type television series and is a popular television personality. Zetterberg was a popular junior star who has kept growing in popularity while starring in the NHL.

"It's nice to come back to Detroit after the summer is over," Zetterberg said, aching for a bit of peace and quiet.

"I've always believed that when you line him [Zetterberg] up against a guy in a series, he'll wear him out, and to me, that's leadership," Babcock said. "I'm proud to be his coach. He's made me a better coach and he's made his teammates better as well."

Some of that will and determination may come from the fact Zetterberg wasn't considered a can't-miss player entering the NHL. Unlike most stars in the league, Zetterberg was drafted in the seventh round, the 210th player drafted overall, in 1999. There aren't a lot of players coming from that low in the draft signing 12-year contracts. Most are headed to the American League for a brief spell, at best.

Most NHL organizations simply saw Zetterberg as too small and frail at the time to ever make the jump to North America. If they ever scouted Zetterberg at all.

"I don't remember too many teams paying all that much attention," Zetterberg said.

But Wings assistant general manager Jim Nill and European scout Hakan Andersson saw potential, albeit long-range possibilities. "He had the skill set," said Nill, who along with his scouts have made careers out of finding unknown talents for the Wings. "He needed to mature physically, get stronger, and we were able to give him that time. We didn't have to rush him."

Many Swedish players are criticized for their supposed lack of grit and tenacity. But that argument never held much stock when

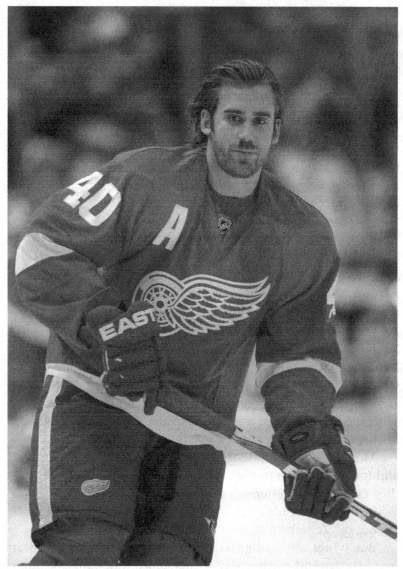

In 2009 Henrik Zetterberg signed a 12-year, $73 million deal to stay in Detroit.

analyzing Zetterberg's skill set, as he continually drove hard to the net, never shied away from physical defenders, and was willing to accept contact if it meant a scoring opportunity.

"You could tell he was an NHL player from the first day he arrived here," Steve Yzerman said.

Actually, it was Yzerman who helped seal the deal when it came to signing Zetterberg to that long-term contract in January 2009. Yzerman was a career Red Wing, a certain Hall of Famer, and a star for Team Canada. The only NHL organization Yzerman will ever be linked to is the Red Wings. Yzerman felt Zetterberg should be the same way.

In an era of professional sports where loyalty is so rare, where there are so few instances of players staying in one city their entire careers, Yzerman and current Red Wings defenseman Nicklas Lidstrom, two of the modern greats, have been able to do that.

Yzerman felt Zetterberg, too, was that type of special player who should be affiliated with only one team, one jersey.

"I had some understanding of what he was going through and what his feelings were," Yzerman said. "What I just wanted to stress with him was that I thought it was important for him, being the type of player and he has that stature, that he should play for one organization his entire career. Actually there were two that I mentioned—the Detroit Red Wings and the Swedish national team. Those are the two jerseys you'll see Hank play in. It creates a legacy for him.

"It's a great reflection for our organization and our city that a player of that stature wants to remain here. He's the type of person we want representing our organization."

During Yzerman's final season, Zetterberg had the locker stall next to him. They often talked after practice, or before games, Yzerman imparting tidbits of knowledge on the league, the Wings, and how to lead a team, as he did so remarkably for so many years.

After talking with Yzerman a few weeks before the contract-extension announcement, Zetterberg knew for certain he wanted to remain with the Wings. "That really turned around the talks, they went faster after that," Zetterberg said. "It's easy to talk to him because he's been on both sides. I sat next to him in the locker room. I respect him a lot. He could have left years ago and didn't. You talk to players on other teams, and they say if you get a chance, you should stay here."

Zetterberg's good friend on the Wings, Pavel Datsyuk, signed a seven-year contract the season before. The two players will likely lead the Wings into the next decade. Datsyuk, too, was a low-round pick (sixth round, 171st overall in 1998).

The two often joke around in the locker room and on the ice during practice. Few organizations are in better hands heading into the future.

"It's as good a one-two punch as there is in hockey, whether you play them apart or together, on the wing or at center," Babcock said. "What separates them from a lot of good players is their determination defensively and their commitment to the team that allows us to win."

PAVEL DATSYUK

Pavel Datsyuk doesn't speak a lot of English, doesn't understand some of it, either. He'll make it through a standard interview, but invariably there will be something he doesn't quite understand—he'll repeat the question and then disarm the interviewer with a quip of his own.

It happens nearly every time.

Like the time someone asked him about the NHL Draft. The Red Wings selected Datsyuk in the sixth round of the 1998 entry draft, the 171st player overall. Another of the mind-bogglingly astute finds the Red Wings' front office seems to collect with regularity.

"Draft? I thought I was drafted to Russian army," said Datsyuk, who didn't have much clue about what an NHL Draft was.

Once, someone asked Datsyuk how he came up with some of his extraordinary one-on-one moves against goalies. It was his daughter of preschool age, Datsyuk said, who created the highlight-reel magic that has turned many a goalie into a pretzel.

In the summer of 2008 Datsyuk finally attended an NHL awards show in Toronto after missing several such get-togethers in the past. "Henrik would never give me any tickets before," said Datsyuk, alluding to friend and teammate Henrik Zetterberg.

It's ironic that Datsyuk and Zetterberg have taken the league by storm the way they have. Both are annual Selke candidates and have drawn conversation about winning a Hart Trophy (most valuable player), which Datsyuk was nominated for in 2009. Like Datsyuk, Zetterberg was a low-round pick (seventh round in 1999), and expectations weren't high.

"They find these guys, who every other team in the league had a chance to get, but didn't," said television hockey analyst Bill Clement. "Look at Datsyuk. He's one of the premier players in the game today. A No. 1 pick [type of] talent. And no one knew about it? Give all the credit to Kenny Holland [Wings GM], Jim Nill [assistant GM], and the scouts in that front office. They beat the bushes and find these players."

All Datsyuk has done in his career since arriving from Russia (not far from Siberia, actually) to Detroit, entering the 2009 season, is win a Selke Trophy (given to the best defensive forward) twice, win four consecutive Lady Byng Trophies (for gentlemanly play), get picked to play in three All-Star Games, belong to two Stanley Cup–winning Wings teams, and sign a seven-year contract in 2007 (worth $46 million) that'll likely keep him a Red Wing for the rest of his playing career.

One other neat statistic: when Datsyuk led the Wings in scoring during the 2008–2009 regular season, he did so for the fourth consecutive season. The only other Red Wings to have accomplished such a feat? How about Ted Lindsay, Gordie Howe, and Steve Yzerman. Pretty heady company for a draft pick who was essentially a shot in the dark. Maybe he'll develop into a player someday, but more likely not. Turns out, the Wings struck gold with Datsyuk.

"When we drafted Pavel, he was something like 5'8" and weighed about 145 pounds soaking wet," Nill said. "You could see the skills, he was a talented player. But you had to wonder if he'd ever grow into an NHL player. That was an issue. So we kept him over there [in Russia] and let him develop."

MILESTONE SHOOTOUT

Who was the first Red Wings player to clinch a victory with a shootout goal? It was Jason Williams, who beat Columbus goalie Pascal Leclaire December 20, 2005, giving the Wings a 4–3 victory over the Blue Jackets.

Has he ever developed.

While expanding on his already elite-level stickhandling and passing skills, Datsyuk has obviously worked on his defensive game to the point where he won a Selke Trophy. Leadership? He's an assistant captain on the team, a player who embraces pressure and is capable of keeping teammates loose with his demeanor. And while not the biggest player in the league (at 5'11", 195 pounds), Datsyuk has come to enjoy playing a gritty, physical game, unlike many fellow Russian players in the league.

"For his size, he's awfully strong," teammate Kris Draper said. "He likes to use that strength."

Fruitful Cancellation

How exactly did the Red Wings land Datsyuk, who should have been anything but a low-round draft pick? As general manager Ken Holland often says, a little luck was involved.

Hakan Andersson, the Wings' European scout, was actually in Russia to see another prospective draft pick when Datsyuk caught Andersson's attention with a dazzling performance. As most good scouts do, Andersson went back for a second look and was no less impressed by Datsyuk. Even better for Andersson and the Wings, there were no other scouts from NHL teams in attendance at these games.

Andersson was scheduled to take a third look, but a snowstorm cancelled the flight he was supposed to board for the game. Ironically, Andersson noticed at least one other scout in the boarding area who was likely headed for the same game, and obviously get an opportunity to watch Datsyuk for the first time.

Andersson and Wings assistant general manager Jim Nill say there's a good chance few other NHL teams even knew about Datsyuk, who at the time, wasn't even well known in his native Russia much less in the NHL. Hence, the opportunity for the Wings to let Datsyuk drop to them in the sixth round.

Major Influence

When Datsyuk arrived in Detroit for the 2001–2002 season, he was fortunate in the fact he had fellow countrymen Sergei

"Chris Osgood, most mediocre goalie to ever win two Stanley Cups."

Not one. But two Stanley Cups.

Backhanded compliment? A total dig? Or, maybe, some sort of a bizarre, twisted compliment? Probably all three. But, when it comes right down to it, keep in mind, yes, Osgood backstopped the Wings to two Stanley Cups after taking care of the Penguins. And maybe he could have led them to a third had coach Scotty Bowman decided to go with Osgood, then relatively untested in 1997, but instead turned to Mike Vernon for the playoffs (Osgood was the regular-season No. 1 goalie).

Probably no player has frustrated Red Wings fans over the years than the boyish-looking Osgood, who has the maddening tendency to follow an acrobatic save with the ability to let in a goal from the (opposing) blue line.

"He's really come full circle, hasn't he?" said forward Kirk Maltby, a teammate of Osgood going back to the 1997–1998 Stanley Cup years.

After being part of those Cup years, Osgood stayed with the Wings until after the 2001 playoff disappointment in which the Wings lost in the first round to the Los Angeles Kings. L.A. defeated the Wings in six games, winning the last four games of a series in which the frustration toward Osgood seemed to mount.

The Wings acquired Dominik Hasek shortly thereafter. Osgood suddenly became an unwanted backup, who was placed on waivers before the 2002 regular season began, beginning an odyssey which saw him land on Long Island, then get traded to the St. Louis Blues the very next season.

But the ironic thing about all this? Osgood never wanted to leave Detroit.

"I loved it here and I didn't really want to leave," Osgood said. "I knew the circumstances. I was hoping to one day return here."

Sure enough, after the lockout ended in the summer of 2005, he returned to the Wings to split goaltending duties with Manny Legace. After a, well, mediocre season, Osgood was retained the following season (Legace was let go), and the Wings signed— drumroll please—Hasek.

Hasek and Osgood, together again, for the next two seasons. Each season Osgood was regarded as the clear-cut backup in the opinion of many analysts. But it never quite materialized that way, as Osgood played just as well—or better—than Hasek, particularly in the 2007–2008 season. Osgood, in fact, was good enough to start for the Western Conference in the All-Star Game.

While others may have thought of Osgood as a backup goalie at this point in his career, Osgood never did.

"I never really looked at myself as a backup, ever," said Osgood during the 2008 Stanley Cup Finals against the Penguins. "You don't want to fall into that trap. I always try to do what I need to do to make myself a better player and just to take what I knew before and add some new stuff to make myself a more complete player. I did that during the lockout and during the last two seasons, and now I'm just seeing the rewards of it."

After that subpar first season post-lockout, Osgood spent the summer reworking his style. He meshed some of the popular butterfly style that younger goalies around the league were perfecting, and incorporated it into his own. Interestingly, one of the young goalies that Osgood wanted to emulate was Pittsburgh's Marc-Andre Fleury, who would be Osgood's counterpart in the 2008 Finals.

John Osgood recalls a conversation he had with his son Chris during the 2005 fathers' trip the Wings host annually. "Marc-Andre Fleury, [Chris] told me on that first father-son trip, he said to me, 'That's how I want to learn how to play,'" John Osgood said. "He said, 'I've got to keep learning.' It's kind of interesting he would say that and think of Fleury.

"He really narrowed his focus after the [2007–2008] regular season. He stayed in his routine and had a goal in mind of winning the Cup. Now he's done that."

The Chris Osgood that won the Stanley in 2008 is much different from the 1998 version. He doesn't get rattled on a goal that maybe shouldn't have gone in. Whatever he's lost in terms of athleticism or quickness, he's able to compensate with a veteran goaltender's guile and knowledge.

And, as coach Mike Babcock has said on a variety of occasions, there are few competitors in the league quite like Osgood.

"I just always knew I could do it," Osgood said after defeating the Penguins in Game 6. "I did the work off the ice and on the ice to be better. I've just got a big heart and I'm strong mentally. I've been through a lot. Sometimes I don't have my A-game, but my mental toughness and my heart get me through it. I definitely needed it in these playoffs."

"Ozzie is a fantastic story," Babcock said. "When you pull your goalie in the first round of the Stanley Cup playoffs, that usually means you're going fishing in about three days, and not 14 more wins or whatever we needed to get it done. You have to give him a lot of credit. He sat in my office at my house two years ago, I guess, after the season and talked about reinventing himself and finding a way, and he did. He learned how to butterfly, and he's improved his game. And he's now back as one of the top goalies in the league because of his mental toughness and his stick-to-itiveness. He showed that in bouncing back and winning."

TOMAS HOLMSTROM

In the long and storied tradition of Red Wings hockey, few players have been as unique as Tomas Holmstrom.

Originally a 10th-round draft choice in 1994 (the 257th choice overall), Holmstrom was the epitome of an afterthought. He was a player the Wings took a chance on with a late pick—something the organization has been successful at doing—in hopes he would turn into a serviceable player. To say Holmstrom was projected to be the player who he's become would be entirely wrong. But given Holmstrom's determination around the net, his willingness to go into the tough areas on the ice, the late-round afterthought has enjoyed a long and successful career.

"He's just a tough player," coach Mike Babcock said. "He's willing to pay the price."

Maybe no player in NHL history has made a living scoring goals and aggravating opposing goalies like Holmstrom. Few come to memory who have been willing to get hit, hooked, pushed, punched, and corkscrewed as consistently as Holmstrom has by opposing defensemen and goalies, and simply gotten up and drawn a penalty, tipped a puck into the net, or screened a goalie successfully so someone else's shot could go into the net, as Holmstrom.

"I enjoy it, someone has to do it," said Holmstrom one afternoon, nonchalantly. "When I retire, someone else will take over my place."

Maybe. But that player likely won't do it as well as Holmstrom.

"He's good at it," said Nicklas Lidstrom, a fellow Swede on the Wings and another Wings veteran with whom Holmstrom has built a strong friendship. It's usually on Lidstrom's point shots on the power play that Holmstrom is screening the goalie or the netminder's vision. "Homer [Holmstrom] has great hand-eye coordination and he's willing to do the hard work in front of the net. It's not an easy job."

Holmstrom played a similar style in Sweden while in junior hockey. Never a fast, graceful skater, he had to use his size and battering-ram style to carve out a place on any team he was on. But it was former coach Scotty Bowman who molded Holmstrom into the NHL player he is. Bowman watched Holmstrom during the player's first training camp and saw an ability to go to the net and not be moved around, or away, once Holmstrom got there.

"I'll never forget it," Holmstrom said. "Scotty told me to just get to the net and stay there. Don't let anyone move you out. Just stay in front of the net."

Fine, thought Holmstrom. *But what if the puck goes to the corner?*

"Scotty said, 'Doesn't matter. Someone else will go get it,'" Holmstrom said. "So I just stayed near the net. I just kept doing what he told me to do. It's worked out pretty good."

The long list of goalies Holmstrom has driven nuts over the years continues to grow. Just in recent years, Anaheim's J.S. Giguere, Dallas' Marty Turco, Pittsburgh's Marc-Andre Fleury, and Calgary's Miikka Kiprusoff have been driven to distraction because of Holmstrom setting up shop around the goaltender's crease.

"When they get mad, you kind of know you're doing your job," Holmstrom said. "I have to go to keep going to the net and doing my job. Create traffic."

Tomas Holmstrom has been a nemesis to countless goaltenders since joining the Red Wings in 1996.

Holmstrom, at 5'11", 205 pounds, doesn't play like your typical Swedish player. Most Europeans are great skaters. General manager Ken Holland and Babcock both say Holmstrom would lose most foot-races against NHL players. "But he's going to get there," Babcock said. "Guys like Holmstrom, you want them on your team."

Holmstrom isn't going to mesmerize with an array of offensive moves. He doesn't have an overly imposing shot and wasn't a great defensive player early in his career. But his willingness to crash the net, a key ingredient in the post-lockout NHL, has made him invaluable for the Wings and their Stanley Cup victories.

"I watch him all the time," said Johan Franzen, a younger Swede whose locker is next to Holmstrom's and has begun to emulate his net-front style. "He's almost fearless around the net. All the abuse he takes, it's unbelievable. But he stays in there and gets the job done."

FRANZEN'S MAGICAL RUN

For Red Wings fans, the 2008 Stanley Cup Finals playoff run will have numerous memories. There were goals, saves, and hits that each individual fan has already ingrained into memory.

Certainly one aspect of that playoff run that Wings fans won't forget was the sudden transformation of Johan Franzen into a version of Wayne Gretzky, Gordie Howe, and Mario Lemieux all rolled into one. Right in front of the eyes of hockey fans everywhere, Franzen—who to that point was a third-line forward whom Wings management was waiting to develop into a more offensive force—suddenly became an impact player.

"I scored some goals, then a few more, and it was giving me confidence," said Franzen, known to his teammates as "the Mule." "I'll never forget it. I've never been part of a streak like that."

Franzen wound up scoring 13 goals with five assists in 16 playoff games as the Wings went on to defeat Pittsburgh and win the Stanley Cup. He missed six games because of a subdural hematoma sustained during the second round. But it was during that second round, along with a magical month of March during the regular season (maybe Wings fans should have seen the onslaught of goals coming), that Franzen's impact was felt most.

THE MULE

Johan Franzen believes it was Steve Yzerman who gave Franzen the nickname "the Mule."

"It's different," said Franzen of the tag, which isn't exactly the most common nickname around.

Yzerman gave Franzen the nickname because of Franzen's strength and the way he used that strength on the ice to not be easily pushed around. It was a compliment, not a criticism or slight.

"I know that," Franzen said. "I like it. I was a little surprised at first, though. I wasn't sure what a mule was."

In that second-round series against Colorado, Franzen established a new franchise record with a staggering nine goals in the Wings' four-game sweep over the Avalanche. The nine goals scored were the most ever scored by a Wings player in one playoff series (breaking Gordie Howe's mark), and his two hat tricks in that series tied a franchise record in one playoff series.

More so, his nine goals were the most scored by any player in NHL history in a four-game series.

"I don't expect myself to score that much," said Franzen, who gave a lot of credit to his sudden offensive prowess to linemates Mikael Samuelsson and Valtteri Filppula. "They gave me some freebies. Every time you get mentioned with him [Gordie Howe] it's a great honor."

How dominant was Franzen against the Avalanche? He matched the Avalanche scoring total by himself in the four-game sweep, 9–9.

"It's not often you see a player score like this. It's fun to be part of it," teammate Henrik Zetterberg said.

"He's a big, big man with lots of skill, and we're lucky to have him," coach Mike Babcock said. "Mule's been good now for a long time. If you're going to break records, you might as well break Gordie Howe's."

During the month of March, Franzen—stepping into the position vacated by Tomas Holmstrom due to injuries—capitalized on an opportunity by scoring 14 goals in 13 games. And he set a

Wings' team record by scoring six game-winning goals during the month.

Franzen kept his clutch scoring going in the playoffs, as he had five game-winning goals in the playoffs—also, incidentally, a new Wings' team record.

"He's a big guy that creates a lot of space around the front of the net," said Dallas Stars coach Dave Tippett during the 2008 Western Conference Finals. "The thing that I'm impressed with the most about him is his ability to find loose pucks, deflect pucks."

An amazing part to this story is the fact Franzen was doing that offensive damage in the Colorado series some of the time with severe headaches caused by a subdural hematoma, which can be caused by minor accidents to the head, major trauma, or the spontaneous bursting of a blood vessel in the brain.

Franzen said the persistent headaches began during the Colorado series. He was forced out of the lineup before Game 2 of the Dallas series in the conference finals and didn't return until Game 2 of the Stanley Cup Finals.

"It's not going to affect him long-term," general manager Ken Holland said. "Basically, in effect, it's a bruise. It's like when you get hit on a part of your body."

Concerned at first, Franzen was reassured by doctors it's an injury that does not reappear again. "I wasn't allowed to do anything and I listened to the doctors when they said that," Franzen said. "I didn't want to jeopardize anything. The doctors said it happens to football players and boxers quite often. It came from a hit, but we don't know exactly when."

UNEXPECTED BONUS

Coming off a Stanley Cup victory in 2008, the Red Wings didn't look as if they needed much on the unrestricted free agent market. They had some money to spend, not a lot, but making their usual big splash didn't seem possible.

General manager Ken Holland kept saying as much. Every team, even the Stanley Cup champion, has a need here or there that it would like to fill. The Wings could use a little more depth up front, if at all possible, or maybe a veteran defenseman might leave (ultimately Brad Stuart stayed, though), but otherwise, the Wings were in good shape.

So, as Holland was pumping gas July 2 at a Mobil station on Woodward Avenue in suburban Detroit, imagine his surprise when Marian Hossa's agent Ritch Winter called, saying Hossa—the best free agent available—wanted to sign with the Red Wings.

"I was stunned," said Holland, who had talked with Winter a day earlier to express interest in Hossa, doing his due diligence but not expecting to get a deal done because of financial constraints. The Wings, in Holland's thinking, simply weren't in a financial position to get Hossa for the long-term.

Shockingly, though, Hossa was willing to help out the team in whatever way he could to make this marriage work. He was willing to take a one-year contract. This, despite the fact other teams were reportedly willing to sign him for a deal worth approximately $100 million over seven to nine years.

Also, Hossa was willing to accept less, in terms of salary, than Nicklas Lidstrom's team-high $7.6 million (Hossa would sign for $7.4 million). All in the name of joining the Wings and playing for a team that Hossa felt presented him with the best opportunity to win a Stanley Cup.

"It wasn't an easy decision," said Hossa after the fact, already in a Wings uniform, by his locker stall and joking with teammate/linemate Pavel Datsyuk, Hossa's locker partner. "I had good friends in Pittsburgh, and the team was a very good team. But, when it came down to it, this team [the Red Wings] has a good chance to win a Stanley Cup.

"And I want to win a Stanley Cup."

Entering the salary-cap era, this was music to the Wings organization's ears. They felt the winning culture would be a selling point, hoping star players would be attracted to Detroit in that respect and bypass teams who could offer more money but didn't have the winning tradition.

The Wings had been interested in acquiring Hossa for some time. Most recently, the high-scoring, dynamic, skilled two-way forward was available in the March 2008 trade deadline when it was apparent the Atlanta Thrashers weren't going to be able to re-sign him. The Wings sniffed around the Thrashers, but Atlanta GM Don Waddell's asking price was too much in the Wings' minds. Pittsburgh won the sweepstakes, giving up a pair of serviceable forwards and several draft picks.

Hossa then helped the Penguins to the Finals, facing the Red Wings, by scoring 26 points (including 12 goals) in 20 games. Forming great chemistry with Sidney Crosby, Hossa seemed to find a home.

But for Wings fans everywhere, this is where Wings forward Tomas Kopecky earns a valuable assist. A longtime friend of Hossa's, Kopecky was consistently extolling the virtues of signing with the Red Wings. There was the commitment to winning by owner Mike Ilitch, the top-flight front office, a dedicated coaching staff, the world-class roster, and, maybe most important after playing in a moribund Atlanta market, the emotion and support of the Hockeytown fans.

On the flip side, Hossa, too, was intrigued by the Wings. Specifically the type of team he saw when playing against them in the Finals. Hossa felt the Wings' defense was the best in the world, and offensively, the puck-possession style suited him, but also was far and above what most other teams could do with the puck.

The chance to play with a good friend such as Kopecky was also a positive checkmark. And Kopecky kept selling what the Wings could provide. "It's a great place to play," Kopecky said. "I knew Marian would fit in real good here. I was hoping it would work out."

Did it ever. Hossa was intent on playing on a potential Stanley Cup team and was willing to do whatever it took financially to make sure he was on a contending team such as the Wings.

Holland, for his part, likely will never get a better morning phone call while he's filling the gas tank.

"A great team, a great organization, everything is about winning here," said Hossa, as the 2008–2009 season began, and his jersey hung in the locker. "Now that I've been here for a while, and have seen what goes on here, what kind of team this is, I know I made the right decision."

THE GRIND LINE

My, how times had changed. And come to think of it, where did the time go?

Kirk Maltby looked around the Red Wings' locker room early in the 2008–2009 season and could only shake his head and smile at all the changes over the years, how many players have come and gone since he arrived in 1996, and Kris Draper in 1994, and Darren McCarty in 1993.

"Amazing how the three of us have managed to stay around," said Maltby, eternally grateful for his good fortune.

Tomas Holmstrom, Nicklas Lidstrom, and Chris Osgood were all still around from the 1998 Stanley Cup–winning team. The front office had pretty much stayed the same. Heck, the feel and atmosphere around Joe Louis Arena hadn't changed much. But other than that, times had changed. Players and entire coaching staffs came and went.

Except for the fact Maltby, Draper, and McCarty—the Grind Line—were still around and kept providing the heart and soul of the team. Experience, leadership, savvy, and a throwback to a decade earlier when the Wings began a journey to rarified status in professional sports.

"They show the way for the young players in the organization," Henrik Zetterberg said.

There was a brief blip when McCarty was bought out of his contract after the 2004–2005 lockout ended and signed with the Calgary Flames. McCarty stayed there for two years, but was out of hockey for most of the 2007–2008 season when the Flames chose not to re-sign him. Realistically, McCarty began wondering if his career was over.

It wasn't. A lunch one afternoon with Draper midway through the season spurred McCarty to begin working out again. Eventually that led to a contract to play with the minor league Flint Generals, a team Draper had a limited ownership stake in.

"He told me he'd help in whatever way he could," said McCarty, a fan favorite because of his rambunctious behavior on the ice (and off, too). "I'll always appreciate that."

Kirk Maltby and Kris Draper have been part of the Wings' famous "Grind Line" for many years.

McCarty and general manager Ken Holland eventually worked out an agreement in which McCarty would get a try-out with the minor league affiliate Grand Rapids Griffins. Ultimately, he would return to the Wings late in the season and was a positive factor in the playoffs.

"It's like coming home," said McCarty, for a long time one of the league's best enforcers, as well as an effective energy player, capable of igniting a team with a thunderous check. "This is where I always wanted to come back to. This is home."

While McCarty left and returned, Draper and Maltby have been stalwarts. They've contributed to four Stanley Cups won by the Wings, been bridges between the Wings' teams of the past to the present, and formed part of the foundation on which the Wings stand today.

Do they garner the most headlines? Hardly. But they've been there for all the victories, all the celebrations, playing a vital role. The Grind Line is what McCarty, Draper, and Maltby have been called, wearing down and frustrating opponents—not grabbing many headlines, but it's a job they have done well over the years.

"The most important things for me are my family and being a part of the Detroit Red Wings," said Draper before the 2008 season began.

Draper gradually evolved into an all-around player and won the Selke Trophy (given to the league's best defensive forward) after having a magnificent season in 2003–2004. Winning a Selke Trophy was a long way from when the Red Wings acquired Draper for $1—that's right, a single dollar—in 1993 from the Winnipeg Jets.

"One of the best moves we've ever made," general manager Ken Holland said.

Draper has supplied the Wings with all the intangibles needed for a successful team. He's an elite penalty-killer, one of the league's premier face-off men, and has been thrown on the ice to stop many of the game's top offensive stars.

But what is normally unseen is Draper's steadying influence in the locker room. "Everybody knows his work ethic, his dedication, and what a stand-up guy he is," McCarty told the *Detroit News*. "But he's the blood flow in this locker room and has been for a long time."

Twice in Draper's career he was headed toward unrestricted free agency (including after his Selke Trophy–winning season) but never made it into the marketplace. Instead, he re-signed with the Wings, maybe at a discounted price looking back, but never wanting to leave Detroit and the Wings organization.

There was a sense of loyalty and contentment that is rarely seen these days in pro sports.

"This is where I want to finish my career," Draper said. "Why would I go anywhere else? Ownership here has always been committed to winning. The fans are incredible. This has become home."

That same attitude is shared by Maltby.

Maltby, too, has had opportunities to test unrestricted free agency but has never come close to testing the process, seeing what his worth could be on the open market. Instead, Maltby has chosen to remain with the Wings, content in his role and the fact his family has settled in Detroit, and not wanting to leave an organization that has been considered a Stanley Cup contender every season Maltby has put a Wings sweater on.

"Any athlete wants that opportunity to win a championship, and in this organization you have that opportunity," Maltby said. "This is a first-class organization. It's a great situation for my family. I wouldn't want to go anywhere else."

It's not often you can mention one of the three players without mentioning the others. Over the years, they've become intertwined. Their friendship is equally close.

"I remember the day Mac returned here [in the 2008 season], he was coming out of the training room and walking into this [locker] room, and it was like we picked up talking right where we

HAPPY BIRTHDAY

Red Wings players are usually a bit careful around the locker room when it's their birthday. You see, Kris Draper is inevitably around somewhere ready to pounce with a pie crust full of shaving cream.

The tradition started several years ago. Draper has been known to even "cream" a teammate on the ice if needed.

"Some guys are a bit tougher to get than others," said Draper, who plots his strategy meticulously. "You just have to work a little harder."

Draper is proud of once getting Dan Cleary while Cleary was doing an interview for several reporters around his own locker.

MCCARTY'S GOAL

Darren McCarty's breathtaking breakaway goal in the series-clinching Game 4 of the 1997 Finals against Philadelphia was ranked seventh best of all time by ESPN one day in those quickie Web polls.

"Not bad," McCarty said. "Could be higher."

It turned out to be the game-winner in the 2–1 victory, and McCarty still remembers it vividly.

"I was just thinking, **Don't lose the puck**," said McCarty, who is noted more for his rugged play than deft stickhandling. "It was one of those moments that you'll never forget. It was exciting. [It feels] like it was yesterday."

left off when Mac left after his last season here," Maltby said. "That was a little weird. But it was as if no time had passed, or he hadn't left at all.

"All three of us pretty much have the same interests, we're about the same ages, we've known each other for so long. It's been a good fit."

NICKLAS LIDSTROM

This still wasn't a conventional route to go for NHL teams. Drafting players out of Europe in 1989 wasn't as casual and done without a blink as it is today. Team executives had so many questions about Europeans, everything from their supposed lack of toughness, to adapting to the NHL style, to language barriers.

To draft a European was a huge gamble.

So, when it was the Red Wings' turn to pick in the third round, with the 53rd pick overall, Jimmy Devellano, then the Wings' general manager, had a mild quandary on his hands.

Granted, it was the third round, and rarely then, or now, does a player make an impact when drafted in that vicinity. But Devellano could have gone with a North American youngster maybe a little more acclimated to the NHL, or a Swedish prospect a Wings scout by the name of Christer Rockstrom was heavily pushing for, along with Neil Smith, the Wings' director of scouting.

A Swedish kid by the name of Nicklas Lidstrom.

"Our scouts really liked him, I remember Christer really pushing to draft Nicklas," Devellano said. "They said he needed to mature physically, but they felt he had good ability, maybe had the talent to play in the NHL. We were confident not many people [in the NHL] knew about him.

"We felt comfortable taking a gamble."

Thus began a Red Wings pattern of going after European prospects in the lower rounds, hoping to strike gold. Going after young prospects that few other teams yet had much interest or information about. Being one step ahead of everyone else.

All Lidstrom has done from the time he entered the league in 1991 is play at a rarified level few defensemen have ever known—and few ever will. Entering the 2009–2010 season, Lidstrom had won the Norris Trophy (given to the league's best defensemen) six times. Only Bobby Orr (eight Norris trophies) and Doug Harvey (seven) have won the coveted trophy more. Most NHL scouts and analysts feel Lidstrom will surpass Orr and Harvey.

"Nick just keeps getting better," said Larry Murphy, himself an NHL Hall of Fame defenseman, current television analyst, and former defensive partner of Lidstrom's.

Along with being the first European to win the Conn Smythe Trophy (playoff MVP in 2002) and the first European captain to lead his team to a Stanley Cup in 2008, Lidstrom's career has been so decorated, so sublime, that to remember he was a relatively lowly third-round draft pick is astonishing.

NORRIS RARITY

Nicklas Lidstrom has won the Norris Trophy six times, but he's only the third Red Wings defenseman to win the prestigious trophy, given to the league's best defenseman.

The only other two Wings defensemen to win the award are Paul Coffey (1995) and Red Kelly (1953 and 1954).

Lidstrom also won the Conn Smythe Trophy as playoff Most Valuable Player in 2002.

"We had no reason to believe Nicklas would turn out to be such a player," Devellano said. "Let's be realistic."

The greatest defenseman to ever the play in the NHL? Lidstrom is definitely in the conversation. Few doubt there have been one, or two, better than Lidstrom, who in his 17 seasons entering the 2009–2010 schedule has appeared in a staggering 97 percent of the Wings' 1,362 regular-season games (he is missed 32).

"That's for others to judge and speculate on," said Lidstrom, who isn't comfortable talking about himself. "That's for the media. It's not for me."

What's interesting about Lidstrom is the simplicity he plays with. He's almost robotic in his perfect execution of plays, situations on the ice, being at the right place at the right time, and slowing the game down when others around him are scattering about. Rarely does he get beaten. Even rarer is the time Lidstrom is flustered.

That calmness permeates throughout the team.

"What a player," says veteran television analyst Bill Clement, himself an 11-year NHL veteran. "He's a pleasure to watch because he's so subtle, so fine. Always in the right place, always making the right play. Smooth, very smooth. The guy doesn't get rattled."

When the Wings drafted Lidstrom, they were intrigued by his graceful skating, his ability to move the puck, and always find the open skater. Granted, he wasn't a physical force and never has been. But Lidstrom doesn't have to be, never needed to be. Positionally, few players may have ever been better. Some of the best forwards who ever played the game have tried to get around, through, or past Lidstrom and failed. Not because Lidstrom is bigger, or punishes them physically, or has athletic gifts that are far superior. Most of the time, Lidstrom simply out-thinks the opposition. He's efficient. "He's always buying himself time, he never seems under pressure," teammate Johan Franzen said. "He's so calm."

In an era of professional sports when money and a me-first attitude have been so rampant, Lidstrom has been the consummate teammate and representative of the Wings organization.

"As good a player as he is, and he's one of the best of all time, he's that good of a person," coach Mike Babcock said. "You don't have to ask Nick Lidstrom to work. He does it. He does it every day. There's not a lot of guys as good as he is [who] are as zero-maintenance.

"To me, he's the best player in the world," Babcock continued. "I've said that time and again. He drives the bus around here. He's the leader. I'll tell you one thing. I'm a lot better coach when he's in the lineup."

There's no reason to believe Lidstrom's performance on the ice will decline any time soon. Because of the way he plays, and his reliance on factors beyond the physical, Lidstrom could play well into his forties.

"We've had guys like Steve Yzerman, Chris Chelios, at the age of [47] still going strong," general manager Ken Holland said. "There's no reason to think Nick can't continue to play at the level he's at [for the immediate future]. Nick plays such a smart game. It's all about positioning, the ability to move the puck. He rarely puts himself in a position where the other team can finish a check on him.

"Beyond that, it depends on health, and I also think it probably depends on passion. Sometimes as players get older, their priorities change and they don't want to play."

Captain Lidstrom
When Steve Yzerman retired, there was some speculation as to whom the Wings would name captain entering the 2006–2007 season.

Lidstrom was obviously a candidate, and the logical successor to Yzerman, an icon in the Detroit community. But a young star such as Henrik Zetterberg, and storied veterans such as Kris Draper and Chris Chelios, were considered possibilities on a Wings team supposedly in transition.

"He doesn't change," says Yzerman, now the Wings' vice president, who has called Lidstrom the best player he has ever played with. "From 10 years ago, he hasn't changed. He comes in and works hard, practices hard, and he's very professional. He's a great representative for the organization."

Taking a chance on Nicklas Lidstrom in the 1989 NHL Draft has paid off handsomely for the Red Wings.

"Whenever we face a little adversity, or controversy maybe, the one guy everyone's going to look to is Nick," Kris Draper said. "He realizes that. He's pretty even-keel. Game in and game out, Nick is going to do what he does. He doesn't have to be a rah-rah guy, either. We've got enough guys in the dressing room that can do that.

"But what Steve did was provide a calming influence for our hockey club. Nick has been a calming influence when he's on the ice. He's going to have to do that in the dressing room, too, now."

At one point in the late-1990s, Lidstrom briefly considered moving his young and growing family back to Sweden. He felt it would be best for his children to be around the Swedish culture, language, and relatives back in Europe. He was adamant about the fact it wasn't anything against the city of Detroit, or the Wings

EXCLUSIVE COMPANY

When Nicklas Lidstrom won his sixth Norris Trophy, awarded to the league's best defenseman, in 2008, that put Lidstrom in some heady company. Only Bobby Orr, with eight Norris trophies, and Doug Harvey, with seven, have more.

Lidstrom passed Ray Bourque, one of the defensemen he had great respect for when he entered the NHL. Bourque had five Norris trophies.

organization, it was just, simply, a family decision. But Lidstrom began realizing that his family was beginning to put down strong roots in Detroit, too.

"We're very comfortable here," said Lidstrom, now with four school-age sons, each of whom is active in athletics, including hockey. "This is becoming home."

Staying with the Wings organization was important, too. Winning the Stanley Cup in 2008 was Lidstrom's fourth with the Wings, and rarely have the Wings begun a season with Lidstrom when the team wasn't considered a serious contender for a championship.

Not many players have been able to thrive in such a consistently positive environment.

"Playing for the Red Wings, you always have an opportunity to win the Stanley Cup," said Lidstrom, voted by the *Hockey News* in 2007 as the best European player ever. "As a player, that's all you can ask for."

"Steve Yzerman was a guy who led by example," Holland said. "Nick's the same way. He comes to the rink every day, works hard, he's a competitor, and throughout his career, when the game's on the line, he's been a guy that's stepped up and really played his best."

Milestone Accomplishment

When the Red Wings defeated the Pittsburgh Penguins to win the 2008 Stanley Cup, Lidstrom became the first European captain to ever hoist the famed trophy.

"It's something I'm very proud of," Lidstrom said. "I've been over here for a long time and I watched Steve Yzerman hoist it for three times in the past, and I'm very proud of being the first European. I'm very proud of being a captain of the Red Wings. There's so much history with the team and great tradition."

More than anything, Lidstrom is humble. In today's sports world, it's a refreshing change of pace. He doesn't talk about himself, he doesn't boast, and he never gets in trouble. He's respectful of his opponents. He takes his role as leader of the Red Wings seriously.

Lidstrom doesn't seek the spotlight. "That's not me," he said.

Others will vouch for Lidstrom's greatness for him, though. Nashville Predators coach Barry Trotz, whose team has had to play against Lidstrom for many years, marvels at the ease with which he plays the game.

Most hockey people will say the same thing. As difficult a game as hockey is, Lidstrom has the ability to slow things down, process, and make the correct play over and over.

Only the truly elite are blessed with that ability.

"So efficient, he always makes the right decisions," Trotz said. "He's what a star should be. He's a classy individual. When you consider all the awards and records, and the type of person he is, what a credit to the game he is."

"You don't appreciate how good he is until you see him day after day, every practice, every game," said Mathieu Schneider, a former teammate now with the Montreal Canadiens.

But, again, Lidstrom shrugs off the praise and plaudits with an uncomfortable smile and a shrug.

"There's a calmness to him," Wings forward Johan Franzen said. "He makes everyone else on the ice with him calm. Everyone knows about the awards he's won. But it's that ability to calm things down, that's another thing that makes him the player he is."

THE BAD

NOT THIS TIME

Strange how similar the ending was. Except this time, it was the Red Wings feeling the sting of defeat and the Pittsburgh Penguins piling onto each other in celebration.

One year ago, the Penguins had come within inches and mere seconds of tying the game—Marian Hossa's shot attempt just missed dribbling past Wings goalie Chris Osgood—and the Wings celebrated a Stanley Cup victory.

The image of Hossa, then with the Penguins but who would sign with the Wings as a free agent several weeks later, sitting sullen along the boards and watching the Wings celebrating stuck in many people's memories. A definition of how close the Penguins had come.

Now, a year later, with Pittsburgh leading 2–1 in Game 7 of a spine-tingling Finals series, the reverse would happen.

The Wings were pressing the Penguins. They had pulled Osgood, had an extra attacker, and were desperate to tie the game and force overtime. Penguins goalie Marc-Andre Fleury was outstanding, as he'd been throughout the game. But with two seconds left in the game, Fleury may have been at his best.

A puck caromed off to Nicklas Lidstrom, who pinched from the point, sensing a rebound may come his way. Few defensemen are better at anticipating this type of play than Lidstrom, one of the greatest defensemen ever.

With the crowd roaring, both benches standing on their feet, the excitement unbearable, Lidstrom fired a shot that seemed to be headed into a vacant area around Fleury until, suddenly, Fleury slid across and made a pad save. A fine save, but under the circumstances, in Game 7 of the Stanley Cup Finals, with the game on the line, a save that will be replayed on future Stanley Cup highlight shows forever and ever.

Two ticks of the clock later, the Penguins were dogpiling. It was the Red Wings sitting on their bench forlornly looking at the joyous scene on the Joe Louis Arena ice.

"It's kind of the exact opposite of the last game last year," Osgood said.

Lidstrom felt he had the game-tying goal on his stick. But Fleury spoiled it.

"The puck kind of squirted to me," Lidstrom said. "Their defensemen and forward came out in front of me. The goalie dove across, and I hit him in the chest."

The fact the Wings had gotten this far, to this ending in Game 7, was a testament to their character. The playoffs had taken their toll. Lidstrom required surgery on his testicles after getting speared in the Western Conference Finals and missed the last two games of that five-game victory over Chicago. Pavel Datsyuk, a league Most Valuable Player finalist, missed the last three games against Chicago and the first four games of the Pittsburgh series because of a charley horse and foot injuries. Brian Rafalski played through a herniated disc. Kris Draper was bothered by a throat injury that forced him to miss games early in the playoffs. Tomas Kopecky was lost after the second-round series against Anaheim after fracturing his orbital bone in a fight.

The Wings were a battered team. And it finally caught up to them against Pittsburgh. "We looked out of gas pretty much all series," coach Mike Babcock said. "We competed, and I thought we tried. But I never thought we got to the level we'd have liked to. The guys that were injured on our team this year never got their game back to the level it could be. And they were significant players for us."

Hossa's Miseries

Around the corner from the Red Wings locker room, there was chaos in the Pittsburgh room, with music blaring, players passing the Stanley Cup one to another, and the victory liquids being sprayed in every direction.

Marian Hossa may have heard some of it wandering in the back of the Wings' room. How tough, how bitter it must have been to hear those joyous emotions.

That's what Hossa wanted to be part of. That's why he came to Detroit, left Pittsburgh as a free agent after the 2008 series, feeling the Wings gave him his best chance at a Stanley Cup.

Or, how about the traditional handshake line afterward? Facing the teammates and friends he spurned, and watching the Penguins hoist the Stanley Cup?

"No, they didn't say anything," said Hossa, of the handshakes with the Penguins.

Pittsburgh players said they didn't have to. Hossa realized he picked the wrong team to be on.

"He's a great guy, and I have nothing but respect for him," Penguins defenseman Hal Gill said. "We wanted him to stay in Pitt, but that's the way it works."

Hossa didn't score in the entire seven-game series. With regular center/linemate Pavel Datsyuk bothered with a foot injury, Hossa couldn't find seams, and scoring chances became rare. Particularly in Game 6, with a chance to win the Stanley Cup in Pittsburgh, Hossa was invisible on the ice.

In Game 7, back in Detroit, Hossa played hard, aggressively, but couldn't help the Wings pull a victory out.

His decision last summer didn't pan out.

"That's life. Sometimes you make choices," said Hossa before a throng of media wanting to find out what went wrong. "It could go both ways. One goal could make a difference. If you score one more, you can celebrate, but if not, they're celebrating. That's life. You just have to move on. It's a great life experience.

"Regret? I don't regret it. It could be different circumstances if I sign in Pittsburgh and they probably couldn't sign some other players and they would be a different team. So we could sit for hours discussing this, but it could be a different team, could be different things, so I don't regret the decision."

Several weeks later, with the Red Wings strangled by the salary cap, Hossa signed a long-term contract with the Chicago Blackhawks.

Duck Warning

Many in the Red Wings' front office, and quite a few Wings players, pinpoint the Anaheim series as the one that did them in.

Sure, the Penguins defeated the Wings in the Stanley Cup Finals, and they give the Penguins full credit for that. But it was Anaheim who delivered the body blows in the second round of the playoffs that ultimately made the Wings stagger and fall to Pittsburgh two rounds later in the Stanley Cup Finals.

Looking back, no one was entirely surprised it happened that way.

The Ducks are a physical, tough, veteran team that had just defeated top-seeded San Jose in the first round. They were entering their series against the Wings playing as well as anyone in the league.

With three minutes left in Game 7, Dan Cleary batted a puck in front of the Anaheim goalie Jonas Hiller through Hiller's legs and broke a 3–3 tie.

The Ducks swarmed in the end, but the Wings and goalie Chris Osgood stood tall.

This wasn't easy.

"I just thought it was a good series, the best series I've been in since I've coached in the league," Babcock said. "For sure, the hardest series."

That was mainly because of Anaheim's experience in these types of situations. "What people don't understand is the people that have won know what it takes to win and they don't give in," said Babcock, alluding to Anaheim veterans such as Chris Pronger, Scott Niedermayer, and Teemu Selanne. "They just keep coming, and that's why they were so hard to get rid of. It was a real tough series and a good series."

No Excuses

For the Red Wings, the scene after the loss to Pittsburgh was unnatural. Usually it's the Wings basking in the glow of another series victory. There's loud celebrations in the Joe Louis Arena locker room.

Not the silence that was excruciating after this loss.

"I don't want to stand here and make excuses. They beat us, that's the bottom line," Chris Osgood said. "We couldn't find a way to win."

Everyone in the city of Detroit was waiting to celebrate. The litany of awful news coming as of late: the endless layoffs in the automotive sector, bankruptcies of General Motors and Chrysler, unemployment at record levels. The city needed some good news.

The Wings were going to provide a brief respite. And they did, during another long, spirited playoff run.

It just didn't ultimately end the way they wanted.

"It's hard for people to believe. We don't take winning for granted," Osgood said. "We know how hard it is. We do have a good team, but it's very, very difficult to win in this league. We were pushed every series. We wish it was us and not them [Pittsburgh]."

Said Kirk Maltby, who like Osgood had been around for multiple Stanley Cup victories, "We've been on the other end of it a lot. To be on the other end of it, to come this far and not finish it off, especially at home, to get one goal in each of our last two games.... No excuses."

THE NORRIS FAMILY

Rarely has an ownership been so welcomed and cheered at the start, and yet end up with so much disappointment, apathy, and bitterness.

When James E. Norris Sr. and his family purchased the Red Wings in 1932, they did so at a time when professional hockey in Detroit was teetering on the brink of extinction. Hockey simply wasn't catching on in Detroit. Interest was minimal, and the organization was floundering on and off the ice.

For sure, success wasn't being achieved. The Falcons, as the hockey team was called, had missed the playoffs four of its first six seasons in operation under Jack Adams.

With the economy still uncertain, Olympia Stadium had gone into receivership, as attendance and revenues sagged. Adams had met payroll with money out of his own wallet on several occasions. Newspaper reports speculated on the Falcons moving to another city, or folding altogether.

To the rescue came Norris, a grain and shipping magnate who used to play junior-level hockey while growing up in Montreal. Norris played on a team called the Winged Wheelers in the Montreal Amateur Athletic Association.

When the opportunity to purchase the Falcons became available, Norris pounced. After purchasing the team, he renamed it the Wings, to represent the city of Detroit's ties with the auto industry. The logo, Norris decided, would be a winged wheel, a tip of the hat to Norris' Winged Wheelers youth team.

Upon taking control, he set down his expectations quickly and boldly. He gave Adams, who was gradually becoming the figurehead of the franchise, one year to turn the fortunes of the team around. Adams, a forceful figure who wasn't afraid to make bold moves, went about changing the culture of the Wings under Norris. What helped was the fact Norris expanded the budget and allowed Adams to better the quality of personnel on the Wings.

The Red Wings finished 25–15–8 in Norris' first season as owner, good for 58 points. The team finished tied for first in the American Division with Boston.

Adams purchased players such as goalie John Ross Roach and forward Carl Voss before the season began, and both made significant contributions—particularly Roach, a Vezina Trophy–caliber goalie, who played all 48 games and had a 1.88 goals-against average. Roach finished second in the voting for the Vezina (Voss, incidentally, had six goals).

Also, Adams passed his own personal test in the eyes of Norris, who expanded the payroll further. Adams rewarded the faith Norris showed by taking the Red Wings into the Stanley Cup Finals.

To expand his footprint in the NHL, Norris purchased Chicago Stadium in 1936 and later the Chicago Blackhawks and began a period that left many Wings fans and players frustrated. The Blackhawks had been one of the dregs of the Original Six era. Rarely were they winners, and interest was low. With Adams running the Wings, this situation actually suited him well. Adams didn't like the idea of keeping a roster identical from season to season, preferring to keep everyone on edge. Trading quality players to an organization like the Blackhawks also strengthened Chicago. Players such as Johnny Wilson, one of the big-name Wings who was traded to Chicago, told Paul Harris in Harris' book, *Heroes of Hockeytown*, that Adams probably ran both teams.

"The Norrises were absentee owners, and Jack Adams ran the whole [Wings] team," Wilson said. "As a matter of fact, I sometimes wonder if Jack Adams didn't run Chicago as well because we were so successful here, they [the Norrises] used to ask Jack about what happened in Chicago. And they funneled a lot of players from here into Chicago because they owned both teams."

The fate of the Wings organization, though, was about to take a dramatic turn.

James Norris Sr. suffered a heart attack and passed away during the 1952–1953 season. The man who saved professional hockey in Detroit and helped take the organization to heights never experienced before left the organization's future in the hands of his children, Bruce and Marguerite (who would become the NHL's first female executive).

Things, as expected, would change. The two Norris children had not been getting along personally, and the conflict would extend into the hockey business. Further, the Norrises had little interaction with Jack Adams before their father passed away, and working with Adams would be an eye-opening experience.

Adams stopped coaching in 1947, leaving the post in the hands of Tommy Ivan, who had been coaching in the minor leagues.

Adams would soon show his tyrannical ways. After Ivan won the Stanley Cup in 1953–1954 with the Wings, he was moved, along with forward Metro Prystai, to the Blackhawks. The move would make the Blackhawks stronger, but was just one of a series of moves that began the Wings' slide.

Bruce Norris took over running the Wings from his sister in 1955. The change further affected the Wings adversely. Norris was unable to harness Adams, who traded players such as Ted Lindsay (whom Adams traded to Chicago to reacquire Wilson), Terry Sawchuk, and others. Adams traded Sawchuk to Boston in 1955, but changed his mind and brought him back in 1957 by sending top prospect Johnny Bucyk to the Bruins. Sawchuk, though still a quality goalie, never matched the level of his early years. Bucyk, conversely, would score 545 goals in 21 seasons with the Bruins after scoring 11 in two seasons with the Wings.

Norris was finally able to remove Adams in 1963 in favor of Sid Abel, a former star player expected to bring stability to the front office. But the constant shuffling of personnel, moving star players from the roster, and the lack of quality young players began to take its toll.

They reached the Stanley Cup Finals three times (1963, 1964, and 1966) and reached the playoffs two other times (1970 and 1978) between 1963 and 1982, when Mike Ilitch bought the team from Norris. When Ilitch took over, he was immediately hailed as a savior, willing to do whatever was necessary to bring winning hockey back to Detroit.

Sounds similar to when Norris Sr. bought the team, doesn't it?

JACK ADAMS

It used to be coaches had all the control, ruling with an iron fist, making decisions without any regard to players' feelings, status, or ability.

Jack Adams was a coach like that. It didn't matter if your name was Ted Lindsay or Terry Sawchuk (future Hall of Famers) or the last man on the roster. Adams didn't care: to him, every player was the same.

The players were going to be pushed and prodded to their absolute best. Usually loudly, and maybe with orange slices being thrown at them between periods. And if a trade was needed, they'd be sent.

Chances are, Adams likely wouldn't be an effective coach today. Not with unions and player associations, multimillion-dollar contracts, and coaches being the ones who are disposable and easy to replace, instead of a team of millionaire players.

Adams would be aghast these days.

The way Adams ruled the Wings at least brought unity into the locker room. "When I played in Detroit there was no dissension among players," former Red Wing Carl Liscombe said. "We all hated Jack Adams."

Adams actually began his Detroit career as general manager/ coach of the Detroit Cougars during the 1927–1928 season. The team became the Falcons three years later, but the name change didn't help. Economically, the organization was a mess, not allowing Adams any flexibility to acquire better-quality players. In fact, Adams was known to meet the team's payroll with his own money, admirably doing what he could to keep the organization afloat.

He would finally get an opportunity to play on a more even field in 1932, when James Norris Sr., a shipping magnate who was born in Canada and played minor league hockey, bought the Detroit franchise.

Norris Sr. changed the team's name from Falcons to Red Wings, changed the team's logo to a winged wheel in part to reflect Detroit's love affair with autos, and most important, was willing to put money into the team.

The downside, for Adams, was Norris' stern laying of the law himself. Norris gave Adams one year to prove himself as a worthy general manager/coach and wanted to see results. Adams proved up to the challenge. The Wings finished 25–15–8 under the first season of the Norris regime, with Adams finding and coaching talent that proved worth the price. For example, before the season began Adams purchased goalie John Ross Roach from the New York Rangers for the price of $11,000, an extravagant sum in the 1930s. Roach proved a successful acquisition. He played all 48 games that season and had a 1.88 goals-against average, while finishing second in the Vezina Trophy balloting. Adams' second season under Norris would see the Wings reach the Stanley Cup Finals.

Having proven himself in the eyes of Norris, Adams would go on to control the Wings with a strong, unyielding hand.

"He was a misunderstood man in some ways, but there was no doubt in the fact he ran the team he felt was best," said Budd Lynch, a longtime Red Wings broadcaster.

Adams coached the team through the 1946–1947 season and was the Wings' general manager until the 1962–1963 season. With Adams as GM, the Wings won seven Stanley Cups (three with Adams as the coach). The Wings finished first overall in the league or division 12 times.

The organization signed and developed players such as Gordie Howe, Sid Abel, Ted Lindsay, Red Kelly, Alex Delvecchio, Terry Sawchuk, Glenn Hall, Harry Lumley, and Jack Stewart under the direction of Adams.

Howe always respected Adams. "The Red Wings' tradition started with Jack Adams," Howe wrote in the foreword to the *Detroit News'* book *Stanley's Back*. "It's why Jack Adams was so great. The pride is always there.... Jack Adams was very demanding."

Still, even with all that talent, Adams wasn't satisfied. He disliked the idea of entering a new season with the same roster from the season before—never mind how successful that season was, even if a Stanley Cup was won. Adams used the formula after the Wings won the Stanley Cup in 1937...and finished last the next season.

After the Wings won the 1950 Stanley Cup, Adams traded Lumley and Stewart to the Chicago Blackhawks. After winning the Cup in 1952, Leo Reise was traded to the New York Rangers. After the 1954 victory, it was Metro Prystai who was shipped to Chicago. After the 1955 victory, Adams dealt Sawchuk, Johnny Wilson, Tony Leswick, and Glen Skov.

That madness probably wouldn't go over in the modern sports world with sports talk radio, Internet forums, chat rooms, and salary caps. But Adams felt he knew better than anyone when a player he had scouted and developed was beginning to lose his skills. He also liked the idea of new players rejuvenating and energizing a roster.

He demanded maximum effort. In the book *Hockeytown Heroes*, Adams is said to have addressed players with train tickets to minor league cities in his coat pocket, easy to see, while berating a team after a bad game. There are also stories of Adams throwing orange slices at players to get their attention, and it would be guys like Howe and Lindsay as often as the checkers who would ultimately smell like orange juice.

For many players and fans, any patience for Adams would disappear when he traded Lindsay in 1957 with the issue being more about politics than anything else. Lindsay was attempting to begin the NHL Players Association, something that irked Adams to no end. Adams felt that would take away his, and every other manager's, authority and wanted to make sure Lindsay knew a union was unacceptable.

"Adams took it upon himself to rid the team of 'disloyal' players," said Howe in his book *My Hockey Memories*. "With Lindsay gone from the dressing room, [the Wings] were left to face down Adams without their spiritual leader."

GOALIE OVERLOAD

The Red Wings had just defeated the Nashville Predators in Game 5 in the first round of the 2004 playoffs, and goalie Curtis Joseph was meeting the media. Joseph had just held the Predators to one goal in a 4–1 win, giving the Wings a 3–2 lead in a series the Wings would ultimately win behind Joseph's shutout in the next game. None of those items were particularly surprising, except the fact Joseph was the starting goalie.

Joseph, a big-money free-agent acquisition just the season before, had found out before the 2003–2004 season the Wings had re-signed Dominik Hasek, who came out of retirement. The Wings attempted to trade Joseph, but found no takers for his $8 million salary (which was what Hasek was making, too) with a lockout in the NHL all but certain in a few months.

The Wings also still had Manny Legace on the roster.

"It's been a different year, no question," Joseph said.

It most certainly was a different year, that final season before the NHL locked its doors for an entire season. One that was as unlikely as it was a soap opera, it seemed, each and every day.

Joseph never really endeared himself to the Red Wings' fans. Cujo, as was his nickname, wept at his farewell press conference in Toronto and consistently went to far lengths to say what a great town Toronto was and how he missed the city. He seemed lukewarm about actually playing in Detroit for the Red Wings.

He followed Hasek, who won a Stanley Cup in 2002 with the Wings. Joseph never could get all the fans on his side with inconsistent play, and a four-game sweep at the hands of the Anaheim Ducks in 2003 didn't help. He wasn't really the reason for the loss to the Ducks, as much as it was the otherworldly goaltending of Anaheim's Jean-Sebastian Giguere. Winner of the Conn Smythe Trophy (playoff Most Valuable Player) that spring, Giguere almost singlehandedly took the Ducks to the Finals. He was particularly sensational against the Wings, with Joseph feeling the heat because of it.

Still, the Wings had signed Joseph to a three-year contract worth $24 million and weren't thinking of sending him anywhere. Until, that is, Hasek contacted the Wings and said he was interested in ending his retirement. Wings coach Dave Lewis flew to Vienna to meet with Hasek and gauge his commitment to returning.

The Wings were satisfied. They weren't worried about Hasek not having played for an entire season and not having worked out that much heading into training camp. The organization remembered his last appearance in an NHL uniform, hoisting the 2002 Stanley Cup. "We made our decision," general manager Ken Holland said.

The Wings were intent on going with Hasek and Legace. They wanted to trade Joseph, but the fact Joseph had undergone ankle surgery complicated trade discussions as much as the salary involved. So the Wings were forced to keep all three through training camp. Then, into the start of the season. And so on, and so on, and so on.

"It made for a real difficult situation," said Legace, who figured he'd get about five to 10 games of action. "Those are two goalies who are used to being the No. 1 guy."

BAD SIGNING

The Wings felt they had signed the shut-down defenseman they'd always been looking for when they picked up free agent Uwe Krupp after the 1998 season.

But Krupp was rarely healthy with the Wings, even allegedly hurting his back one season because of a supposed dog-sledding incident.

Krupp and the Wings went to court over various issues relating to his injuries.

The day the two finally met wearing the Wings jersey was one to remember. Joseph was sitting near his locker when Hasek came walking down the hallway leading into the locker room. Both were startled to see each other. They attempted a bit of small talk—Hasek asking Joseph about the ankle surgery, Joseph asking Hasek how he felt—but it was all terribly awkward. Especially with several reporters still in the locker room after a midweek practice.

According to several Wings players, that may have been the first and last time the two goalies spoke to each other. The three goalies' lockers were rearranged to have Legace in the middle between the two veterans. "Jimmy Buffer," Legace would call himself.

The Hasek experiment didn't nearly go as well the second time around. He was limited to 14 games the entire season because of lingering groin problems and never could get completely healthy. Then, one afternoon in January, after practice had ended, Hasek skated out to the ice to presumably test his groin. What was odd was the fact some players seemed to be aiming shots high, at Hasek's head. It seemed they were trying to hurt him, rather than help him back into the lineup. Evidently, the Wings already knew. Hasek was about to call it a season.

"That's it for the season," Hasek said by his locker to a large media throng. "I cannot handle any more. My groin, it cannot handle it. I hoped for two months it would get better every day. But it didn't get better. It got even worse last week."

So the Wings were left with Joseph and Legace. Suddenly, the team was more than happy to still have Joseph, who was putting together a fine season. "We're very, very lucky that he's been a real pro through this," Holland said. "And luckily for us that nobody claimed him [on waivers at the start of the season]."

Joseph had certainly gone through a lot. He was sent to the minor leagues and was playing for the Wings' minor league affiliate in Grand Rapids on December 8 after clearing waivers. The next day, Joseph was on a bus to Cleveland, along with the rest of the Griffins, when news of Hasek bothered with his groin filtered down.

With Legace also unavailable at the time because of injury, suddenly the Wings needed Joseph back. Associate coach Barry Smith called Joseph and said he'd be returning with forward Jiri Hudler, a 19-year-old forward who spoke little English at the time. They were to meet up with the Red Wings in Buffalo.

So Joseph rented a Chevy Cavalier (it was the only vehicle available) by the Cleveland hotel the Griffins were staying in and drove with Hudler to Buffalo.

"I remember that real good," said Hudler, years later. "The car was so small, he could barely put his equipment in it. He didn't have a suit, either. Just a sweat suit. I didn't talk much, and I was pretty tired. The way I remember it, I slept most of the way. He just kept driving.

"I do remember I scored my first NHL goal in that game [in Buffalo]."

And Joseph backstopped the Wings to a 7–2 victory.

"It's a challenge certainly, but you have to rise to the occasion," Joseph said.

Soon after reclaiming the starting job, Joseph twisted his other ankle and was forced out of the lineup again.

Legace wound up as the starter all the way into the playoffs, until Game 4 of the Nashville series, when Joseph replaced a struggling Legace.

Joseph would carry the Wings past Nashville, but Calgary defeated Detroit in six games. Calgary goalie Miikka Kiprusoff, like Giguere the season before, simply outplayed Joseph, who again, didn't play altogether badly...just not good enough.

After the lockout ended, the Wings didn't re-sign Joseph, who wound up heading to Phoenix. After a brief stop in Calgary, Joseph returned to Toronto as a backup on July 2, 2008, some six years after leaving for Detroit.

"If I had to do it all over again, I probably would not do it," Joseph told Toronto reporters about leaving for Detroit. "I didn't play well my first year in Detroit. Maybe my heart was still in Toronto."

PLANE HORROR

The road trip looked imposing even on paper, one that would certainly be tiring and test the Red Wings mentally and physically. The Wings were scheduled to go from Dallas to San Jose, to Vancouver, spend a few days in Phoenix, then play in Edmonton and Calgary.

What made the January 2001 trip more eventful, memorable, and even downright scary, though, was a plane scare on the flight from San Jose to Vancouver.

"Everything was normal, and then all of a sudden you hear [what sounded like] an engine stalling," said forward Darren McCarty, who was on that nerve-wracking flight.

The Wings' plane is a DC-9 called Redbird II. To that point, the team had never experienced any problems with it. No malfunctions, no real maintenance issues. But approximately 30 minutes into the flight from San Jose to Vancouver, there were real issues. Players heard rattling, bumping noises. One engine apparently stalled. Then it came on. Then, the other engine came to a standstill. The entire saga didn't last long, mere minutes, but seemed terrifyingly long.

"Some guys were screaming, some weren't, but there were a lot that were [screaming]," said McCarty, who considers himself a calm flier, normally, but was admittedly a bit nervous during this particular instance. "I was as calm as you could probably be at that point. Some guys weren't very calm."

Just not knowing what exactly was happening was the worst part. The pilots were giving as much information as possible, but obviously had larger problems to correct.

Wings players, coaches, training staff, and broadcasters were all hoping for the best. Some players clung to their seats. Others, according to several players, were holding pictures of their wives and kids, just in case the plane was going to go down.

"It's one of those things where you're thinking, *Is this it?*" said McCarty, noting the plane was essentially gliding through the air at one point, as pilots raced to start and restart the engines. "You begin to wonder whether that'll be it. Everything seemed fine, and then when the other one [engine] went out, you really begin to wonder.

"But I can't say enough about the job the pilots did. They kept us abreast of what was going on. Once everything kind of settled down, that's when a lot of beers came out. I didn't [drink], but everyone else did."

"I don't think anyone could believe this was really happening," said Ken Kal, the Wings' radio broadcaster.

McCarty never really felt or noticed the plane dip or fall. "But it was gliding, that's the best way I can describe it," McCarty said. "Just going through the air. It's something you don't want to experience again, that's for sure."

When the Wings finally did land, that's when more of the hoopla took shape. The plane made an emergency landing at the Sacramento airport. The Associated Press had sent out a story about the Wings having a major in-flight emergency, which was picked up by local northern California television stations, but also by Detroit television. Each of the local Detroit stations cut into their 11:30 PM regular broadcasts to announce the Wings were experiencing problems on their flight and were about to make an emergency landing.

When the plane landed without incident, the passengers were greeted by television trucks, fire trucks, and the police, all making it seem very surreal—maybe like something off a movie set. "I always compare it to the *Die Hard* movie," McCarty said. "It really was amazing. You had all these ambulances and fire engines and stuff like that. It really was like *Die Hard*. Lights everywhere. I guess they were prepared for the worst.

"But like I said before, the pilots did an incredible job. You never know what'll happen, that's for sure. You see what the guy flying the plane onto the Hudson [River in 2009] did, how calm he was, and that's an amazing story. You see how calm he was, listening to the tapes. I guess those guys are trained for stuff like that. You just hope you're never part of it."

Once on the ground, it was up to John Hahn, the Wings' director of media relations, to find a hotel capable of housing the Wings that evening. Hahn found the Sacramento Hyatt was available, and off the Wings went...in several taxis.

For all this commotion, though, the Wings had another game that very next evening (actually, at this point, later that evening) in Vancouver. They were able to get another chartered plane to arrive in Sacramento late in the morning, and the team arrived in Vancouver at approximately 2:00 PM for a 7:00 PM game.

"Not the way you want to prepare for a game," said defenseman Mathieu Dandenault, who agreed the original San Jose to Vancouver flight was "challenging."

Talking to the media before the game, coach Scotty Bowman, typical of his straightforward approach and lack of emotion (at least in public), said the entire saga was ultimately a minor inconvenience. Captain Steve Yzerman said the experience wasn't as scary as was being portrayed in the media.

The Wings appeared tired and little shell-shocked as they prepared their equipment about two hours before game time against the Canucks.

Amazingly, the Wings won.

"It was kind of a strange game day for us," Brendan Shanahan said. "But we knew a lot of people would be ready to make excuses for us if we didn't play well. We took it as challenge to come out and have a big game."

They flew to Phoenix shortly after for a little sunshine and deserved relaxation. There were no problems on the flight. The flight was smooth, without incident, and the Wings could savor a victory that was as impressive, considering the circumstances, as any the team ever had.

There were no problems with the flight, whatsoever.

"But we kept looking out the window, just in case," defenseman Steve Duchesne said.

2006: WINGS STUMBLE AGAIN

After such a record-breaking season, with so many breakthrough performances, the overwhelming scene of 2006 will be of Steve Yzerman walking through the tunnel at Rexall Place in Edmonton after another terribly disappointing Wings playoff exit.

The Red Wings trudged single file through the tunnel to their locker room, the crowd noise growing louder by the second.

The Wings were the No. 1 seed, the Oilers the No. 8 seed.

The Wings earned 124 points, dominated throughout the season with 58 victories (including a record 31 road wins), had the best record in the league. But for the third consecutive playoff season, they were eliminated in either the first or second round.

The first round, this time.

"I'm disappointed and I'm stunned," general manager Ken Holland said.

"I'm shocked we're in this situation," said coach Mike Babcock, echoing the thoughts of many of his players. "We felt we had done a lot of great things to prepare. That was our focus, to build a foundation for this part of the year. But we didn't do enough good things. They [the Oilers] found a way to win, and we didn't."

Losing was one thing, but seeing Yzerman go off the ice for the final time, without an opportunity to play in a Stanley Cup Final, that hurt the most.

Yzerman missed both Games 4 and 5 with a back injury and was arguably the Wings' most dangerous forward in Game 6. He nearly tied the game late against Oilers goalie Dwayne Roloson, who clearly outplayed the Wings' Manny Legace in the series.

Yzerman would retire later that summer. But as he stood in the emptying Wings locker room after this game, the pain of this loss sunk in by the second. "It's such a fun game to play, the more times you're in situations like that, the more you come to enjoy it," he said. "I don't know that I'm ever not going to want to play. But I'll have a decision soon."

Babcock admired what Yzerman gave the Wings in the series. "He has, obviously, been a great leader in the sport and a courageous competitor," Babcock said. "He probably should not have played [Game 6], but he perceives this as his team, and he wanted to lead them, and he did a good job for us tonight. There's no way you can win three Cups and be as dominant in the league as he has without having something special about you. The good players have something extra."

How did the Wings inexplicably lose this series to Edmonton?

First, the goaltending. The Wings outshot the Oilers 238–156, but Roloson, a late-season acquisition, was much more effective than Legace, who earned his first opportunity as a No. 1 goalie in the playoffs.

Legace was despondent in the locker room after Game 6. "I feel like going home and hanging myself," Legace said. "It's hard to take."

Legace seemed capable of taking the Wings deep into the playoffs. A career backup, he was headed to unrestricted free agency and was confident a good run in the playoffs would earn him a big contract from the Wings. Instead, the first-round loss convinced the Wings Legace wasn't the starting goalie for them. The team brought back Dominik Hasek in the summer to form a tandem with Chris Osgood.

"Manny played fine, but obviously we're all judged on wins and losses," Holland said.

Babcock gave lukewarm support, at best, of Legace's performance after the Game 6 loss. "The guy who is good enough wins, and their guy was better, he won," Babcock said.

Then, there was the lack of scoring up front. Aside from Henrik Zetterberg, who slashed any thought of his not being a prime time player with six goals in the six games, no other key Wings forward produced offense. Pavel Datsyuk, Brendan Shanahan, Tomas Holmstrom, Jason Williams, Mikael Samuelsson, and Kris Draper combined for three goals (one each from Shanahan, Williams, and Holmstrom).

"A lot of guys up front didn't score for us," Babcock said. "We don't want to be about winning in the regular season and not being able to get it done in the playoffs. We'll take a good look at our team. You have to score more goals than we did, but we didn't keep it out of our net, either."

Datsyuk and Shanahan received the brunt of the criticism from media and fans after the loss, but Holland stood behind the pair. Datsyuk was returning from a deep thigh bruise and didn't return until Game 2 of the series (after having missed the last three weeks of the regular season). Datsyuk also saw his goalless streak in the playoffs extend to 26 games. Holland reiterated his confidence behind Datsyuk, though. "I can tell you right now, today, there are no plans to trade Pavel Datsyuk," said Holland about the player who was speculated as trade bait for an elite goalie. "With Pavel and Hank, we have a 1-2 punch that are great players, that really care, that compete, and they love hockey."

Shanahan was a linemate of Datsyuk's, but the chemistry they had during the regular season (Shanahan was a 40-goal scorer) didn't reappear quickly enough in the Edmonton series. Shanahan, then 37, would leave the Wings and sign a free-agent contract with the New York Rangers in the summer.

Holland felt there were plenty of positives to take out of the 2006 season. While Datsyuk and Zetterberg continued to turn into dominant NHL players, the Wings also found players such as Mikael Samuelsson, Niklas Kronwall, Dan Cleary, and Andreas Lilja, all of whom turned into effective regulars for low salaries—a must in the new salary-cap era. Chris Osgood was a steady performer in net.

Holland preached patience.

"I look back to 1996, when Scotty Bowman was our coach, and we won 62 games during the regular season, then lost in the playoffs [to Colorado]," Holland said. "We stuck with it, and we went on to win the next two Stanley Cups, working around the core of that team.

"I like the core of this team."

2001 ODYSSEY

This was going to be another breather. The Red Wings opened the 2001 playoffs with a first-round series against the Los Angeles Kings, a team the Wings had swept the previous year and certainly looked primed for another quick exit again.

The Wings were coming off an 111-point season, had what appeared to be a fine mix of veterans and young players, and seemed on a collision course to meet archrival Colorado in the Western Conference Finals again.

And, after defeating the Kings in two straight games to start the series, another sweep looked entirely possible.

But there are no guarantees in professional sports. And, especially, in hockey.

The Kings would win four consecutive games, win the series, and cause the Wings organization to do a fair amount of soul-searching.

"It was stunning. That series loss hurt," said Jimmy Devellano, the Wings' senior vice president, in his book *The Road to Hockeytown*. "That series loss also resulted in us really examining our roster to see why we had failed so quickly."

Devellano said the organization was moving further away from the Stanley Cup, instead of closer.

Where did it all turn in this series against Los Angeles? Many point to the final minutes of Game 4, at the Staples Center. The Kings had won Game 3 to cut the Wings' series lead to 2–1. Though the Wings were again controlling Game 4 and had a 3–0 lead, Los Angeles scored three times in the game's final six minutes (5:14 to be exact) to send the game into overtime, where Eric Belanger won it for the Kings.

"We got what we deserved," said goalie Chris Osgood, as the Wings failed to kill off two Martin LaPointe penalties, then watched as the Kings' Bryan Smolinski scored the game-tying goal after Los Angeles pulled goalie Felix Potvin.

The Wings looked shell-shocked after that game, as did most every fan in the Staples Center, to be accurate. But, heading back for a Saturday afternoon game at Joe Louis Arena, most analysts felt Detroit would regain control of the series. The Wings hadn't lost at Joe Louis Arena in a team-record 19 games (17–0–2).

Ziggy Palffy gave the Kings a quick 1–0 lead not even two minutes into the game, and the Wings found themselves scrapping to come from behind the rest of the day. Ultimately, the Wings lost 3–2. That Game 5 frustrated Osgood the most. "Some guys didn't show up tonight," Osgood said. "It makes me [angry]. The big boys gotta play, but whether you've only scored one goal this year, the other guys have to pick it up. Honestly, I can't believe we've lost three in a row. From my angle, we've got to play a heck of a lot better.

"Really, we put out a silver platter for them. We've got to make them work harder for goals. We're just handing it to them. We've got to come out [Monday in Game 6 at Los Angeles] and play a totally different game from the way we have been playing. We've got a day and a half to wake up and win a game. If not, we're out. It's frustrating because we're losing. We got a little momentum [in scoring twice in the third period in Game 5], but we're handing it to them. We've got to show more passion."

The Wings were without Steve Yzerman, who was bothered with an ankle sprain, suffered in Game 1. But they did get Brendan Shanahan, who missed the previous three games with a broken left foot. Shanahan played heroically, playing over 21 minutes, but wouldn't play in Game 6. Yzerman couldn't, either, after trying to give it a go during the pregame skate.

Without the two veterans, the Wings couldn't stem the momentum that was headed in the Kings' direction. Kings forward Adam Deadmarsh, who tormented the Wings when he was a member of the Colorado Avalanche, tied the game in the third period and won it in overtime, slapping back a rebound past Osgood, to give the Kings a dramatic, series-clinching 3–2 victory.

"I happened to be a bit backdoor and had half the net to shoot it," Deadmarsh said. "We wanted to get it done [in Game 6]. They're a good team at home, and we wanted to get the job done."

There was an eerie silence in the Wings' locker room after the loss. There was a real sense an era was closing out, as Wings management likely wasn't going to accept this playoff nightmare so easily.

"It's very disappointing, especially when you're a No. 2 seed and had high hopes," Yzerman said.

General manager Ken Holland felt the nucleus of this roster—Yzerman, Fedorov, Shanahan, Lidstrom—was still in the prime of their careers. Pavel Datsyuk was a young player on his way to the Wings' roster in 2002 whom the organization had high hopes for.

But Osgood's disappointments in the playoffs the past couple of seasons likely would see the Wings seek goaltending depth in the summer, along with more scoring depth up front.

"It was apparent we'd have to make some pretty drastic additions to our team," Devellano wrote in *The Road to Hockeytown*. Which the Wings would do that summer, acquiring goalie Dominik Hasek in a trade and signing free agents Luc Robitaille and Brett Hull.

Devellano said it was important to do something dramatic that summer because fans were beginning to get upset with the Wings' three consecutive playoff failures.

Signing Hull, Robitaille, and Hasek pushed the payroll to $65 million (up from $55 million just two seasons prior).

"Those signings saved us from losing many season-ticket renewals, definitely made us a better hockey club, brought our payroll to a record high for the NHL, and made us the clear-cut favorites to win another Stanley Cup. On paper, that is," Devellano wrote.

The moves proved beneficial and correct. It was money well spent. The Wings did win the Stanley Cup the next season.

THE UGLY

CELEBRATION ENDS EARLY

Three days, only three days after they were on top of the world, in the midst of one of Detroit's great celebrations.

There was a parade with about a million fans celebrating the Red Wings' 1997 Stanley Cup victory. Calling it unbridled joy would be a classic understatement. The Wings were on top of the world. Detroit was drunk on its favorite team's triumph. Life couldn't have been better for everyone involved.

And then, three days later, on a Friday night in suburban Detroit, Wings defensemen Vladimir Konstantinov and Slava Fetisov, and team masseur Sergei Mnatsakanov were severely injured in a limousine accident.

Pain and sorrow and despair replaced joy. Fans who had been celebrating the Wings' triumph were now gathering at an accident scene and lighting candles.

The limo, driven by Richard Gnida, veered off Woodward Avenue going approximately 50 miles per hour and rammed into a tree. Gnida, 28 at the time, pleaded guilty to a misdemeanor second offense of driving on a suspended license and was sentenced to nine months in jail and 200 hours of community service. According to reports, he had fallen asleep at the wheel.

The result: Konstantinov suffered severe physical and mental injuries, small bruises to spots on the brain that have left him able to walk only with the assistance of a walker. He speaks haltingly these days. His hockey career, once so promising, ended the moment of the crash.

Mnatsakanov was left a paraplegic, bound to a wheelchair, although his mind is attentive and sharp.

Fetisov was the most fortunate. He suffered a chest injury and bruised lung, but returned to play on the Wings' 1998 Stanley Cup team.

"To this day, you just can't believe it happened," said teammate Kris Draper. "Just an unbelievable tragedy."

The accident occurred shortly after 9:00 PM. About 45 minutes later owner Mike Ilitch, and many of the Red Wings, including Steve Yzerman, Brendan Shanahan, Sergei Fedorov, and many, many others, began arriving at Beaumont Hospital.

Most of the players had been at a players-only golf outing earlier in the day. Limousines were hired by the players to take them home if needed. Konstantinov, Fetisov, and Mnatsakanov left the golf course early, but were planning to attend a party at Chris Osgood's house.

Then the tragedy occurred.

A physical, snarling, combative defenseman, Konstantinov was developing into a Norris Trophy–caliber player. He was excellent throughout the 1997 Stanley Cup run, frustrating young Philadelphia star Eric Lindros to no end.

"I don't care if I'm a dirty player or not," Konstantinov said in the book *Hockeytown Heroes*. "I play for my team; not for stars."

Konstantinov was an 11th-round pick in the 1989 draft, the 221st player selected that season.

His leadership qualities made him a captain on the Russian national team. "That's the thing that struck me about him when he played with the Wings, the leadership and the competitiveness," said Paul Woods, the Wings' radio analyst. "Vladimir Konstantinov played the game so hard, so competitively, he was an incredible teammate. A lot of people talk about his hits and the physical play, but his offensive game was superb. The passing, the Russian puck-possession style. He was an all-around player."

A car accident in 1997 cut short the career of Vladimir Konstantinov, just days after the Wings had won the Stanley Cup.

Konstantinov was plus-60 during the 1995–1996 season, best in the league, and a testament to his sound play at both ends of the rink.

While the tragic accident immediately put a startling damper on the Wings' celebration, at the same time it brought that team closer than it ever was. There was a patch with the word "Believe," written in English and Russian, which the Wings wore on their sweaters throughout the season.

Konstantinov's locker was prepared as if he'd come back and jump into the lineup at a moment's notice.

The few times during the 1997–1998 season when Konstantinov and Mnatsakanov would arrive at Joe Louis Arena, there was a unique sense of caring and resilience in the locker room.

"We never tried to exploit the accident as a way of motivating our team," Yzerman said. "They're two really special guys for different reasons, really loved by the team. If anything, our team has grown closer through all this."

At the 1997–1998 season opener, Konstantinov and Mnatsakanov sipped out of the Stanley Cup at the hospital. Their wives wheeled both to the ice for the banner-raising, bringing goose-bumps and tears to everyone in attendance.

"With no No. 16 in the lineup, it was a sad moment," Igor Larionov said. "Vladie and Sergei would have loved to been part of the ceremonies."

Even more emotional, though, was the Western Conference Finals, when Konstantinov and Mnatsakanov were shown in the private box of owner Mike Ilitch. Konstantinov's quasi-theme song, "Bad to the Bone," blared, and immediately everyone looked up to Ilitch's box. The crowd at Joe Louis Arena erupted, and both the Wings and Dallas Stars tapped their sticks on the ice.

The Wings continued to march through the playoffs, inspired by Konstantinov and Mnatsakanov. In the 1998 Finals, the Wings swept Washington in four games. Rarely has a team gone through a season with such a single purpose and accomplish what it wanted to achieve so perfectly.

"The guys weren't trying to win it for them, because that doesn't make Vladie's or Sergei's lives any better," said Wings trainer John Wharton, who was instrumental in the rehabilitation of the two injured men. "They wanted to win it because of them. It was a silent rallying point, an internal thing."

Media who were there for the celebration on the ice after the Wings won in 1998 have called it one of the most tear-jerking scenes they've ever seen.

Yzerman raised the Stanley Cup, then immediately presented the Cup to Konstantinov. The team then pushed Konstantinov around the ice in his wheelchair, the former defenseman clutching the Stanley Cup. "That was something special," Larionov said. "I have goose-bumps."

Konstantinov chomped on a cigar and raised two fingers to symbolize the back-to-back championships. A championship cap on his head.

Like Larionov said, it was something special.

SEPTEMBER 11

Traverse City is the perfect resort town. Located in northwest Michigan, on Grand Traverse Bay, the gorgeous hideaway is close to beaches, Lake Michigan, sand dunes, wineries, and a vibrant shopping/bar district that draws visitors, not just in the summer, but year round.

And particularly when the Red Wings hold their training camp in early September.

This camp in 2001 was going to be particularly exciting. The team signed future Hall of Famers Dominik Hasek, Luc Robitaille, and Brett Hull in the summer. Excitement was at an all-time high. There was a buzz throughout the tiny town—the entire state, for that matter—that has yet to be replicated.

But on the morning of September 11, that energy dimmed considerably. Hockey became a secondary issue for a period of time, just like everything else did at that point in time. Many Red Wings players were unaware of what was happening in New York, as two hijacked airliners slammed into the twin towers of the World Trade Center.

Many players were taking their physicals in the upstairs workout room overlooking the newer rink of two that comprise

Centre Ice Arena. Some veterans, notably Chris Chelios and Steve Yzerman, were doing some light skating. It was, for all intents and purposes, a typical first day of training camp.

But, soon, as news spread about those incidents, everything changed. They became increasingly aware of a plane having gone down in rural Pennsylvania and the Pentagon having been hit by a hijacked airliner, as well.

"You watch all of this, what's going on, and you just can't believe it," Robitaille said. Robitaille's wife was flying back from Detroit to Los Angeles that morning, which worried him to no end until he received a phone call from her saying she was safe.

Several of the young prospects in camp were worried about family members or friends who worked either in New York or Washington, where the incidents took place.

Suddenly, training camp took a back seat to reality.

There was one television at the arena, and it was near an open space by the concession stand. What was staggering was the pot-pourri of people sitting or standing, watching the events that were unfolding on the screen above them. The quiet near that television was noteworthy. Nobody said a word. Down below, through the windows, you could hear pucks being shot. The only sound near the concession stand, though, was of the newsmen reporting on this unthinkable tragedy.

You had Hall of Fame hockey players. You had reporters. Volunteers from Traverse City who gave up their personal time to help around the rink that day, and the entire week. Mothers and fathers. There were young players who weren't ever going to play in the NHL. Some minor leaguers who had a chance, maybe not. Millionaires and middle-class people. But all of them, mesmerized, sad, shocked, over what was happening hundreds of miles from where they were, in northwest Michigan, on a beautiful, blue-sky day.

That day, the Wings still had obligations that went on.

A golf tournament benefiting former Wings player Vladimir Konstantinov and masseur Sergei Mnatsakanov, both of whom were seriously injured in a 1997 limousine crash, went on as scheduled. A dinner was held afterward.

Some Wings front-office types, and Robitaille, were further saddened to hear Garnet "Ace" Bailey, who was a former Red Wing in his playing career, and at the time of the incident director of amateur scouting for the L.A. Kings (where Robitaille had played) was on one of the planes that hit the World Trade Center.

"Words can't express how I feel," said Mickey Redmond, the Wings' television analyst, who was a teammate of Bailey's.

The next day, the Red Wings decided to go back on the ice. There was talk of maybe taking a day off, letting everything sink in, to mourn what had happened in New York, Washington, outside of Pittsburgh. But the Wings felt it was right to go back to work. There wasn't a right or wrong decision. Life had to go on.

"It's a delicate issue," Holland said. "Where's the line? How long do you grieve? We're here, but I don't know how much everybody's into what we're doing right now. Our hearts and minds are elsewhere."

Life in Traverse City had to get back to normal, though.

ROCKET RIOT

A road game in Montreal is never a bad thing for a hockey team. It doesn't matter if it is the 1950s, 1990s, or 2000s.

Montreal is one of the greatest hockey towns ever, with passionate fans in an area that worships hockey. Along with that, the restaurants are top-notch, entertainment is plentiful, and there's good ice to play on, whether it was the old Montreal Forum or the new Bell Centre.

But when the Wings visited Montreal on March 17, 1955, this wasn't one of those leisurely, enjoyable visits. This turned out downright scary. Even life-threatening.

Montreal star Maurice "Rocket" Richard lost his temper and attacked linesman Cliff Thompson in a game March 13 at the Boston Garden. Richard felt he wasn't getting the type of calls other stars were around the league, and exploded after this particular non-call.

The league, somewhat surprisingly, came down hard. NHL president Clarence Campbell suspended Richard for the remainder of the regular season and, most surprisingly and where it hurt the

Canadiens the most, for the playoffs. Predictably, Montreal fans were livid. Already not pleased with the league for what they felt was an anti-French bias, the Canadiens felt this was the ultimate slap.

Richard was leading the league in scoring—an individual title he had never won—and this particular season appeared to be his best opportunity (he wound up second to teammate Bernie Geoffrion).

On an immediate level, Montreal was about to play the Wings in a home-and-home series with first place at stake.

When the Wings arrived, there was a sense Montreal fans were boiling.

"They were angry with Richard being suspended," said Budd Lynch, the Wings' radio play-by-play man at the time. "The Forum was buzzing."

What made the scene even more volatile was the fact Campbell was also in attendance. From the start of the game, fans noticed him and threw objects and insults in his direction.

The Wings jumped out to a 4–1 lead in the first period. Without Richard, the Canadiens lost an immense offensive talent, as well as his fiery emotion and leadership. As the horn sounded to end the period, fans became more riled. A tear-gas bomb went off, and the Forum suddenly became a war zone, with fans rioting and showing their displeasure toward Campbell.

"We watered down some towels and pressed them into the crack of the door so none of the gas would come in," Red Wings trainer Lefty Wilson said in Richard Bak's *Detroit Red Wings: The Illustrated History*.

Lynch could sense something was going very wrong. "Being an old army guy, I could smell tear gas," Lynch said. "It was just an unfortunate situation. They scrambled us out of there. We got on the bus and took off to the train station. You looked behind you, and people were throwing rocks, rioting. I'll never forget it."

The Canadiens did forfeit the game to the Wings.

"We were all surprised. And then Jack [Adams, the Wings' general manager] says, 'It's time to get out. Go out and the back way,'" coach Jimmy Skinner told Rich Kincaide in *The Gods of Olympia Stadium: Legends of the Detroit Red Wings*.

Calm finally arrived when Richard went on the radio to ask fans to stop the unlawful behavior. Eventually, the fans stopped.

Police were in high alert three days later at Olympia, when the Canadiens arrived to play the Red Wings. But there was no repeat performance. The Wings won 6–0, and there were no incidents out of the ordinary in the crowd.

The teams did meet in the Stanley Cup Finals, and the Wings won in seven games. Montreal played gallantly even without Richard, but had no answer for the Wings' Gordie Howe, who set a new playoff record with 20 points.

Richard, Howe's career rival, could only watch from home in Montreal.

JIRI FISCHER

The morning of November 21, 2005, Jiri Fischer was getting prepared for a hockey game that evening against the Nashville Predators, as he would any other game in his rapidly progressing career.

Fischer was taping his sticks while talking about a past fight against the Predators' Scott Hartnell. He talked about the Red Wings' defense. He helped a reporter with some information about Fischer's native Czech Republic.

Fischer, as always, seemed like the picture of health. Robust, young, athletic, healthy. Few Red Wings were in better shape physically, it seemed, certainly from a conditioning standpoint. Fischer would stay extra time in the weight room. It was a practice he learned from an early age. His discipline to be better than the next player, from every possible angle, was admirable. He didn't eat the wrong foods. Everything he put into his body was healthy and was going to help him achieve the best possible results in his chosen career of hockey.

Fischer, age 25 at the time, was smiling and joking that morning, a scene completely opposite from what the day's events would bring. Because later that evening, his young hockey career hit an unbelievable end.

With 7:31 remaining in the first period, there was sudden panic on the Red Wings' bench. Coach Mike Babcock and several players nervously, frantically, began waving their arms toward the direction of the Zamboni entrance to get emergency personnel.

Players stopped on the ice. Gradually, the fans at Joe Louis Arena realized something wrong had happened, and a hush descended like no one has ever heard, despite 20,000 people being in the arena.

Something had happened to someone on the Wings' bench, and no one knew exactly who it was and what had occurred. Up in the press box, reporters tried to figure out who had become stricken, but amid the bodies scurrying around, it was difficult to take a head count of who was up and standing.

Was it one of the Wings' assistant coaches? Maybe one of the equipment guys? Possibly a fan falling over the railing and getting seriously injured?

Then, word from the broadcast side began to filter down that it was Jiri Fischer.

"Fear," said Steve Yzerman afterward of the emotion that was rampant on the Wings' bench.

Suddenly, a couple minor pieces began to fit. Fischer had missed several practices during training camp in 2002 when he was diagnosed with a heart abnormality. He did pass a stress test, and brushed off the scare as nothing that would stop him from continuing what looked like a very productive NHL career. "There is a little abnormality, but nothing that will stop me from playing," Fischer said in September 2002. "It's nothing that will bother me emotionally. I wasn't scared about the abnormality. But I was scared about not playing hockey again. That was a shock for me."

Doctors and emergency personnel raced to the Wings' bench to revive Fischer. Team doctor Anthony Colucci jumped down from his perch behind the bench and quickly began CPR. Dr. Douglas G. Plagens, another team physician, and trainer Piet Van Zant also jumped into action.

Fischer had suffered a cardiac arrest and was mere moments from dying, if not for the heroism of the Wings' medical staff.

Fans were told of Fischer's condition and some of what had occurred at approximately 8:45 PM. About 15 minutes later, the game was officially postponed for a future date. A polite applause shattered the eerie, incomprehensible quiet in the arena. No one was thinking about playing hockey at that point.

Fischer required CPR and the use of a defibrillator, an instrument that would thankfully gain a lot of attention in the days, months, and years ahead.

"He had a seizure and he fell forward and ended up on his side," Red Wings head coach Mike Babcock told reporters afterward. "They started doing CPR on him, and his heart had stopped. There was no pulse, so they hooked up the auto defibrillator, and it shocked him."

Brendan Shanahan escorted Fischer's fiancée, Avery, across the ice to get closer to the bench. Avery had been in a family lounge in the bowels of the arena. "Obviously, she was very worried and concerned," Shanahan said. "She just wanted to be next to Jiri."

Shanahan said defenseman Brett Lebda, who was seated at the far end of the bench next to Fischer, immediately began shouting that Fischer had collapsed and something was seriously wrong.

"He saw Jiri lean forward, and he was the one that alerted the rest of the team that something was wrong," Shanahan said. "I stood up and saw Fish. So I jumped on the ice and I knew...you can just tell when it's urgent like that. A couple of us jumped on the ice and started screaming for the referees to blow the whistle, and they were confused."

Yzerman had been involved in professional hockey for over 20 years but could never remember such an incident. "Everybody is definitely caught by surprise," he said. "We turn and see Jiri laying between the boards and the bench, and we're not sure why. You see the guy laying there, and the doctors are doing what they're doing. You fear for the guy's life at that moment. I cannot remember anything like that. You're just sitting back, hoping that this is going to work out all right. You're not really sure of what is going on, what his condition is, or what he is suffering from at that moment, so you're just wondering what is going on."

The confusing thing for everyone was the fact Fischer wasn't complaining of feeling badly. He also hadn't been involved in any major hits or collisions during that first period.

"Incidental contact," Babcock said. "Nothing that would seem to lead to something like this. What happened basically is, Fish was out on a shift, he came off, he was standing there with his teammates, or sitting on the bench, and he had a seizure.... Right away, as soon as we got aware of what was going on, we got it stopped."

By the time Fischer had been transported to Detroit Receiving Hospital, news began getting to the Wings that Fischer was fine and in good spirits. Teammates visited him and were relieved to see him alive and spry.

Just a little before then, Wings and Predators players were talking in the hallway between the two locker rooms. Wings forward Robert Lang, a Czech, was talking with Czechs on the Predators such as Tomas Vokoun, Marek Zidlicky, and Martin Erat, all acquaintances of Fischer.

Predators coach Barry Trotz said his team was also affected by the tragedy. "We were trying to get some updates for our players," Trotz said. "We have some players that are good friends with Jiri Fischer, and the players all know each other. They've become friends from playing over in Europe, world championships, things like that. They were very upset."

Yzerman and Shanahan let the Predators know what was going on.

"Obviously a scary situation," Trotz said. "One of the things we wanted to do was clear the ice right away. That was a smart move by the NHL. Detroit came to their locker room through ours so they could make the proper medical procedure happen."

What was it like in the locker room?

"It was very quiet in there, and everybody wanted to get news as quickly as possible," Shanahan said. "We were trying to get news. We had everyone in management and staff down there. Just the players on the team, and Nashville's team as well, we were all very rattled. Jiri has some friends on the Nashville team that he's played with on the national team. I don't think any one of the players felt it was right to finish the game, and I think Nashville felt the same way. A hockey game shouldn't be played tonight."

Trotz echoed the Wings when he said playing the game was best saved for another day. "It was very disturbing to both sides, and I think the NHL recognized it, the players recognized it," Trotz said. "To be quite honest, the game became very secondary."

In the days and months later, it was revealed how very lucky Fischer was.

If it weren't for Colucci and the rest of the medical personnel, and their medical equipment and quick response, Fischer likely would have died.

"Whenever someone stops breathing, or their heart stops, no matter how much you know or have to aid you, you are concerned you can't get it going again," Colucci said.

Fischer appeared at an emotional news conference about a week later to publicly thank Colucci and express how thankful he was to be alive.

"I'm extremely lucky," Fischer said.

At first, he felt the idea of playing again was possible. He didn't feel he needed to let the dream of playing again disappear. "I don't see a reason why I should," said Fischer at Joe Louis Arena after one of his frequent visits to teammates the next season after the cardiac arrest. "I'm 26, and even if it takes longer than I would like it to, it's something that keeps me motivated and something that I love. I just don't really see a reason saying right now, 'Hey, my time is done.' Absolutely not."

But the insurance complications, the risks involved, the fact teams would likely be scared off, were all factors working against Fischer. "I have to get healthy first, but by being healthy I have to be healthier than everybody else to really even think about coming back to hockey," Fischer said.

Not being able to skate, and not being able to train as religiously as he once did, Fischer's dream of returning to the NHL as a player gradually disappeared.

Ultimately Fischer settled into a role in the Red Wings' front office as director of player development. Working with young players, teaching and counseling them, as well as scouting, seems to have helped Fischer come to grips with what has happened in his life.

"I love working with the young players," Fischer said. "They're so eager, wide-eyed, and they want to learn and get better. It's very inspiring. They see guys like Zetterberg and Datsyuk and Lidstrom on the big team, and they want to get there. They want to know what they need to do to get better. It's a great feeling to be a part of that process, having a part in it."

It took over two years, but Fischer put the skates on again and began doing some light skating. In the 2008 playoffs, after practice ended, Fischer would skate with the healthy scratches. He's scrimmaged with some recreation teams for charity.

All of it is a far, far cry from what he used to do, playing in the NHL, earning millions of dollars, enjoying a career many would love to have.

Fischer is still trying to figure out why everything happened the way it did. How in a matter of seconds his world turned upside down. "I believe things happen for a reason, and I'm still figuring out my reason or why the reason it happened to me the way it did," he said. "I treasure every day. Every day, for me, is about learning. I appreciate everything. My family, my life. I pay attention to everything nowadays."

RED WINGS VS. AVALANCHE: BLOOD FEUD

Here we were, 12 years later, and Claude Lemieux was still being hated.

Lemieux, an agitating forward who had come out of a five-year retirement, was now skating for the San Jose Sharks. Not the Colorado Avalanche, where the dislike of Lemieux began in the minds of Wings fans.

But here it was, February 25, 2009, and Lemieux was still getting it from the Joe Louis Arena faithful.

"They love me here," said Lemieux afterward, a slight smile on his face, insisting they weren't booing him. "They were saying, 'Le-mieux.'"

Sure sounded like booing (and a lot of it) to everyone else. And in a roundabout way, it showed the leftover passion from that bitter Red Wings–Avalanche rivalry in the 1990s and into the early 2000s.

UGLY EXIT

It was the Red Wings who were responsible for legendary goalie Patrick Roy leaving Montreal.

The Wings defeated the Canadiens 11-1 on December 2, 1995, with Roy allowing nine of the 11 goals. He didn't like being left in net for so long, and immediately stormed to the team president seated behind the Montreal bench and demanded a trade, saying he had played his last game for the Canadiens.

Several days later, Roy was traded to the Colorado Avalanche, where he would make several more memories involving the Wings in one of hockey's greatest rivalries.

Few rivalries in professional sports had a similar hatred.

Add to that the incredible array of talent on both sides, and the fact the teams were annually battling for the Stanley Cup, and the games were must-see television.

Lemieux, in his inimitable style, had much to do with lighting the spark.

The 1996 Western Conference Finals saw the Red Wings and Avalanche pitted against each other. The Wings were favored, after having won 62 games in the regular season and having reached the Stanley Cup Finals the season before, but getting swept in four games by New Jersey.

There was anticipation that Detroit's time had come and a fairly young Colorado team was a mere roadblock.

In Game 3 of the series, though, Lemieux sucker-punched Wings forward Slava Kozlov after Kozlov had laid a questionable hit on Avalanche defenseman Adam Foote. Lemiuex wound up being suspended one game, and the match was lit.

Bad blood was beginning to boil.

"[Bowman] thinks so much, the plate in his head causes interference in our headsets," Avalanche coach Marc Crawford said of Wings coach Scotty Bowman, who had issues with Lemieux's hit.

The Wings didn't look comfortable in the series. They found themselves trailing 3–2 in the series heading to Game 6 in Denver and one game, obviously, from elimination. They would get eliminated but saw their season, also, end with violence and one of their own badly hurt.

Thanks to Lemieux.

Lemieux nailed Kris Draper from behind into the boards in front of the Wings' bench early in the game. Draper suffered a broken jaw and nose, his teeth were displaced, and on top of everything else, he had a mild concussion. In all, 30 stitches were required to repair his face.

For several weeks, Draper only was able to drink his meals from a straw.

"Not necessarily the hit, but the way he [Lemieux] responded, or reacted, to it or didn't react to it, that the was biggest thing [that bothered the Wings]," said Draper of Lemieux's cavalier attitude to the entire matter. "In hockey, things happen, it's a fast game, a physical game, and things happen."

Lemieux was ejected for the hit, but returned on ice for the postgame handshakes. There were no apologies, no asking how Draper was.

And the Wings, fed up with Lemieux's antics, were livid. "I can't believe I shook his friggin' hand," Wings forward Dino Ciccarelli afterward "I hadn't seen Kris' face. It's shit. Kris was one of our best players, and Lemieux blindsided him. The poor kid was right by the door, he had his back to him, and he didn't have a chance. He was at his mercy. Lemieux could have broken his neck. Hey, they beat us, they had the better team—but that's just b.s."

Lemieux was suspended for the first two games of the Finals, a series that saw Colorado go on to win over Florida in four straight games.

But several Wings said there would be retribution the following season. And it would come, all right, on an evening that still lives in Wings lore: March 26, 1997.

People just know where they were on certain days or nights. You know where you were when Kennedy was shot, when 9/11 occurred, when the *Challenger* exploded. From a sports perspective, in Detroit anyway, you knew where you were on March 26, 1997, when the Wings hosted the Avalanche.

Lemieux missed the first two games between the teams that season because of injuries. The third game, in Denver, passed without incident. Then came March 26, 1997, an evening when the Red Wings earned retribution for what happened to Draper, and to a much broader and larger sense, became a team in every sense of the word.

And, to think, Igor Larionov and the Avalanche's Peter Forsberg set off the timebomb in the first period with an innocent-looking collision, not really looking to fight, but really, nothing more than a collision.

Chaos would break out.

"The smallest of things could have ignited the biggest thing, and who would have thought it was those two guys," Draper said.

Darren McCarty found Lemieux amid the clutching and grabbing all over the ice and began to absolutely pummel Lemieux unmercifully. Lemieux assumed the turtle position as the crowd began to roar. McCarty would drag Lemieux to the front of the Wings' bench, maybe symbolically, as Joe Louis Arena erupted with ear-piercing venom.

"An opportunity presented itself, and something happened," McCarty said.

As McCarty toyed with Lemieux, Avs goalie Patrick Roy left his crease, and Brendan Shanahan came flying through the air to intercept him. Shanahan thought Roy was only attempting to stir the pot further. "When I was three feet in the air, I was thinking, *What am I doing?* When I was five feet in the air, I said, 'What I am really doing here?'" Shanahan told the *Detroit Free Press.*

Roy did get paired up with Wings goalie Mike Vernon in a battle that lives on in pictures in nearly every sports bar in Detroit.

Everywhere on the ice, there was equipment and players engaged in battle. The Wings had finally exacted some revenge.

It also may have had a lot to do with bringing that particular Wings team together, and leading that team to the first of three Stanley Cups later that spring.

"It brought the whole team together," Draper's linemate Kirk Maltby said. "It wasn't like we were playing poorly, but we were

The rivalry between the Wings and Colorado Avalanche has become one of the most heated in the entire NHL.

just going about our business, and that night just ignited us as a team. It definitely turned our season around. The camaraderie of it, and we just became that much more of a team. It was a season-turning game for us."

Of course, the Draper-Lemieux incident was foremost on everyone's mind. But the Wings' failure in the two previous play-offs, the Avalanche winning the 1996 Stanley Cup, and looking like favorites again in 1997, and Lemieux never showing remorse for severely injuring Draper, well, yes, everyone expected something to happen.

"Everyone expected it to happen, and how we got there wasn't good, but it was an accumulation of a lot of games," goalie Chris Osgood said. "It was probably more fun for the fans [than the players]. But it was kind of necessary. It was probably one of the last steps for us to take, to come together as a team and the fact we stood up for each other, going into the playoffs."

The build-up heading into the game, and the war of words between the teams, led everyone to believe something memorable was going to occur. Someone in the media compared it to kids talking in school of a fight in a schoolyard after the final bell sounds. The anticipation was unbelievable.

"There was hatred between the teams," Osgood said.

"They were a great hockey team, and we were a great hockey team, and they had the one thing that we wanted, the Stanley Cup," Draper said. "They had beaten us the year before, and New Jersey had beaten us in the Finals in 1995, and we had to find a way to get over that hurdle.

That night really helped us and excited us, especially because it was so close to the playoffs."

Wings coach Mike Babcock remembers watching that game, and those highlights, as a hockey enthusiast at that point in his career, and relishing the emotion. "Sure I watched it, and it was competitive playoff stuff, and that's what sells hockey," Babcock said. "It was great. Now, did you want anyone ever getting hurt? No. But it was a competitive rivalry and those teams in the pre-[salary] cap days were four lines deep, six defensemen deep, with good goaltending. Those rivalries in those days lasted. If you went to the Finals one year, the next year those guys were going to come back [to your team]."

"Just think of all of the Hall of Famers on both teams when you go down the list," Draper said.

And all those incredible images of that evening those Hall of Famers produced.

"The fact it was Forsberg and Larionov that started it, I guess it just shows you the entire thing needed a little spark like that," Maltby said. "But then, Claude and Darren fighting, and Darren scoring the game-winning goal, that was great. In today's game, Darren would have been kicked out.

"People tend to forget, after all the other stuff that happened, the fact it was a great game that night, 6–5 in overtime. Going back and forth. That was just a fun game to be part of."

"I'll never forget coming into the locker room after overtime, after Mac had scored, and the excitement in everyone's eyes,"

Draper said. "Not only that we won the game, but what we accomplished on the ice, and then Mac kind of put a stamp on his career, going out and doing what he did, and scoring the winning goal. It was something no one will ever forget."

For Osgood, his favorite memories centered on the goalies.

"Vernie skating to center, and I thought he'd be exhausted just skating all the way there," Osgood said. "I remember pictures of Vernie's head fitting into Roy's glove. Remember, at that time, there was no rules on equipment, and Vernie's head fit entirely in Roy's glove. Roy getting cut, and saying he'd won the fight. Vernie was so tired. Vernie skated off the ice and he was exhausted and was hoping they'd kick off out of the game, but they didn't, and he had to go back there and play. He could barely move. And Shanny flying through the air [before the melee started] to get after Roy."

It was more than ten years ago, but everyone in Detroit remembers it as if it were yesterday.

"For everyone involved, it was an unbelievable night," Draper said.

The Avalanche, incidentally, didn't forget either. "That team has no heart," Colorado forward Mike Keane said after the game.

FREDRIK WHO?

There were so many stars in the Red Wings–Colorado Avalanche playoff series in 2002. But one who scored a key goal for the Wings in Game 3 wasn't a star at all.

Defenseman Fredrik Olausson, a less-heralded free-agent acquisition than the likes of Hasek, Robitaille, and Hull, scored a Game 3 overtime winner past goalie Patrick Roy that gave the Wings a 2–1 victory and 2–1 series lead.

"They were caught in a line change," Olausson said. "Patrick saw the shot. I got in a good spot."

It was Olausson's first playoff goal in more than 10 years.

"I don't know if it's my most important goal," Olausson said. "It's nice to get one."

"Detroit had the opportunity to do that in our building, but they didn't. They showed their true colors tonight. Everyone is gutless on that team, and I'd love to see them in the playoffs."

They did. But as Draper, Maltby, and Osgood, among others, had predicted, the Wings had become too much of a team by then. They had been galvanized and united. But not before some more theater.

In Game 4 of the Western Conference Finals between the teams, there were 236 penalty minutes (by comparison, 148 penalty minutes were called on March 26).

Crawford climbed the glass to scream at Bowman in the final stages of the game. Bowman, who knew Floyd Crawford, Marc's dad, from junior hockey, would only belittle Crawford. "I knew your father before you did, and I don't think he'd be too proud of what you're doing right now," Bowman told the younger Crawford.

The Wings would go on to win in six games.

After the final game, Draper didn't shake Lemieux's hand as Lemieux declined to make eye contact. Lemieux simply refused to shake McCarty's hand.

Post Mortem

Gradually, as the years passed, players were traded or simply retired. New faces appeared but had no link at all to the mayhem that occurred in the 1996–1997 season.

Skill on both teams overtook the physicality. But, every once in a great while, a spark ignited a little taste of such craziness. Such as in 2002, in a regular-season game in Denver.

The trouble began at 9:56 of the third period, when Maltby was pushed into the net by Avalanche defenseman Martin Skoula. Maltby took out Roy's legs, and Roy took exception, punching Maltby inside the net.

"I was going to the net, and Skoula took me in," Maltby said. "I was just trying not to hit my head. Then it became a wrestling match."

"What I didn't like is that he tried to take my knee out," Roy said.

Players from both teams began to gather around the Avalanche net. Suddenly, out of nowhere, skating the length of the ice, was Hasek, apparently wanting to get after Roy. Skating furiously, with a purpose, determined, Hasek was set to engage, only to...slip and fall on the ice.

In the process, Hasek took out Roy. Dazed and momentarily confused, Roy didn't know who had done that. Roy refocused, saw it was Hasek, and half-heartedly invited Hasek to fight before reason took over.

"I felt it was my responsibility to go there and help my teammates," Hasek said. "I was ready to fight."

Said Roy, "It would have been interesting if the refs had not been there."

Later that spring, the Wings and Avalanche met once more in an epic series. This wasn't about dirty play or cheap shots. This was about pure hockey with talent galore on both teams.

Colorado had taken a 3–2 series lead on Forsberg's overtime goal, and could have clinched it at home in Game 6. But Roy pulled one of the biggest blunders of his career, attempting to make a Statue of Liberty–like save early in the game, only to see the puck drop and Shanahan bang in the goal for a 1–0 lead. The Wings would win 2–0, Hasek was superb in net, and the teams would go to Joe Louis Arena for Game 7.

The excitement for that game, on a beautiful spring night in Detroit, equaled any of a Stanley Cup game.

Interestingly, many favored Colorado in this game. Roy was 6–5 in Game 7s heading into that game, while Hasek was 0–2.

All the pressure, because of the Hall of Fame roster, was on the Wings. So Bowman tried to calm nerves before the game. "I just told them before the game a few stories about Game 7s that I'd been involved in," Bowman said. "And I told them that no matter what happens, it will be memorable—that I remember every one of them whether we won or lost."

Players like Luc Robitaille, Shanahan, Draper, and Hasek all said afterward that Bowman was tremendous in his approach. Bowman was even-keeled, provided a sense of humor, and lessened the anxiety level in the locker room by a huge amount.

A relaxed Wings team completely destroyed the Avalanche from the opening drop of the puck. The Wings chased Roy out of the net after two periods and won 7–0.

"You imagine something like this, but you don't necessarily expect it to happen," Brett Hull said.

The Wings would go on to win the Stanley Cup over the Carolina Hurricanes.

Glory Days

Now, this was 12 years later, and Lemieux and Draper were still in the news.

"I'll try to work on my clichés for you guys," Draper said.

Actually, Lemieux barely played seven minutes as the Wings defeated the Sharks 4–1. Lemieux made no impact whatsoever.

A long time had passed, but fans remembered Lemieux and what he'd done. The pain he caused. Time had passed, but the emotion was surprisingly fresh.

"People want to bring up the old incidents of the mid-'90s," Lemieux said. "That was a long time ago, a lot of water under the bridge."

But what a time it was.

"We've been watching some of the stuff on YouTube," said Henrik Zetterberg, who was teenager at that point. "It was great stuff."

Yes, it was.

LEGENDS

STEVE YZERMAN

There are many examples of Steve Yzerman's legendary leader-ship, but one instant really showed the essence of what, and who, Yzerman was.

It was, of course, the 2002 season, when the Red Wings had a roster of stars but found themselves struggling after two games of the first round of the playoffs to the no-name Vancouver Canucks.

This was shocking. The Wings lost both games at Joe Louis Arena and suddenly had to travel to Vancouver—with no momentum, goalie Dominik Hasek plagued by an incredible streak of bad bounces going against him, all the pressure of the world on the Wings' shoulders, and several big names slumping.

Yzerman, himself, had just returned for the playoffs after missing half the season with knee problems. Still, he was playing courageously. And as he met the media after Game 2, he wasn't down on his team. He believed in them. "I don't think we've been outplayed in either of the two games we've lost, but we're just not quite there," Yzerman told a large group of reporters. "Our power play isn't there. Maybe we're not as sharp as we should be. We're not as cohesive as we should be.

"I've been through it before [in Detroit]. There's high expecta-tions. So I'm not really concerned about it. We know when to shoot the puck [fans had been getting on the Wings for not shooting the puck on the power play]. You want to shoot the puck, but you can't shoot it into three people."

Yzerman wasn't worried about the psyche of Hasek, who had been acquired before the season to solve the Wings' goaltending woes, but seemed to be crumbling under the pressure. "I'm not concerned about the goaltending at all," Yzerman said. "Before the series is over, you're going to say, 'That Dom, he's an unbelievable goalie.' He's a fantastic goalie and he'll prove it."

Then some reporter asked Yzerman whether he felt the series could still go seven games. Yzerman lowered his eyes and looked at the floor. His face looked determined, angry, challenging. "Maybe not," Yzerman said, and then paused a few more moments. "Doesn't mean we're going to lose, either."

To anyone who was in that room for those few minutes, you could sense Yzerman was still about to make a huge, huge impact on that series.

Before the next practice, he gave what amounted to a pep talk to his teammates—not necessarily a Knute Rockne, passionate talk, just that he still believed in this team. "Let's just relax," Yzerman said was the essence of what he told his teammates. Whatever he said worked. The Wings won the next four games against the Canucks. The series, like Yzerman vaguely predicted, didn't go seven games.

And Yzerman, limping badly off the ice, doing everything in his power to skate, played better than anyone on the ice.

"He inspired everybody," forward Kris Draper said. "He said he believed in every guy in there, and he believed we were going to win the series."

"Just seeing what he had to go through night in and night out with the knee, it was inspiring to see a guy like that go out there and lead," Draper said. "He'd address the team, then be the first guy out there leading, and he did it so many nights here."

"For sure, he was a great captain and a great leader on this team," goalie Dominik Hasek said. "He always had the right thing to say."

Retirement Ceremony

Yzerman had his No. 19 retired on January 2, 2007, in a wonderful ceremony at Joe Louis Arena.

Actually, it was more like Steve Yzerman Day in the state of Michigan, with Yzerman receiving various gifts throughout the day, recognized from various dignitaries for different achievements.

He received a key to the city of Detroit from then–Detroit mayor Kwame Kilpatrick. "I find it somewhat ironic that I'm presented with a key from the mayor's office today but I still don't have a key to my office at Joe Louis Arena," Yzerman joked, turning to GM Ken Holland seated on the dais.

"Actually, I just got one," Yzerman admitted later, laughing. "But I've got to get another one, because I'm constantly getting locked out."

His speeches were, obviously, almost legendary, and someone asked whether Yzerman would give one more speech to the Wings players' before this evening, the night the No. 19 would be raised to the rafters. "Well, I made a lot of speeches and we didn't win, too," he said, laughing. "So my record isn't necessarily perfect. "

Coach Mike Babcock only had one season working with Yzerman, a 2005–2006 season in which the Wings set numerous team records for excellence but ultimately fell to the Edmonton Oilers in the first round of the playoffs.

It was a crushing loss. The Wings were the No. 1 seed, Edmonton the No. 8 seed in the Western Conference. Yzerman missed one game with back problems, Game 5 at Joe Louis Arena with the series tied 2–2, but returned for Game 6 and was arguably one of the best Wings forwards despite his pain.

"There's a lot of really good hockey players in the NHL, but there's some guys that are special—they make their teammates better, they make their team better, and they win championships because of their will," Babcock said. "Skill only gets you so far. And obviously he had a lot more to him than that."

Yzerman was humbled by seeing his name and sweater raised to the rafters of Joe Louis Arena with the likes of Gordie Howe, Alex Delvecchio, and Ted Lindsay.

One of the most decorated hockey players of all time, Steve Yzerman won three Stanley Cups during his 20-year run as captain of the Red Wings.

"It's a tremendous honor for me. I don't think about myself as being amongst them," Yzerman said. "Those are the players that built the league and guys that I admire, and I don't know that I could ever reach the level they're at in my own eyes."

One intersection outside Joe Louis Arena was renamed Yzerman Drive. "I kind of wish my name was Smith or Jones. In 20 years, people around here aren't going to be able to pronounce it. It took 20 years for people to learn it. But I have three young children, and I think they'll really get a kick out of it," Yzerman said.

Canadian Recognition

Hockey Canada announced before the 2006 Olympics that no one would wear No. 19 out of respect for Yzerman, who turned down an opportunity to play on that team because of lingering pain in his knee.

Yzerman also declined to participate in those Olympics, because of the large number of deserving young players in Canada.

He was instrumental for Canada as it won the 2002 gold medal for the first time in 50 years, in Salt Lake City.

"There's a lot of potential No. 19s on that team, so they're saving themselves from controversy," said Yzerman, with a smile.

"I don't really know how to answer that," said Yzerman, when asked about his number being put aside by the Canadian team.

Babcock attempted to put the honor in perspective.

"Can you imagine how good you must be for them to do that?" Babcock said. "This is Canada. They're saying you can't wear that number. You must be pretty good, and pretty good for a long period of time. How good must you be? There's a lot of respect, and there's the same respect here."

Babcock talked about the pictures of many former and current Wings that line the hallway outside the locker room. Wings legends such as Chris Chelios, Nicklas Lidstrom, and Brendan Shanahan line the hallway, along with Yzerman.

"Steve has been at another level because he's the leader of that group," Babcock said.

It was Yzerman's leadership and character that has impressed Babcock, who didn't know Yzerman personally before being named the Wings' coach. "I didn't know how classy he is, and I didn't know he has such a good big picture look at things," Babcock said. "He really does. He has a good feel for what's going on. He has the leadership and he finds ways to help guys. That's the thing that I've been impressed with, he finds a way to help people. [But] you couldn't do what he does in [terms of] leadership without being a player first. You can't. But he's been the player."

Until you've been around the area and understand what Yzerman means to Wings fans, it's impossible to comprehend otherwise, according to Babcock. "Until you've either lived here, coached, or played here, you have no idea what he means to this community, the state of Michigan, and the organization," Babcock said.

The fact Yzerman remains in the organization and around the team, said Babcock, is an important benefit to the Wings.

"There are very few athletes who are as revered by his teammates as he is," Babcock said. "His ability to play through the pain and deliver when it counted, his ability to do the right thing, and his ability to make teammates accountable [are what impress me]."

Caring Teammate

The best times for Sergei Fedorov were when he was on the same line with Yzerman.

"The most fun I had was when we were on the same line because he was easy to read off," said Fedorov, who won three Stanley Cups with Yzerman before signing a free-agent contract with Anaheim in 2003. "He played and skated so well, it was easy to play with him. I scored my first goal with Stevie assisting on it. Those kind of memories stick with you forever.

"[Goalie] Tim Cheveldae passed the puck to the red line, and we were able to break down against Slava Fetisov [on New Jersey then] two-on-one, and Steve passed the puck, and I had almost an empty net against [goalie] Sean Burke."

When Fedorov left Russia to play for the Wings, he was young, didn't know the country or language that well, and was scared.

Fedorov appreciated the support Yzerman provided. "He was a veteran on the team, and I was just breaking in completely to a new country, a new league, North American hockey, understanding a new game and a different rink, and just the way he understood my game and passed the puck, he gave me a little bit of confidence," Fedorov said. "He looked after me that first training camp so nobody shaved my head. Those days were fun and exciting."

And those stories of a rift between Yzerman and Fedorov?

"I don't remember our relationship being bad," Fedorov said. "People want to speculate because we were producing points and goals and would elaborate without our opinion. In my mind, we had a great relationship. I ran into him at a few golf courses in Detroit over the summer. I was happy to see him. He looked great.

"I just basically never really cared about them [the rumors of not getting along] or paid attention to them. I don't think two top players can play together for such a long time if they would have a problem."

The Goals

Ken Kal, the Wings' radio play-by-play voice, was fortunate to call many of Yzerman's historic goals. To name just one that left an imprint with Kal would be too difficult.

"There were so many of them," Kal said.

So there's actually a few that stand out for Kal. "His 500th goal, it came against Colorado in 1996," Kal said. "He had gone a pretty good stretch without scoring a goal, and then to do it in that game, against a rival like Colorado and [goalie] Patrick Roy, that was a huge goal in a big rivalry game, and again, it kind of showed what kind of player he was.

"And, then, the goal against [goalie] Jon Casey in Game 7 of the playoffs [in 1996, double overtime]. Stevie going over the line and just firing the puck and beating Casey just under the crossbar. There was so much riding on that game and Stevie just stepped up and came through with such a big goal.

"Great players do that. He was a great, great player.

"Steve was a joy to watch. I can't recall him ever taking a night off. He competed hard whenever he took the ice, and fans all over the NHL who paid to watch him play over the years sure got their money's worth. Like Howe, Lindsay, Sawchuk, and Abel, Steve will be remembered as one of the Red Wings greats of all time."

Impact on Young Players

At the time, forward Jason Williams was a junior free agent in Traverse City on a try-out. He was far from making the Red Wings, an unknown. But Yzerman knew about him, even on the first day veterans arrived in camp.

"I just happened to pass him in the hallway at the [Centre ICE] rink," Williams said. "He stopped, shook my hand, introduced himself, and told me to keep working hard and doing what I'd been doing. I couldn't believe Steve Yzerman knew who I was."

For Williams, it was the first example of the kind of player and leader Yzerman was. "Those first few seasons, whenever I would be sent down [to the minor league], Steve would be one of the first guys who would come over and tell me to go down there and work hard, and do my job, and I would eventually be back here. It meant a lot to me, it really did, it gave me some confidence," Williams said. "And the thing is, he would always know how you did, how you'd been playing. He has a good sense of humor and he'd know you had 15 goals, but he'd remind you about the minus-7, or something like that, too."

Sean Avery was one young player who got to know Yzerman's sarcastic humor quite well. Avery has grown into one of the most hated players in the league, a pest on and off the ice. But Yzerman had a way of keeping Avery in check while dishing out medicine Avery would understand.

"He isn't one to hide his feelings in that way," Avery said.

Avery's favorite player growing up was Brett Hull.

RETIRED NUMBERS

There will be several more to come in the future, no doubt, but currently there are six numbers retired by the Wings organization.

They are:

1	Terry Sawchuk	10	Alex Delvecchio
7	Ted Lindsay	12	Sid Abel
9	Gordie Howe	19	Steve Yzerman

"But being around Yzerman on an everyday basis, I went from No. 16 to No. 19," Avery said. "He's an amazing player. Just the way he carried himself, the guy was an unbelievable leader. He's a pretty humble guy."

Avery switched to No. 19 when he was traded to the Kings. He called Yzerman in the summer that off-season to tell him about the switch in numbers.

"In his own sarcastic way, he asked me not to do it," Avery said.

League-Wide Acclaim

Former teammates, or opponents—it's amazing to almost hear the awe in their voices when talking about Yzerman.

"He showed up every game, every shift," said Martin Lapointe, most recently with the Ottawa Senators.

Larry Murphy is a Hall of Fame defenseman who played a lot of years in the NHL with equally Hall of Fame–caliber players. But while sharing the locker room with Steve Yzerman while both were with the Red Wings, there was something about Yzerman that struck Murphy. What you see is what you get with Yzerman. There is no fake. There is no Steve Yzerman in front of the camera and another one behind closed doors

"He's the real deal," said Murphy, himself an everyday Joe–type who appreciates modesty, humility. "I've played with players, in certain instances, the media builds them up bigger than they really are. But Steve, he lives up to the hype. This guy, he was the ultimate competitor."

"It was an inspiration just being on the same team with him," defenseman Niklas Kronwall said. "It was really something to be part of, being on the same team with him, and it's nothing that I'll ever forget."

"He's the toughest player I ever played with," said Nicklas Lidstrom, who succeeded Yzerman as the Wings' captain.

"Steve will always stand out for me because, on a team filled with All-Stars, he was the guy everyone followed," said Luc Robitaille, who won his only Stanley Cup in 2002 on a Wings team captained by Yzerman.

"On the ice, we all know what a great player he is. Off the ice, he's a quality guy, a super guy," said Colorado Avalanche forward Joe Sakic, a teammate of Yzerman's on Canadian national teams. "I was fortunate enough to play with him in the Olympics and World Cups, and I got to sit beside him [in locker rooms] at a couple of those. He's just a great man, one of the smartest I've ever seen on the ice."

The way he carried himself, what was best for the organization and team. All that was important to Yzerman.

"He had all the intangibles. He's not an athlete you look at and say he's had moments. He didn't. He's classy. He's a leader. And a guy who's dedicated to the city. When you think about Detroit and hockey, it's Steve Yzerman," said defenseman Aaron Ward, another former Red Wing who won a Stanley Cup with Yzerman.

In the Front Office
Yzerman rather quickly moved into the front office of the Wings after retirement.

A vice president, Yzerman offers input into personnel matters. He sees it as the first step toward possibly some day being a general manager of a team.

"For me initially, it gives me an opportunity to see how I fit in a little bit and really learn how it [the front office] operates," Yzerman said. "I've always wanted to stay in the game and with this organization. I get a chance to slowly learn and see how it works and I'm very pleased with that."

In the Wings' locker room, players were pleased to see Yzerman back in the game. "It'll be good to have him back in the organization," Lidstrom said. "It's a big job for him. I'm happy for Steve."

Babcock wasn't surprised to see Yzerman stay in the game. "You can't be as good as he is without passion for the game," Babcock said. "He's not working in hockey because he needs the money. He has a burning desire to be here. He loves hockey and he's good with people and he's results oriented. He understands who can help and who can't, and having Kenny Holland, Jimmy Devellano, and [assistant GM] Jimmy Nill to help along the way, he'll carve out a niche for himself."

GORDIE HOWE

There was a gleam in Gordie Howe's eyes that only Mr. Hockey has. Howe has always had that talent, something in his eyes that makes a chance meeting with him, or interviewing him, just that much more of an enjoyable experience. More personal and friendly, as if you've been a friend for a lifetime.

This time, there was a small group of reporters surrounding Howe in the media lounge at Joe Louis Arena. Howe was beaming. He'd just received a leather jacket from the Red Wings, a gift on his 80th birthday, during a pregame ceremony honoring him.

Remember, it was a Wings team jacket he received in 1945 as a signing bonus.

"I've still got the original [hanging back at home]," said Howe, a warm smile creasing his face, and those eyes making contact with a reporter who asked a question. "It's a corduroy. It still fits. But this one is leather. It's probably worth more than what I got paid my first year [with the Wings]."

There was laughter from the small media throng. Howe smiled, satisfied his joke got a positive reaction. That's another thing with Mr. Hockey. He's a man of many one-liners, funny anecdotes, and great stories, collected after decades of being in the game and knowing so many hockey characters.

And there are so many people who would gladly listen to everything Howe would tell them.

"It's great when Gordie comes into the room," said Chris Chelios, the veteran defenseman who made it his mission to at least come close to Howe's all-time games-played record. "He'll always crack a joke, say something funny. It's great for the younger guys on the team to see hockey history like that. You're talking about one of the greatest, if not the greatest, player of all time."

Chelios said he'd stop short if there was ever a chance of his eclipsing Howe's record of 1,767 games played. When reporters tell Howe about Chelios' intention of being at most No. 2 to Howe's record, Howe snickers. If anything, Chelios plays with the passion Howe did. There is the same sense of love for the game of hockey.

HOWE HAT TRICK

Gordie Howe is known as "Mr. Hockey" for all his contributions and greatness surrounding the game of hockey. It figures Howe would bring into the game's vocabulary the Gordie Howe hat trick.

Normally, of course, a hat trick is scoring three goals in a particular game. But Howe, one of the most physical offensive players the game has ever seen, would usually add a twist to the accomplishment. A Howe hat trick includes a goal, an assist, and a fight.

"He lies," said Howe, giggling, knowing Chelios would miss the game too much. "No, it'd be nice to see the kid do it. Kid, what is he, 46? His feelings will change. When you have a feeling you're losing it, then you start missing it. He's an athlete who takes care of himself. If he keeps that going, he can go forever."

Just like Howe seemingly did for so many years.

A staggering 25 seasons with the Wings to be exact. In that span, he played 1,687 games in a Wings uniform (no one has played more), and scored 786 goals and 1,023 assists, for 1,809 points. No one has scored more goals and points, either, although Steve Yzerman's 1,063 assists bettered Howe.

Six times Howe won the Hart Trophy, given to the league's Most Valuable Player.

When you combine Howe's work with the Hartford Whalers, the totals rise to 1,767 games, 801 goals, 1,049 assists, and 1,850 points.

At the age of 52, in his final season with the Whalers in 1980, Howe had 41 points.

"I felt good at midseason," said Howe of playing at age 52. "I always tell people they sat me on the bench too much. You stay awake some nights and think, *How the heck did it ever happen?* It was my love for the game."

Howe scored more than 20 goals a staggering 22 consecutive seasons, more than 30 goals 14 times in his career, and surpassed the 40-goal mark on five occasions.

Five times Howe led the league in goals.

Generally speaking, hockey fans either have Howe or Wayne Gretzky to debate as to who was the greatest player of all time. Mario Lemieux comes up for discussion, also, but Lemieux's not being able to stay healthy for long periods of time hurts him in any debate. So usually it's Howe and Gretzky.

For a debate such as that one, it's always interesting to hear what Scotty Bowman says. Bowman's coaching achievements speak for themselves, but further, no other individual has probably studied or watched the game more.

In Bowman's estimation, as told to USA Today once, Howe was the greatest player who has ever lived. "I don't think there is anyone even close to him," Bowman said. "Some say Bobby Orr, but he only played 10 years. Gordie was the ultimate forward, and he could play center. He could play wing and he could play defense."

Ken Holland, the Red Wings' general manager, said Howe is the greatest player of all time and certainly the best power forward who's ever lived.

Howe could score goals, and his skill level for a man his size (a sturdy 6', 205 pounds) was off the charts. But it was Howe's physical nature, his ability to fight and protect his teammates, and his willingness to drop the gloves against some of the best fighters the league has seen that separates Howe from so many other talented offensive players.

"I saw guys fighting on the train, how bad was that?" said Howe of how the game was played back then. "[Ted] Lindsay was one of them. He'd fight his mother if we lost."

The present-day NHL is much different from the time Howe played.

"It's hard to play both ways," he said. "If you hit, you get tired, and if you skate, you get tired. I think individuals who can skate can take the puck and go up ice, more power to them. Some of the kids from Europe, some of them I think their mom and dad taught them how to play with the puck before they were three. To get somebody to play with them is difficult, because you almost have to have a guy with two sets of eyes. It'd be an honor to play with them."

Howe actually almost became a member of the New York Rangers. When he was 15, he attended a tryout camp of the Rangers in Winnipeg. In those days, the NHL didn't have a draft system. Teams could talk to young players and claim them as the organization's property.

"I remember feeling homesick before I even got there," said Howe in his book *Gordie Howe: My Hockey Memories*. Howe said he'd never ventured that far from home before without any friends or family close by. "No one from the Rangers came to meet me at the [train] station, but I managed to make it to the rink on foot. As soon as I got there, they sent me to the equipment manager to be fitted out. He asked me what I needed. I told him I needed everything because I only brought my skates."

There was a further problem when Howe got the equipment. He'd never owned shoulder pads before, not to mention garter belts, and the like, so he watched veteran players put them on and mimicked their every move.

Despite his age and being homesick (Howe was from Saskatoon, Saskatchewan), Howe impressed the Rangers' front office and coaches to the point where they wanted to make him part of the organization.

But the homesickness was too much to overcome. Howe declined the opportunity and returned to Saskatoon. "Looking back, I guess if I wasn't shy, I would have been a Ranger," Howe wrote.

The next year, Howe attended a Red Wings camp and signed at the urging of Wings scout Fred Pinckney, a part-time scout and timekeeper for the Saskatoon Quakers senior club.

After a year-long stay in the United States Hockey League, with Omaha, Howe joined the Wings in 1946. His first contract was worth $5,000 and included a stipulation that it would be cut to $3,500 if Howe were to be sent to the minors.

"To be honest, I wanted to play so badly, I likely would have signed on for whatever [Jack] Adams offered," wrote Howe, alluding to the Wings' bombastic general manager/coach.

Adams concentrated solely on GM matters after Howe's rookie season, and Tommy Ivan (who coached Howe in Omaha) took

Gordie Howe spent 25 years with the Red Wings, won the Hart Trophy six times, and will forever be known as "Mr. Hockey."

over. That lightened the mood in the locker room and seemed to boost Howe's confidence even more. "The presence of Ivan helped to lower the level of tension that Adams liked to cultivate," Howe wrote. "Ivan was a breath of fresh air."

Howe's career began to take off.

Life or Death

Howe almost died on the ice during the opening round of the 1950 playoffs against Toronto.

He sized up Toronto's Ted Kennedy for a hit as Kennedy carried the puck up the boards. Just before the players collided, Kennedy pulled up, and Howe went crashing into the boards head-first. All the while, Howe's teammate Jack Stewart also had a read on Kennedy and simultaneously hit Howe from the side, making Howe's impact into the boards that much more severe.

Some accounts say Kennedy butt-ended Howe in the face at the point of collision, causing Howe to fall awkwardly into the boards.

In the end, Howe had a fractured skull along with a broken nose and cheekbone. He was rushed to the hospital, and a hole was drilled into his skull to relieve pressure on his brain. His parents were called to come in from Saskatchewan, with the doctors not confident Howe would make it.

But he did. And the Wings went on to win the Stanley Cup that season, with a little motivation from the Howe incident, no less.

"If you ask players who have been lucky enough to win the Cup a few times which one they remember best, they usually say the first one," Howe wrote. "Well, I spent most of my first one flat on my back."

Retirement

Howe retired in 1971 at the age of 43 after the Wings had finished last twice in a four-year span and injuries began to accumulate.

Howe was intent on retiring from playing and beginning a career in the front office—the Wings and owner Bruce Norris had created a vice president position for him. Figuring he'd do scouting and offer input on personnel decisions, Howe was disappointed to learn, as he put it, he'd become "vice president of paper clips. Essentially, my duties consisted of attending banquets and functions as a representative of the Red Wings."

There was something missing, something unfulfilled, but that void was soon going to be filled with the advent of the World Hockey Association (WHA).

An expansion league with teams in many growing markets, the league recruited many NHL journeymen and never-weres, but also several big names such as Bobby Hull, Dave Keon, and Bernie Parent, among others.

Howe came out of retirement before the 1973–1974 season to play with his sons Mark and Marty for Houston in the newly formed World Hockey Association. Neither son was draft-eligible by the NHL—in terms of age, they were too young—but the WHA felt that didn't apply to them.

Houston Aeros coach Bill Dineen, a former teammate of Howe's with the Wings, and assistant coach Doug Harvey, a Montreal Canadiens rival, were able to convince Howe—who didn't need much convincing—to make it a package deal of Howes. The three Howes would earn in four years what Gordie had earned in 18 years in the NHL: $2.5 million.

At the age of 45, in his first season in the WHA, Howe played in 70 of the 78 games and put up 31 goals and 100 points. Howe was also named the league's Most Valuable Player.

In 1977 with the league encountering financial problems, the Aeros folded. Howe's wife, Colleen, who had become the family's manager/agent, contacted the Wings about possibly reuniting the Howes with Detroit. But a deal couldn't be reached. The Howe trio would eventually land with the New England Whalers.

Howe's last season with the Whalers was the team's first in the NHL after the WHA folded, but four teams (including New England) were absorbed by the NHL.

Howe had 15 goals and 26 assists during the 1979–1980 season and didn't miss a game.

ALL-STAR EVENING

Gordie Howe returned to Detroit for his 23rd All-Star appearance before a record-breaking crowd of more than 21,000 people on February 5, 1980.

Joe Louis Arena had just opened, and the ovation was ear-rattling for Howe, who collected an assist in the 6–3 Wales Conference victory over the Campbell Conference.

Considering how his final season with the Wings was disappointing in terms of injuries and playing with a team on the decline, Howe had a glorious final season with the Whalers. Playing with his sons, and on a team with Hull and Keon, Howe wrote "my last go-around in the NHL with Hartford almost made up for that [season with the Wings]. I truly played the game for the love of it; that's what kept me on the ice for hours as a boy and brought me back to the NHL as a grandfather."

Hero and Friend
Wings coach Mike Babcock also grew up in Saskatoon, just like Howe. As a child growing up, Babcock couldn't get enough of Howe. "Gordie's been a hero of mine forever," said Babcock, who remembers meeting Howe once when Babcock was a teenager— Babcock's friend was Howe's nephew.

One of the perks of being head coach of the Red Wings is the procession of Hall of Famers, including Howe, who walk through the hallway that leads right past the coach's office.

Howe often stops by to say hello and crack a joke.

"Getting to know Mr. Hockey, that's pretty cool," Babcock said. "To come to Detroit and meet him, I met him when I was a kid, but to meet him and to know him and to be around him— he comes into my office a lot. It's kind of special. I get to know Mr. Hockey. That's cool."

MICKEY REDMOND

As popular a player as Mickey Redmond was while wearing a Red Wings sweater, it's been his work as a television analyst that has catapulted Redmond to cult status among Wings fans.

Those darn "Mickeyisms." Redmond will say something, comment on a particular play or player, and it'll be just so down-home Canadian that it'll stick in your front lobe until the next broadcast. At which point, Redmond will say something again that'll blow a hockey fan away, and the legend of Redmond continues to grow.

"I've been blessed and fortunate," said Redmond, who has had to battle cancer scares from 2003 through 2007, but hasn't lost any of his vigor, passion for the game, or love of interaction with Wings fans. "You can't call this work. It's too much fun."

There are a slew of drinking games out there that honor Redmond. Especially come playoff time, when games are on a seemingly nightly basis, household parties abound with fans hanging by Redmond's every word. So what are fans waiting to hear? What follows are some of Redmond's best, or most popular, Mickeyisms:

- "Wow": pretty self-explanatory, Redmond will get excited over a big hit, a beautiful pass or goal, a terrible call.
- "Bingo Bango": a tape-to-tape pass punctuated by a goal.
- "Holy Mackerel": used in a variety of ways, but usually when Redmond is exasperated.
- "Oh, boy, here we go": a favorite of many Wings fans, usually there's a fight about to take place.
- "This is no place for a nervous person": the game is on the line.
- "Hey Gang": listen up, fans.
- "Look out": some unsuspecting player is about to get clocked.
- "That was a tic-tac-toe play": a pretty passing play.
- "You be the judge": Redmond disagrees with a penalty call.

There are many more, all of which have made Redmond an institution among Wings fans.

But for his level of popularity as an announcer, it's sometimes easy to forget Redmond also had a distinguished playing career, although cut short by injuries with the Wings.

Redmond was traded to the Wings by Montreal during the 1970–1971 season and had two 50-goal seasons with the Wings before back problems began forcing him into the training room on a regular basis. In 1973–1974 Redmond set a Wings single-season record for power-play goals (21) and was named First Team All-Star.

Redmond also became the answer to a trivia question, one that is sure to stump at least several Wings fans.

Who was the first Red Wings' player to score 50 goals in a season? No, it wasn't Gordie Howe or Steve Yzerman or Sergei Fedorov. It was Redmond, during the 1972–1973 season.

"I was very proud of that achievement, but like I've often said, very disappointed in the fact we didn't make the playoffs," Redmond said.

Alex Delvecchio, a linemate of Redmond's, enjoyed having a shooter like that as an outlet. "Mick could really fire the puck," said Delvecchio, one of the game's better passers. "When you have a guy like that on your line, you get the puck to him. It made my job easier."

Redmond was forced to retire in 1976 at the age of 28 because of a ruptured disc. He said he probably waited too long to have surgery, and by that point, some permanent damage had been done to nerves and his legs. "In those days you were encouraged to play through injuries," Redmond said. "That's just the way it was."

A few years later, Redmond found himself in the broadcast booth. A second equally successful career began.

Wings fans everywhere have been glad of that ever since.

RED KELLY

Scouting is a difficult profession in any sport. It's such an inexact science, attempting to project where a young player will be years into the distance, how good the young athlete can become, without any guarantees.

Scouts will get nearly as many hunches wrong about young players as they will get right. Actually, more wrong than right. It's just part of the business.

Sometimes, though, you just can't help but scratch your head and be baffled about how wrong a scout can be. Could they really miss that badly? Misjudge talent so far off base? That comes to mind when considering the case of longtime Red Wings defenseman Red Kelly.

There were scouts with the Toronto Maple Leafs who felt the Simcoe, Ontario, native wouldn't, or couldn't, handle professional hockey because of the physical nature of the game, and that Kelly didn't have the physicality or aggressive nature to succeed in the National Hockey League.

Uh, wrong.

The Wings gladly snapped Kelly up and placed him among a team of other greats. During his 12-plus-year stay with the Wings, Kelly became one of the greatest defensemen the NHL has ever seen.

He was durable, technically sound, and revolutionized the defenseman position. The player some scouts felt couldn't become an NHL performer became a Hall of Fame inductee in 1969.

Joe Falls, the *Detroit News'* prestigious longtime columnist who followed the Wings during their glory years of the 1950s, wrote this about Kelly: "A remarkable player. He could handle the puck better with his feet than most players could with their sticks." Falls felt Kelly was the fifth-best Wings player he'd ever seen behind Gordie Howe, Steve Yzerman, Terry Sawchuk, and Ted Lindsay. "He could have been a great soccer player; instead he was a great defenseman—Bobby Orr before there was Bobby Orr."

Kelly's way of playing wouldn't raise an eyebrow these days, but in his day, he was a curiosity—a defenseman who would actually rush the puck into an opposing team's zone. That would be called an offensive defenseman in present-day hockey terminology.

"He could defend with the best of them and move the puck ahead better than anyone, except for Montreal's Doug Harvey," Falls said.

Kelly was an offensive force, from his position, like no one in the NHL had ever seen before. It was absolutely unheard of for a defenseman to crack the top 10 in scoring in the 1950s. But Kelly did it three times: in 1950–1951, 1952–1953, and 1953–1954. And after the 1953–1954 season Kelly became the first winner of the Norris Trophy, awarded to the league's best defenseman. On October 21, 1954, Kelly became the first Detroit defenseman to ever score three goals in a game. Not unheard of anymore but, obviously, a historic accomplishment in Kelly's day. From 1949–1950 to 1956–1957, Kelly was a named a first-team All-Star six times and second-team selection twice.

Occasionally, he would be used up front to take advantage of his skating and playmaking ability. The player who some scouts felt couldn't compete in the NHL also played on four Wings Stanley Cup–champion teams.

Kelly was a gentleman on and off the ice. Few of his teammates or peers ever recall him uttering a cuss word. "Nobody ever heard him use a swear word," Falls said.

"Red Kelly is the greatest man I've ever met," said Marcel Pronovost, a teammate of Kelly's both in Detroit and Toronto. "He's the most honest, most dedicated, and possibly the most intelligent."

Kelly won the Lady Byng Trophy—given to the player who exemplifies gentlemanly play—four times.

The fact some would feel Kelly wouldn't be tough enough for the NHL is rather strange, considering he was an accomplished boxer in his childhood. At 5'11" and a stocky 193 pounds in his hockey prime, Kelly was less heavy as a youngster but no less competitive or durable. "He could stand up for himself when he had to," teammate Marty Pavelich said.

Kelly only missed 64 games in his career and never missed more than 12 in a season. With Detroit, he missed only 24 games over his 12 years spent in a Red Wings sweater and was known to play as many 50 minutes per game in key games.

Still, despite the impeccable credentials, Kelly was another of the Wings' veterans during the 1950s who was deemed expendable by general manager Jack Adams late in their careers.

There was also some ill feelings from Adams' perspective when Kelly went public with the fact Adams asked Kelly to play with a broken ankle late in the regular season while the Wings failed to qualify for the 1958–1959 playoffs.

After some testy contract negotiations, and feeling Kelly was beginning the downside of his career at age 32, Adams traded Kelly and Billy McNeill to the New York Rangers during the 1959–1960 season for defenseman Bill Gadsby and forward Eddie Shack.

Kelly was devastated. He considered himself a Red Wing through and through and didn't report to the Rangers. He retreated to his tobacco farm and bowling center in Simcoe and contemplated retirement. Adams was forced to void the trade (upsetting the Rangers, who felt they had a deal), and NHL president Clarence Campbell threatened that Kelly would be put on an NHL retirement list unless he reported back to Detroit (in those days, getting off the retirement list meant unanimous approval from all six teams, which was not easily done).

Two days before Campbell's ultimatum, Toronto coach Punch Imlach informed Kelly the Leafs would be interested in acquiring him. The idea of playing for the Leafs, who were a haven for older players under Imlach during that era, appealed to Kelly. The Leafs acquired him for defenseman Marc Reaume, certainly not one of the Wings' best trades. Kelly would go on to win four Stanley Cups in Toronto, while at the same time moving to center and dominating at forward positions, as well.

His final statistics would read like this: eight Stanley Cups won with two different teams, 281 goals, 542 assists for 823 points, in 1,316 games over 20 seasons.

You have to wonder how the poor scout who thought Kelly wouldn't be an NHL player felt.

TERRY SAWCHUK

How's this for intimidating if you're a present-day Red Wings goalie?

A picture of Wings Hall of Fame goalie Terry Sawchuk hangs over the stalls where the Wings goalies sit and dress these days in the locker room. Sawchuk is poised to stop a shot, looking square at the shooter, a confident look on his face, and likely about to make another stop in his illustrious career.

Chris Osgood sits somewhat under that picture. Not directly, but he knows that picture of Sawchuk looms overhead. Osgood is the first to say because of the age differences, and the fact Osgood didn't follow the Red Wings growing up, he's not a resident historian on Sawchuk. But he understands the history and intrigue surrounding what many historians and analysts say was the greatest goaltender ever. No Red Wings goalie, it's generally regarded, was ever better.

"Everyone knows he was one of the best of all time," Osgood said. "Just look at the numbers, the awards. And all the stuff he went through, he had so many injuries. It's tough to think of many who were better."

The numbers certainly are impressive. Four times Sawchuk won the Vezina Trophy as the league's best goalie. And given Sawchuk played in the Original Six days, that accomplishment spoke for itself.

"Consider the talent in that era," said Mickey Redmond, former Wings player and current television analyst. "Every night you were facing Hall of Famers."

Sawchuk set NHL records for games played (971), minutes played (57,194), and shutouts (103). He led the league in victories his first five full seasons.

Just with the Wings, Sawchuk played in 734 games and posted a 352–243–132 record with an astounding 85 shutouts, 2.45 goals-against average, and three Stanley Cups (Sawchuk also won a Stanley Cup with Toronto late in his career).

"You couldn't throw a pea behind him," said former team-mate Ted Lindsay.

Sawchuk turned in one of his most memorable Stanley Cup playoff runs with the Wings during the 1951–1952 season. The Wings swept both Toronto and Montreal with Sawchuk allowing a measly five goals in the eight games (0.62 goals-against average). Sawchuk had four shutouts among the eight victories.

"A lot of people think he was the greatest goalkeeper who ever played the game. I include myself in that group," said goalie Glenn Hall, who succeeded Sawchuk in net for the Wings as a talented young prospect himself. Jack Adams, the Wings' general manager, traded Sawchuk to Boston in 1955 to make room for Hall.

The Hockey Hall of Fame waived its five-year wait period to induct Sawchuk in 1971.

Although the numbers are spectacular, it's really what Sawchuk went through in achieving those numbers that is extraordinary. It was the death of his brother Mike (16 at the time, due to a heart condition), also a goalie, that put Sawchuk into goalie pads. Terry was 10 at the time, but he inherited Mike's pads and instantly warmed to the sport and position.

That Sawchuk would even attempt to play hockey was a somewhat of an upset considering he was often ill as a child.

Sawchuk took to the position like few players ever have. He became the first goaltender to crouch and look for the puck through screens and traffic in front of the net, simply for the fact he wanted to get a better look at the puck.

Once in those pads, maybe no player endured so much physical suffering. The list of injuries connected with Sawchuk is astounding. A right elbow injury that Sawchuk suffered in childhood while playing football never properly healed, and he needed surgery in which 60 pieces of bone were taken out. He also had a

Goalie Terry Sawchuk spent 14 seasons in Detroit and recorded 103 career shutouts.

right arm injury later in his hockey career that ultimately made his right arm shorter than his left.

During his career Sawchuk had his lungs punctured, his appendix removed, ruptured discs, a blocked intestine, a ruptured spleen, infectious mononucleosis (Sawchuk's weight dropped to 166 pounds and he was hospitalized for 12 days), severed hand tendons, and a broken instep. Sawchuk, it's estimated, also had 600 stitches during his career stemming from cuts caused from flying pucks and slashing sticks. He was one of the last goalies to play without a face mask.

He temporarily retired during the 1956–1957 season with Boston, after returning from his mononucleosis, because of tension from the abuse he took from Boston sportswriters for his substandard play.

Sawchuk played the next seven seasons with the Wings, and though still an elite goalie, he didn't match the level before he was traded to Boston.

He eventually went to the Toronto Maple Leafs, where he won a Stanley Cup, teaming with fellow goaltending legend Johnny Bower.

Why did he go through so much to continue playing? Many say he did so because of the fact there were only six teams, six starting goalie positions, and Sawchuk didn't want anyone to take his spot. Not that anyone really could.

"He'd always say to the guys, 'Get me a couple and we'll win,'" former Red Wings coach Jimmy Skinner told the Red Wings' website. "He didn't say it in a bragging kind of way. He was just that confident. I saw a lot of the greats, but to my mind, I haven't seen anyone better than Sawchuk. Reflexes, angles—he had it all and he also had a lot of guts. He was fearless in the net and extremely confident."

Sawchuk's death was as tragic as much of his life.

On May 31, 1970, then a member of the New York Rangers, Sawchuk died at the age of 40 from complications resulting from internal injuries after an alleged fight with teammate Ron Stewart.

The two shared a home and allegedly got into an argument on April 29, supposedly over housecleaning chores. Stewart said Sawchuk tripped over a barbecue grill and allegedly suffered serious internal injuries. Sawchuk had his gall bladder removed following the accident. Instead of recovering, he relapsed and underwent a second operation, this time for his liver.

He died of a blood clot in the pulmonary artery.

SID ABEL

There weren't many parts of the Red Wings organization that Sid Abel didn't make an imprint on.

Playing? He was one of the best who ever wore a Red Wings sweater.

Management? He was a general manager, and the head coach, at various junctures for the Wings.

Broadcasting? Abel did that, also, doing color on television and radio broadcasts along with play-by-play man Bruce Martyn for 10 seasons.

It was on the ice, though, where Abel stood out, best known for centering the Production Line with Ted Lindsay and Gordie Howe. From 1947 to 1952, the line was arguably the most dominant in its time in the NHL.

Abel was 29 and just returning from war duty when Red Wings coach Tommy Ivan decided to try him in the middle between the two physical, younger wings (Howe was 19, Lindsay was 22). Hardly a bruiser, Abel was 5'11", approximately 155 pounds, and was a shifty player who had a keen sense about himself on the ice and melded well with the rambunctious (but skilled) Howe and Lindsay.

"I remember Sid would joke often about just dumping the puck in and letting the two young guys go get it," said broadcaster Budd Lynch, who watched the Production Line dominate.

During his 12 seasons with the Wings, Abel was a four-time All-Star and won the Hart Trophy, as the league's Most Valuable Player, in 1948–1949, when he scored a league-high 28 goals.

"With Sid, you never played under pressure, even though it was there," said Johnny Wilson, former Wings player and coach, in *Hockeytown Heroes*. "It [pressure] was lying there, but he made you feel like, 'Hey! You know this is just another game. A back alley game. Let's go have some fun.' It took a lot of pressure off."

Abel—nicknamed "Bootnose" because of the shape of his nose after getting it broken by Montreal's Rocket Richard—was part of three Stanley Cup championship teams with the Wings, and five times the Wings finished first overall during the regular season with him.

With Howe, in particular, Abel struck an immediate chemistry on the ice, and strong relationship off it. Like Howe, Abel was from Saskatchewan. For the shy, reclusive Howe, having someone, anybody, whom he could relate to proved invaluable.

That bond was evident on the ice. The trio dominated the league scoring races, particularly in 1949–1950, when Lindsay led the league with 78 points (23 goals, 55 assists) in 69 games, while Abel was second and Howe third.

Eventually, general manager Jack Adams, as was his custom, felt Abel was beginning to slow and wanted to get younger players into the lineup. Adams released Abel, who would land as a player/coach in Chicago.

In 14 years with the Blackhawks and Red Wings, Abel had 189 goals and 283 assists for 472 points.

ALEX DELVECCHIO

You could tell immediately the man was speechless, and really, although he was so thankful for the ceremony, somewhat uncomfortable.

The Red Wings were honoring one of their greats this evening. In this instance, it was Alex Delvecchio, one of the greatest, maybe somewhat underappreciated Red Wings of all time. The organization was doing so with a statue in the concourse of Joe Louis Arena.

The only other players to have statues at Joe Louis Arena are Gordie Howe and Ted Lindsay, who happened to be Delvecchio's linemates. "Not bad company," said Delvecchio with one of his trademark grins.

But as he kept glancing at the statue, a good likeness, too, as it turned out, the amazement was awash over his face.

There shouldn't have been. This was a player who played 24 years, played in 1,549 games (all with the Wings), and had 1,281 points (456 goals and 825 assists). Three times Delvecchio won the Lady Byng Trophy, given to the player who exhibits gentlemanly play. For 12 seasons, Delvecchio was the Wings' captain.

Another statistic on a lengthy hockey résumé that could be easily overlooked, or sneered at: Delvecchio played in 13 All-Star Games when it was actually an honor and a privilege to be a part of it.

"That is unbelievable," said Mickey Redmond, a current Wings television analyst who also benefited from a 50-goal season with Delvecchio as his center in 1972–1973. "Think about that for a moment. That's 13 All-Star Games in an era when there were many, many real good hockey players. Just six teams, remember. Each and every team had a lot of talent. To play in 13, that's a real tribute to Alex Delvecchio the player."

Then there was Delvecchio's durability. In those 22 seasons Delvecchio starred for the Wings, he missed only 43 games. "A lot of that is luck," Delvecchio said. "I never really got hit that bad [to be injured]. But in those days, you just kept on playing. You didn't want to lose your spot [in the lineup]. We all loved to play."

All the numbers, the gaudy statistics, the durability, those are all admirable. But Delvecchio would see it somewhat differently from most folks, who heaped praise on him. Delvecchio felt a lot of his success came about because he played with some great players.

Just take a look at those other statues. Howe, Lindsay, Sid Abel.

"This wouldn't have happened had I not played with some great players," said Delvecchio, looking over at Howe, who was part of this ceremony and was signing autographs for a legion of fans. "Like that guy over there. Playing with guys like that helps your career immensely."

Many of Delvecchio's contemporaries beg to differ. Along with being humble, what Delvecchio was, according to several Wings teammates, was one of the most creative players of his day. "A great artist, that's what he was," Howe said. "I had no idea how much of one until I played with him. Lindsay and I would sit on the bench when Alex was just a rookie and talk about what a good player he could become."

Ted Lindsay, Gordie Howe, and Alex Delvecchio comprised one of the greatest lines in NHL history.

Delvecchio replaced Abel when he was released by the Wings after the 1951–1952 season. Abel, Howe, and Lindsay formed one of the greatest trios ever put together. It was the Production Line, don't forget. The trio had the perfect mix of strength, ferociousness and finesse. Delvecchio was able to replace Abel because of his deft passing ability and hockey acumen.

"Everyone knew the Production Line," Delvecchio said. "I had heard of them [while preparing for the NHL]. But I had played with them at times during my first season, while Sid was still with us. That made things easier."

The infamous line never lost a beat in terms of chemistry—or production.

"We read each other very well," said Howe, matter-of-factly and sternly, to make sure everyone around him would know how important Delvecchio was to the line's success. "I played with some great hockey players, but none came to his order. They put us together, and things kept moving right along. If something maybe didn't work at first, we'd talk about it on the bench or between periods, and we worked it out. Jack Adams had a way of doing things. He sat us next to each other in the locker room, on the bus, and we'd trade stories. Alex knows every story I have.

"Nobody does it alone. I can thank Alex for a lot of good years."

Redmond would learn the facets about Delvecchio later in their careers. "You hear about players who make other players better, and Alex was one of those players who made people around him better," Redmond said. "He was an extremely unselfish player. The game slowed down for him. He was a top-notch, excellent passer. Very few could deliver in the game like he did."

Obviously Howe's legend in the game, his place among the all-time greats, has long been secured. His critical eye of the game is amazing, even today noting some segment of a particular player's skills that others may not entirely focus on or appreciate.

When it comes to Delvecchio, there was undoubtedly something that Howe was struck by. "He was such a thinker on the ice," said Howe, almost in amazement. "If he wasn't feeling good on a particular evening, he played his position so well. Alex always knew the right place to be, where he needed to be in any given situation. I could count on that. Not many players can think the game like that."

Then, there was the durability. Delvecchio played in 1,549 games.

"The style he played with was conducive [to being able to play so long]," Redmond said.

Of course Delvecchio brushes off the praise.

With Delvecchio, it always goes back to the sense of team and the fact he was surrounded by some of the greatest Red Wings to ever wear the famed sweater. "With guys like Teddy and Gordie, with the horses we had and I played with over the years, my job was to get the puck to them," Delvecchio said. "Get the puck to them, and they'd get the job done. I learned that quick. They helped me become a better passer, shall we say."

Typical Delvecchio, to be sure. Always deflecting the praise to other teammates, never giving himself credit.

"He's a real gentleman on and off the ice," Redmond said. "Maybe some can say he was underrated because he was so unassuming. Maybe he fell under the radar just a bit because of that. But you look at the numbers and you say, 'Wow.' I can't help but pointing to those numbers and accolades [such as the All-Star Games], and he accomplished that in an era when there was an awful lot of good competition. The stuff Alex accomplished, it's a great tribute to how good a hockey player he really was."

Delvecchio remained in the Detroit area after retiring. He became the team's general manager from 1974 to 1977 but eventually turned to private business.

Although he doesn't have the status of a Howe or Yzerman in Hockeytown, Delvecchio still has a secure spot in Wings fans' hearts.

"People in Detroit have been real good to me," Delvecchio said. "Playing here has opened a lot of doors."

All those accomplishments are mentioned on the statue, the one that looms large in Joe Louis Arena these days. It's the statue that Delvecchio can't stop taking gazes at, somewhat sheepishly, maybe a little embarrassed.

"It looks great, they did a heckuva job with it," said Delvecchio, a little satisfied smile appearing on his face. "To have that done for you, it's a special honor. You never dream about these types of things happening to you. All we wanted to do was play hockey and try to win some games."

TED LINDSAY

A reporter asked Red Wings coach Mike Babcock right before the holidays one season about the NHL thinking of playing on Christmas and taking advantage of a potentially huge television audience.

144

TERRIBLE TED

Some people called him Terrible Ted or Teddy, while others called him Scarface in honor of the multitude of stitches on his face. Either fit for Ted Lindsay, one of the toughest but also skilled players in the Original Six era.

Lindsay, who started the NHL Players Association, holds a rather dubious honor. No other player has led the NHL in both scoring and penalty minutes.

In the 1949–1950 season, Lindsay led the league in scoring with 78 points. Nearly a decade later, during the 1958–1959 season, Lindsay had a league-high 184 penalty minutes while with the Chicago Blackhawks.

Babcock just shook his head and nodded toward former Wings great Ted Lindsay, a tremendous player in his time but also the man who began what is now the NHL Players Association. Lindsay, as he quite often does, was spending time in the Wings locker room that morning.

Babcock said it's because of Lindsay that the league shuts down on Christmas, and players get to spend the day with families, as Babcock believes they should. Lindsay fought for many things, fought for what he believed was fair and right for NHL players in the 1950s. "Quite a man," Babcock said.

Whether for beginning the Players Association, or his accomplishments on the ice, Lindsay left an indelible mark on the game. A member of the Hockey Hall of Fame, Lindsay's rough style of play, ability to score goals, and his refusal to lose, all rolled into a 5'8", 165-pound ball of fire, made him a favorite among Wings fans.

And still do. Lindsay made Detroit his home and is a frequent visitor to Joe Louis Arena, attending games and practices.

"You must have done something right if they still remember you," said Lindsay, whose statue, along with former linemates Gordie Howe and Alex Delvecchio, stands on the Joe Louis Arena concourse.

Howe's eyes light up when he talks about Lindsay. The two were teammates were for a decade, and Howe appreciated the way Lindsay played the game.

It was Howe, Lindsay, and center Sid Abel who formed the Production Line, unquestionably one of the greatest trios to ever play together. Lindsay's role was digging the puck out of the corner, playing policeman, and doing his part offensively on a line that was nearly unstoppable.

Eight times Lindsay was named first-team All-Star, an incredible accomplishment given the quality of talent in those years of the Original Six.

"He was a miserable little bastard," said Howe, cracking a sly smile and saying those words in the respectful tone any tough hockey player would say about another. "Tough as nails. Mean and aggressive. He would take care of a guy who was trying to go out of his way to get me, and I would do likewise for him. We got along real well."

Which is a good thing, not necessarily just for hockey reasons. "Teddy was my landlord for a lot of years," Howe said. "I had to be in his good graces."

Lindsay was the Red Wings' captain from the 1952–1953 season to the 1955–1956 season, an honor he took to heart. He played with a passion that few players ever have.

"I don't think a lot of guys in here would like to face him even now on the ice," said current Red Wings forward Darren McCarty, whose style is somewhat reminiscent of Lindsay's.

The best Lindsay story may be the first round of the 1956 playoffs as the Wings were playing the Toronto Maple Leafs. The Wings were leading the best-of-seven series 2–0, and it was headed back to Toronto. But, as the teams were heading to Toronto, a

BALANCED SCORING

For all the offensive talent the Red Wings have had, there haven't been many league leaders in scoring.

In fact, Ted Lindsay and Gordie Howe are the only two Red Wings to ever lead the NHL in scoring. Lindsay did it during the 1949–1950 season. Howe, Lindsay's linemate on the Production Line with Sid Abel, won the scoring title six times.

death threat was phoned in to the hotel where the Wings were staying. The caller said Lindsay and Gordie Howe were going to be shot if they took the ice for Game 3 at Maple Leaf Gardens.

Instead of shying away from the action, being preoccupied with the threat, Lindsay and Howe excelled in the game. Lindsay, in fact, scored the game-tying goal in the third period and the winning goal in overtime. Further, with Maple Leafs fans booing, Lindsay went to center ice after scoring the winning goal, made his stick like a rifle, and began to pretend to shoot it into the rafters at Maple Leaf Gardens.

"Nearly the entire arena was booing because it was all Leafs fans," Lindsay said. "But after I went to center ice and did what I did, they started clapping. They figured, 'This Lindsay guy isn't that bad.'"

That type of fearless attitude is what made Lindsay a prototypical captain.

"He was real talkative, much more than Alex or I," said Howe of Lindsay's leadership ability. "He'd get after guys if he felt those guys weren't playing to their ability. If the team wasn't playing well, if it was playing badly, Teddy made sure we were aware of it. He was a good captain."

"I was a Red Wing through and through," Lindsay said.

Which made the Wings' trade of Lindsay and goalie Glenn Hall after the 1957 season to Chicago for Johnny Wilson, Hank Bassen, Forbes Kennedy, and Bill Preston that much more difficult to absorb for Lindsay.

The Wings traded him, the belief is, for beginning the Players Association. The trade really made little sense because Lindsay was playing some of the best hockey of his career and was in his prime. Trading him to the Blackhawks for players who would make little or no impact weakened the organization.

And devastated Lindsay.

"It was difficult to leave," Lindsay said.

Lindsay would retire as a player in 1960. But four years later, while applying for a radio analyst's job with the Wings, Abel—then the Wings' general manager—asked Lindsay whether he'd be interested in making a comeback.

Always a physical fitness nut, Lindsay continued to be in hockey-playing shape. So at the age of 39 Lindsay played with the Wings during the 1964–1965 season, scoring 14 goals (28 points total) and amassing 173 penalty minutes.

Terrible Teddy hadn't lost his edge after all those years.

Lindsay's frequent appearances in the Wings' locker room these days are welcome.

"You think about the sacrifices that guys like Ted made, and it really humbles you," Kris Draper said. "He paved the way for the players ahead of him."

"What a great guy," said Chris Chelios, another player with similar rambunctious qualities on the ice and who shares Lindsay's passion in terms of the Players Association. "You listen to the stories he has, and it just amazes you."

SERGEI FEDOROV

Prior to the 1989 draft, then–Red Wings general manager Jimmy Devellano was in the midst of a rebuilding project and wanted to speed it along.

The Wings needed talent, players who could make an impact, and Devellano knew the best way to accumulate talent was through the draft. He also knew that much of that talent resided in Eastern Europe, where the NHL had not yet treaded.

But Devellano felt it was time to change. And, if need be, the Red Wings were the ones to force the change. "We all knew that Russia had a wonderful supply of hockey players. Czechoslovakia, too," Devellano said. "But you couldn't get the buggers out. It really bothered me when we'd be drafting in the third, fourth, fifth round and we'd be taking North American players and really our scouts weren't that high on them. Finally, I remember sitting with Kenny [Holland] and Neil Smith, who were our lead scouts at the time, and saying 'Who's the best 18-year-old player in the world?'

"They both said, 'Sergei Fedorov.'"

Of that, scouts had little question. Fedorov was a young player with sublime speed and skating ability, and coming out of the Russian system, he was as responsible defensively as he was skilled offensively.

But, like Devellano mentioned, how do you get those Russian players out?

"Our question to Jimmy was, 'Are you prepared to waste a draft pick? Are you prepared to draft a player and never see him?'" Holland said. "Jimmy said, 'Get the best player, and we'll worry about that later.'"

In July 1990 then–executive vice president Jim Lites and then–assistant general manager Nick Polano helped Fedorov defect while the Russian national team was competing in the Goodwill Games. Lites and Polano discreetly arranged a plan with Fedorov to sneak away after a game late at night. Fedorov still talks about the anxiety and exhilaration he felt that evening, especially while in a rental car with Lites and Polano and heading to owner Mike Ilitch's private jet.

For the Wings, this entire episode was an example of how they were going to do whatever it took, under Ilitch's ownership, to win.

"We've extended ourselves more than anybody else in the league," said Ilitch, who would, in the years ahead, grab several other European stars such as Vladimir Konstantinov and Petr Klima. "Don't take this the wrong way, but I think we have vision. I mean, we were trying to get players out of Russia when it was a Communist country.

"I remember when Sergei was going to defect [in 1990] in Vancouver. I had a pilot for my plane, and it was his first day on the job. And I said, 'I've got a player who's going to defect from Russia and you've got to go pick him up.' His eyes got like saucers, and he said, 'I've got to go to Russia?' And I said, 'No, no, no. Just Vancouver.' He was petrified—probably ready to quit right away."

All the work involved getting Fedorov paid off.

Detroit is a long, long way from Hollywood. But there was something about Sergei Fedorov that bridged the gap a little bit. Fedorov, for whatever reason, had that Hollywood mystique about him. And that helped him reach a stardom level, particularly in hockey-mad Detroit, that few players have achieved in the last couple of decades.

Now not all the time would Fedorov be loved. But good or bad, few players have stirred the passions of Wings fans like the

DEFENSIVELY DOMINANT

Red Wings forwards are beginning to stake a regular claim to the Selke Trophy, the league's award given to the best defensive forward.

Since the 1993–1994 season, four different Wings forwards have won the award.

Sergei Fedorov won it twice, while Steve Yzerman, Kris Draper, and Pavel Datsyuk each won the award once. Datsyuk had to beat out teammate Henrik Zetterberg for the award in 2008 and won the award again in 2009.

Russian star who won a Hart Trophy in 1994, Selke Trophy in 1994 and 1996, and the Lester Pearson Award (given to the most outstanding player as selected by the Players Association) in 1994.

"He's one of the best players I've ever had as a teammate," said Nicklas Lidstrom, himself one of the game's all-time best defensemen.

Why did Fedorov invoke such myriad emotions?

Maybe it was his involvement with Anna Kournikova, the Russian tennis goddess who had an on-again/off-again relationship with Fedorov that included a brief marriage. They would be seen together in many hot spots in Detroit, and Kournikova was a semi-regular at Wings games when the two were a couple. Spotting Kournikova in the crowd became a nightly occurrence for television producers hoping to get a brief shot for that evening's game.

Or was it the European movie-star looks that made Fedorov the favorite player of many a female Red Wings fan, particularly the younger ones? Young fans, male or female, still wear the No. 91 jersey that remains popular in local hockey rinks.

Or was it the moodiness that could, and would, take over Fedorov, and make him disappear in some games. Nothing raised the ire of Wings fans more. How could a player with so much wondrous talent be invisible so often on the ice? Fedorov's subpar playoff performances bothered Wings fans to no end.

Or was it a contract dispute to start the 1997–1998 season, in which Fedorov (who was an unsigned free agent) sat out until he was tendered an offer sheet by the Carolina Hurricanes (six years, $38 million) which forced the Red Wings to initiate movement and re-sign him?

So many different events, and wide-ranging emotions on the spectrum. You either were for or against him.

But, oh, that ability. More than one NHL scout marveled at the athleticism, the skating ability, his ability to play on defense (then-coach Scotty Bowman would put Fedorov on defense on rare occasions), and his savvy on the ice.

"You look at the things Sergei Fedorov can do on the ice, the skating, his strength, the shooting, and there are few athletes in any sport that are better all the way around," said Rick Dudley, a former player, and now front-office executive in the NHL.

Fedorov left the Red Wings as an unrestricted free agent after the 2002–2003 season, signing with the Anaheim Ducks. He ultimately was traded by the Ducks to the Columbus Blue Jackets, and then to the Washington Capitals.

Since leaving the Wings, Fedorov hasn't come close to matching his average statistics with them. He hasn't come close to winning a Stanley Cup, of which he won three with Detroit.

When returning to Joe Louis Arena as an opponent, Fedorov has been heavily booed whenever he has the puck. The abuse is more for Fedorov than any other opposing player at Joe Louis.

Is Fedorov sad or angry about his treatment?

"I'm on the other team now," Fedorov said. "It doesn't surprise me."

HULL AND SHANAHAN

Every team needs a talker—someone with a quick wit to defuse a potentially bad situation or keep the team loose. The media enjoys that guy, also, because of his ability to deliver great quotes.

The Red Wings had two of the very best in the league in the early 2000s with Brett Hull and Brendan Shanahan.

What made the situation even better for the Wings was that along with their vocal abilities, both were Hall of Fame–caliber players, players with vast offensive abilities who were key factors in the Wings' 2002 Stanley Cup championship, with Shanahan playing a significant role in the 1998 and 1999 titles, as well.

Shanahan played with the Wings from 1996 to 2006, instantly becoming a fan favorite as the power forward the organization had yearned for while building a powerhouse team.

"You see what he's accomplished throughout his career, all the goals [more than 600], his presence on the ice, he's one of the best power forwards the game has ever seen," Shanahan's former teammate Kris Draper said. "He definitely has a place in Red Wings history."

Shanahan left the Red Wings after the 2005–2006 season, one season after the lockout ended, and a season in which he was the team's leading goal-scorer with 40 goals. The Wings, posting a sensational regular season, were upset in the first round of the playoffs by the Edmonton Oilers. Steve Yzerman retired just a few weeks earlier.

Shanahan said it was a gut instinct to leave the Wings and move to the New York Rangers.

"It's nothing that was said to me," Shanahan said. "It's just I felt I was identified with the past rather than the future."

That doesn't mean he didn't strongly reconsider returning and signing with the Red Wings. Shanahan still had, and has, strong feelings for former teammates he played with on the Wings, and appreciates the organization.

But the fact his wife is from Boston and he wanted to relocate to the East, the chance to play with the Rangers (he signed with the New Jersey Devils during the 2008–2009 season) was an opportunity Shanahan couldn't refuse.

"It plays a role," Shanahan said. "We were very comfortable in Detroit, we had a nice home there. But what makes New York attractive is it's closer to home, which is the South Shore [of Boston], and also with the schedule, the road trips aren't like what you have in the West."

As for Hull's stay with the Wings, it was much shorter than Shanahan's, but nevertheless enjoyable and noteworthy.

Hull came aboard the Wings the eventful summer of 2001 when general manager Ken Holland acquired Dominik Hasek in a trade, then signed Hull and Luc Robitaille as unrestricted free agents, the prelude to the Wings winning the Stanley Cup in 2002.

Hull stayed with the Wings for three seasons, leading up to the lockout in 2004. But winning the Stanley Cup in 2002, among a few other notable highlights during the stay, was the most memorable for Hull.

"They were like my years in Dallas, they were great organizations, just like St. Louis," Hull said. "I wish everyone could play for an Original Six team. It was definitely different."

Hull called the 2002 Stanley Cup team the best team he's ever played on.

"What, nine or 10 Hall of Famers?" said Hull of the All-Star dominated team. "That was unbelievable."

Hull lived up to his advertised billing during his stay with the Wings. The media loved him—he was quotable about any subject thrown his way, not necessarily just hockey. The shot was as lethal as it was in Dallas or St. Louis or Calgary, stops before he wore a Wings jersey. The Hull one-timer was a sight to behold.

"We knew he was a little bit lazy, and he was a little bit overweight," said Dominik Hasek, with a sly grin crossing his face. "But we knew he could play. Nobody before him, and nobody after him, had the same type of shot like him."

Hull also scored his 732nd career goal while with the Wings, moving past Marcel Dionne at that point, and trailing only Wayne Gretzky (894 goals) and Red Wings legend Gordie Howe (801). Fittingly, it was a game-winning overtime goal, a lethal one-timer that was a signature Hull goal. Many die-hard Wings fans of that era will always enjoy the mental picture of Hull unleashing one of those blasts.

"I have nothing but good things to say about my time in Detroit," Hull said. "Great memories."

CHRIS CHELIOS

He wouldn't have expected it would turn out this way. Few people really would have, given the ill will Red Wings fans had toward

Chris Chelios. He wouldn't have expected this love affair that materialized over the years, Chelios suddenly becoming more than just a fan favorite. Chelios, in his time in Detroit, became a Red Wing.

Even more so, a Detroiter. When you think of Chris Chelios now, hockey fans in Detroit first visualize Chelios wearing a Wings jersey, being a Red Wing...and certainly not a Chicago Blackhawk.

On a bitter opponent such as the Blackhawks, Chelios was the player passionate Red Wings fans hated the most. They disliked his smirks, his (dirty) stick work against the Red Wings, the fact he bled Blackhawks red and was Chicago through and through.

"A lot of arenas were like that, they'd be booing me, but in Detroit it seemed like there was a little more of it," Chelios said. "I mean, Chicago and Detroit, that whole thing, two great cities, a great sports rivalry."

Know what really peeved Wings fans? That Chelios also didn't hide that he disliked the Red Wings. After a ton of regular-season and playoff games between the two old Original Six rivals, there was a lot of hate to share. So if there ever was a player who likely would never wear a Red Wings sweater, it had to be Chelios. No way, no how.

"You wouldn't think," Chelios said.

RESTAURANT OWNER

Chris Chelios has a good idea what he'll do with most of his time when he finally retires. He is the owner of Cheli's Chili Bar, with two locations, one each in Detroit and Dearborn, a Detroit suburb.

In his youth, Chelios helped his father, Gus, run restaurants in Chicago. Chelios said it was a natural to one day own his own restaurant, which he first did in Chicago before being traded to Detroit. The Chicago location closed shortly after Chelios became a Red Wing.

"It's something I enjoy," said Chelios of the restaurant business. "I'll definitely spend time doing it when I stop playing. Hopefully that won't be for a while longer."

But in professional sports, never say never. The impossible seems to occur every day. Even the possibility of Chris Chelios, the ultimate anti–Red Wing for so many years, suddenly wearing a Wings sweater and protecting the likes of Yzerman, Brett Hull, Pavel Datsyuk, and Henrik Zetterberg. For Red Wings fans, the impossible occurred March 23, 1999, the day Chelios arrived from the Blackhawks for defenseman Anders Eriksson and first-round picks in 1999 (who turned out to be Steve McCarthy) and 2001 (Adam Munro).

One of the most hated players Wings fans loved to torment suddenly was one of their own.

"It was pretty strange," said Chelios of his arrival to Detroit. "They loved to give me the business whenever I used to come in here. But from the first game, the ovation they gave me, it didn't take all that long to get comfortable.

"It's been pretty amazing to be allowed to stay with one team this late in your career. Usually you have to move around a lot. They've kind of accepted me here as family. I'm one of the last guys from that group of faces like Yzerman, Hull, Shanahan. And from where I came from, and the way they felt about me, I'd never thought it would be possible. But it's been a great situation for me and my family. I can't say enough about the city and organization."

Talk about a lopsided trade.

Considered a top prospect with the Wings, Eriksson never reached his promise with the Blackhawks and was soon traded. Those draft picks never materialized in Chicago, either, never making a huge impact in the NHL.

And Chelios?

He's been part of two Stanley Cups, including being an integral part of the Wings team as late as the 2008 Stanley Cup championship. At the ripe old age of 46, no less.

Through the 2008–2009 season Chelios had played in 266 playoff games (more than three regular seasons' worth), more than any other player had ever played in.

"I've never really kept track of the individual things I've done. I've always been more proud of the team stuff," Chelios said. "But it's a pretty good accomplishment. My kids and family think it's pretty cool. I'll look back at it someday and consider it an accomplishment. I've been blessed, obviously, to play on some pretty good teams, and play with some great players."

"When you consider what this guy has done in his career, what he's accomplished, it's pretty remarkable," said Wings coach Mike Babcock, who is a year younger than Chelios and played against him in junior hockey. "At our age, it's a lot of mind over body."

A trade that appeared to be a bit of a gamble on a memorable 1999 trade-deadline day by general manager Ken Holland and the Wings organization (the team also acquired Wendel Clark, Bill Ranford, and Ulf Samuelsson the same day) turned out brilliantly.

"He's a unique athlete," Holland said. "You can't judge him by the birth certificate."

Chelios has continued to excel for the Wings because of a work ethic off the ice that is extraordinary. No player comes in earlier, puts out more in the weight room or on the ice, or is more dedicated.

There are stories of Chelios biking to Joe Louis Arena on certain spring or summer days. Then there's Chelios working on the stationary bike in the sauna, and of course those grueling, legendary off-season workouts in Malibu.

Chelios has been an eye-opener for future Hall of Famers, or minor leaguers, alike. "He's an inspiration to me," said Dominik Hasek, then at the age of 42, jabbing a good-natured needle to his one-time teammate. "Cheli had to change his style to keep playing. He works so hard off the ice. You see his dedication and you want to keep working hard, too."

The fact Chelios has remained free of serious injuries and playing for an annual Stanley Cup contender such as the Wings has kept his incredible competitiveness sharp. Few players can match his will to win.

But overlooking all that, to be able to play into his late forties, there's the mind-blowing workouts Chelios endures almost 365 days a year.

Chris Chelios has been a steadying presence and a workout warrior since the 47-year-old defenseman joined the Wings in 1999.

"Nobody works out like that guy," said Wings defenseman Brett Lebda, half the age of Chelios and a Chicago native, who happened to have a poster of Chelios hanging in his bedroom growing up.

"I've kidded him about it," Lebda said. "My first game, I was able to play with him [on a defensive pairing]. Yeah, it was a bit surreal. It was a thrill, too."

Malibu Mob

So how does someone the age of Chelios still continue to be an effective NHL player?

Give some of the credit to noted Southern California trainer T.R. Goodman. The trainer to the NHL stars has worked with Chelios for more than 15 summers. Chelios was actually one of Goodman's first pupils, and the success Chelios has achieved has inspired many other NHL players to train under Goodman's watchful eye.

The workouts usually begin before dawn and don't end until much later. Goodman is a former college hockey player, so he understands what individual players need.

"He knows what he's talking about and he knows how to push you," said Chelios of the Venice Beach–based trainer.

The two now have a relationship where Goodman designs a specific workout for Chelios for the summer. But it's in Goodman's Gold Gym that Goodman believes Chelios exhibits a unique fierceness, fighting through a non-stop 60-minute circuit training session.

"It's his competitiveness: that's the reason he's still willing to do the work that you have to do to sustain yourself," said Goodman, calling Chelios a "machine" in his ability to power through.

When Goodman's techniques began to get noticed by the rest of the NHL, Chelios felt it was time to try something else.

"Even as other guys caught on, it wasn't a big deal, because I was still in my thirties," Chelios said. "Then it got to the point where guys 20 years younger than me were using the same techniques, and I really didn't feel I had an advantage anymore. But that's when I met Don and Laird."

That would be Don Wildman, now 76, the founder of Bally Total Fitness, and Laird Hamilton, 45, the renowned surfer, a pair of guys more Chelios' age. They are part of the Malibu Mob.

Any talk of Chelios these days has to include something in regards to his legendary summer workouts with the self-proclaimed Malibu Mob.

It's a motley collection, to be sure. You have Chelios, in his late forties, a future NHL Hall of Famer and icon in the game. And, on any given day, you have the likes of Chelios' son, Dean, currently playing junior hockey; Hamilton; former NFL linebacker Bill Romanowski; Wildman ("There's maybe 5 percent of the guys in the world his age that are doing the things he's doing," said Chelios, shaking his head. "Probably not even that."); and actors such as John Cusack, John C. McGinley, and Tony Danza; and occasionally former tennis great John McEnroe.

"Just a bunch of guys who work out and hang out together," Chelios said.

The workouts, too, are rather startling. They'll open the day pedaling a dirt bike uphill through mostly dirt roads in the blazing sun with no water. "Water? Nah, that's not how we do it," Chelios said. Then, all the way down.

And have some breakfast.

Then, when they're done with breakfast (remember, he started the day at Goodman's gym), Chelios will do some weightlifting, followed with a little mountain biking and surfboarding in the Pacific (with pals from the Mob).

"I don't know anything about hockey," Hamilton said. "But with me, my first impression is usually instinctual. You either like

STAYING IN SHAPE

During the lockout, Wings defensemen Chris Chelios and Derian Hatcher played for the United Hockey League's Motor City Mechanics.

The team also had Sean Avery, one of the most rambunctious players in the NHL, and who happened to begin his career with the Red Wings. Chelios housed Avery for a brief period of time during the lockout. Ultimately, though, Chelios had to kick him out.

"He was driving all of us nuts," Chelios said. "The kids were getting out of control because of him."

CELEBRITY SIGHTINGS

Who are some of the hockey-loving celebrities who've attended Red Wings games, either at Joe Louis Arena or on the road?

Kid Rock, a good friend of Chris Chelios, is a fairly regular visitor. The Detroit-area native was frequently in attendance during the 2002 Stanley Cup run.

Cuba Gooding Jr., Glenn Frey, Tara Reid, and John Cusack are several other celebrities who are noted Wings (and Chris Chelios) fans.

'em or you don't. You can smell it. It's like, why does a dog bark at one person and lick somebody else? It's all about trying to keep it interesting and keeping you inspired. I just like guys that work hard. There's no secret: you just do the work. And there's a certain humility with people like that. That's one of the things I like about Chris: he's a humble guy and he's super-cool. He's comfortable."

They all seem to have the same mindset—to take your body to its limit—but Chelios doesn't quite see it that way.

"I don't know about like-minded," Chelios said. "What I did is I found some extreme guys and I mixed a little of their mentality with mine. I mean, they go flying down the hill. I don't. Because there's an element of real danger with what these guys do.

"Every once in a while, guys will show up and just want to train with them," Chelios said, laughing. "And they'll take 'em and just bury them, then come down here to breakfast and have a good laugh about it.... They really get a kick out of that."

DOMINIK HASEK

This was a typical practice, a day after a weekday night game, and all several Red Wings wanted to do was get off the ice, get their work done in the weight room, and head home.

But Dominik Hasek wouldn't let them. Hasek didn't like a certain aspect of his game, something in his technique wasn't quite right the night before. Hasek allowed a goal he didn't like.

And, when Hasek gave up a goal he didn't like, there was work to be done the next day.

"I've never seen a goalie work as hard as Dom does," defenseman Niklas Kronwall said.

To watch Hasek at practice is to watch a perfectionist make sure every detail is just right. Each movement is self-analyzed and critiqued. Mentally, he's facing shots that aren't even there. Up, down, up, down. Facing imaginary shooters only Hasek sees in his mind.

And don't even try to score on Hasek in practice. Never mind it's practice.

"No, he doesn't live to give up goals," Tomas Holmstrom said. "He gets pretty mad."

That work ethic paid dividends for Hasek during his career, and particularly when he was the Wings. Playing a position that had become an incredible source of consternation for the Wings, Hasek came in and stabilized the position, strengthened it like no goalie had since Terry Sawchuk was in net. Hasek gave it a Hall of Fame presence.

Actually, Hasek did it twice.

The first time, the summer before the 2001–2002 championship season, the Wings were in a state of flux after being eliminated in six games in the first round of the playoffs against the Los Angeles Kings. The second time, heading into the 2006–2007 season, was when the Wings signed Hasek as an unrestricted free agent. Again, they had suffered an inglorious first-round playoff loss, this time to Edmonton.

Hasek, in Ottawa, suffered a groin injury during the Olympics and was unable to help the Senators go deep in the playoffs. Ottawa chose not to bring back Hasek.

The Wings, who had lost confidence in Manny Legace, decided to take a chance on Hasek the summer of 2006 to share the net with Osgood.

"Dom's accomplishments in the game speak for themselves," Holland said.

The Trade

The need for a change in the goaltending position came about after the 2001 playoffs.

The Wings lost the last four games of that infamous 2001 series to Los Angeles after winning the first two. And, while injuries to Steve Yzerman and Brendan Shanahan played a significant part in the slide, the inconsistent goaltending of Chris Osgood seemed to affect the psyche of the team.

Osgood had won the Stanley Cup with the Wings in 1998, was an adequate No. 1 goalie, but his tendency to let in a deflating goal was beginning to unnerve the Wings, as well as a restless fan base. While Osgood and Manny Legace was a seemingly fine goaltending tandem, there was room to upgrade.

Hasek would be a dream come true. When general manager Ken Holland received a call from Buffalo GM Darcy Regier a short time before the NHL Entry Draft, telling Holland of Hasek's interest in the Wings, it was an opportunity Holland couldn't resist.

"There are no more questions regarding the goaltending," said Holland after acquiring Hasek.

Time had run its course in Buffalo for Hasek, as the Sabres weren't able to financially compete against some of the NHL's bigger markets like Detroit, New York, Toronto, and Philadelphia.

The lack of a Stanley Cup on his résumé gnawed at Hasek. He came close in 1999, but a controversial overtime goal by Dallas forward Brett Hull in Game 6 clinched the series for the Stars. There would be no more chances with the Sabres.

Hasek informed Regier of a desire to be traded in June 2001. The Wings and St. Louis headed his short list of places he would allow a trade to.

The more he thought, the more the possibility of playing in Detroit appealed to him. "Look at the team," Hasek said. "There was so much talent. They had come close before. And it was an organization that seemed committed to winning."

Playing in a hockey-mad environment such as Detroit also held some intrigue. Buffalo was fairly similar, to an extent. But the passion the sport—the Wings, actually—had in Detroit excited Hasek. Every game, every news item, was big news. Hockey was important every day of the year.

Never more so than during the 2001–2002 season, as the Wings' roster consisted of nine future Hall of Famers. Hasek was a big part in taking that collection of Hall of Fame talent to a Stanley Cup, with Hasek hoisting the Cup for the first time in his career.

"With Dom back there, it gives a team so much confidence," Kris Draper said. "You just see what the guy has done throughout his career, it's a good feeling having him on your team."

After a sluggish start to the regular season, and adjusting to a roster much more talented and poised than the one he played in front of in Buffalo, Hasek was tremendous the rest of the way (save for a hiccup the first two games of the first round against Vancouver in the playoffs).

The fluky, back-breaking goals previous Wings goalies had given up disappeared with Hasek in net.

But just as quickly as Hasek arrived in Detroit and delivered on a Stanley Cup, he left. There were rumors throughout the season that Hasek was likely to retire after the 2002 season, despite his relatively young age (37 at the time). He wanted to return to the Czech Republic. He and his wife wanted to raise their teenaged son and daughter in Europe, rather than the United States.

Also, professionally, Hasek felt he couldn't give any more. Much of Hasek's game depends on his personal competitiveness. He loves the challenge of stopping a shooter, winning the personal battle within the game. But after winning the Stanley Cup, a goal Hasek had been pursuing for his entire NHL career, there was no more carrot to chase.

At his press conference announcing his retirement, Hasek said, "Winning the Cup has been everything I could ever ask for. After 12 years of playing professional hockey at the highest level, I do not feel I have enough fire in me to compete at the level I expect of myself. I achieved my final goal and now I want to spend time with my family and move on to new challenges."

The Return
When Hasek retired, skating off into the sunset with the Stanley Cup, there was every sense he was done with the NHL. He had achieved everything he'd wanted, there was nothing left to prove.

Soon, though, that Hasek competitiveness began rearing its head.

An altercation playing roller hockey landed him some unwanted media attention in the Czech Republic as well as North America. He also jumped wholeheartedly into a sports clothing line, putting his name behind it and involving himself in nearly every aspect of the business operation. He was seemingly looking at every avenue, every angle, to fill the void of hockey.

When Hasek returned for the Wings' Stanley Cup banner-raising ceremony in October 2002, although he said the right things and said the NHL was the furthest thing from his mind, the answers weren't heartfelt. The competitive juices, once so bright and fierce, were beginning to burn again.

Hasek would return to Detroit at times during the 2002–2003 season to promote his clothing line, all the while watching his replacement, Curtis Joseph, not play up to his level of dominance.

Fans, spoiled by Hasek's success, never fully gave Joseph a chance. And, playing in an almost no-win situation, Joseph couldn't deliver on a Stanley Cup, in fact coming second-best to an almost superhuman performance by Anaheim goalie J.S. Giguere in a four-game first-round sweep of the Wings by Anaheim in April 2003.

A couple months later, Hasek informed the Wings his retirement was over. He wanted to play hockey. He missed the game. "I missed the game, missed my teammates," he said.

But from the start, the comeback seemed flawed. It also created personnel problems for the Wings, who couldn't find a taker for Joseph's $8 million contract. The league was one year away from a lockout, and no teams were willing or able to take on a contract of that magnitude.

So the Wings' goaltending depth chart had Hasek, Joseph, and Legace in that order.

"We have depth at a lot of positions," said Steve Yzerman, before the season began. "We have a lot of depth in terms of goaltending."

Hasek, though, was troubled nearly from the start with nagging groin-pull problems.

Dominik Hasek led the Wings to the Stanley Cup in 2001–2002, his first season between the pipes in Detroit.

At first, the team felt optimistic he would get healthy, get comfortable, and carry the Wings as he did in 2002. During brief stretches, Hasek would show that level of dominance, but it would be too few and far between.

Hasek would appear in only 14 games (8 victories), playing his last game of the season on December 8 in an overtime victory over Los Angeles. Early in 2004 he announced he was ending his season to rest a nagging groin injury that would ultimately require surgery in April in Prague.

Hasek's announcement he was ending the season was typically unexpected, much his like his entire return to the Wings. He went onto the ice after the Wings had concluded practice, seemingly to test his groin. Most of the players on the ice seemed unaware Hasek was going to even come out to the ice. A few shots, from players who had grown frustrated by Hasek's on-again, off-again groin problems, were high and buzzed Hasek's helmet.

His return had created divisiveness in the Wings' locker room. The team was nearly split on who should be the No. 1 goalie—Hasek or Joseph. The amazing thing was, Joseph also was battling a series of nagging injuries himself, and ultimately, it was Legace who got the majority of the starts during the strange 2003–2004 season and even began the playoffs as the Wings' No. 1 goalie.

"I didn't even think I would play 10 games that season," Legace said. "It was amazing. No one would have predicted it. I mean, those are two Hall of Fame goalies to be stuck behind."

After returning as a hero, Hasek was suddenly cast a villain by many Wings fans. Many wondered whether he was actually hurt

WRESTLEMANIA

Dominik Hasek was thrilled. Not just because the Wings had won that afternoon, but because there was plenty of time to get back to Detroit and take in the 2007 Wrestlemania at Ford Field.

The schedule worked out perfectly for Hasek. They had a Sunday afternoon game in Columbus, but it would end early enough for Hasek to easily arrive for the 6:00 PM start for the professional wrestling megashow.

Hasek was a fan of the sports entertainment empire for some time.

"They put on a good show," Hasek said. "They're good athletes, too. The way they fly through the air. I know it's not real, though. But it's fun to watch."

that bad. Some wondered whether he was actually in shape when training camp began (a legitimate question that likely contributed to Hasek's undoing). Still others wondered whether he returned to the NHL only to promote his clothing line.

Interestingly, amid the arrows being thrown at Hasek, he told Holland to suspend his salary. Hasek said he didn't want to be paid if he wasn't playing and contributing. But even that news came out late and sloppily and only muted fans slightly.

He vowed heading into the summer before the lockout he would return and play somewhere, not wanting to see his career end the way it did. But, for now, the Red Wings weren't likely to be interested in revisiting the Hasek saga.

The Return II

Hasek would ultimately sign in Ottawa, and enjoyed a spectacular 2005–2006 return to the NHL (after the lockout ended) only to injure his groin during the Olympics. He would not appear in another regular-season or playoff game for the Senators.

That summer, the Senators parted ways with Hasek, who thought his career was over. That is, until he received a message from his agent Ritch Winter, who informed Hasek the Red Wings were interested in bringing him back.

The Wings had just been eliminated in the first round of the playoffs by Edmonton, and goalie Manny Legace was the culprit in the eyes of the fans. Legace also didn't inspire huge confidence from coach Mike Babcock, who wanted more experience in net.

Holland felt Hasek had played as well as any goalie in the league the previous season, up to the point Hasek was hurt. A tandem of Hasek and Chris Osgood, felt Holland, would be good enough to make the Wings serious Cup contenders as well as maintaining Hasek's health.

"I really thought my career was over," Hasek said. "To have an opportunity to return to Detroit, play for the Red Wings, I didn't expect that. But I was happy."

Hasek wound up playing 56 games (winning 38) during the 2006–2007 season and rebuilding his relationship with Wings fans. He was in superb shape from the start of training camp, and the troublesome groin that had derailed his previous two NHL seasons never was a serious problem his final two seasons with the Wings.

Hasek was a key factor in taking the Wings to the Western Conference Finals during the 2007 playoffs. But he again contemplated retirement after the series loss to Anaheim.

"I had to talk it over with my family," said Hasek, who this time was leaning toward returning to play from the start. "I felt this team had a good chance to win a Stanley Cup."

The Wings seemed poised on making Hasek's prediction come true right from the start of the 2007–2008 season. Hasek and Osgood handled the goaltending chores evenly and superbly, with Osgood actually outplaying Hasek during the course of the season. Osgood even was the starter for the Western Conference in the All-Star Game.

But as the playoffs began, Hasek was crowned the starter by Babcock, who valued Hasek's big-game, playoff-pressure experience. From the start of the first-round series against Nashville, though, Hasek didn't look comfortable. There was a bad tendency of allowing quick back-to-back goals, forcing Babcock to pull Hasek in Game 4 and inserting Osgood.

Ultimately, it was Osgood who drove the Wings to the Stanley Cup. Hasek was in the unfamiliar position of being the backup goalie.

"It was different," Hasek said. "But Ozzie was playing well, the team was playing well. It was different to watch the games instead of playing. But, of course, the key is to win the Stanley Cup."

Which the Wings did. Hasek celebrated with his family after the Game 6 victory in Pittsburgh, and there was little suspense or question this was going to be it in terms of Hasek's career.

He bore the look of a man content and relaxed with his future. Hasek retired days later.

When he returned to the 2008 Stanley Cup banner-raising ceremony, he received as loud of applause as any present Wing. He was trim and looked ready to don his goalie pads at a moment's notice and make his customary sprawling saves.

But, no, said Hasek, he had no desire to do so.

"I'm very comfortable with my decision [to stay retired]," Hasek said. "I don't miss it at all."

He said he had taken up beach volleyball and mountain bike racing. He wasn't planning on watching any NHL games back in the Czech Republic.

This time, Dominik Hasek was retired for good, it seemed. Don't count on any more returns.

MEN IN CHARGE

MIKE ILITCH

No, it wasn't like the entire room went silent, but certainly everyone took sudden pause.

The words, the way Red Wings owner Mike Ilitch described the way he feels about his employees, both his hockey team—Ilitch also owns major league baseball's Detroit Tigers—and those of his Little Caesars pizza empire among myriad interests, wasn't the way many other businessmen feel about their employees.

"I love my employees," said Ilitch during a press conference announcing the signing of star forward Henrik Zetterberg to a 12-year contract worth $73 million.

Love? His employees? What employer would say such a thing? Amid a raging depression, with thousands of layoffs being announced every day, and especially in the world of professional sports, where loyalty usually lasted until the next defeat?

But Ilitch wasn't ashamed to say it. He was heartfelt and sincere. He was proud of it.

And if there was one more reason why the Red Wings organization stands where it does these days—among the best in the National Hockey League, even in all of pro sports—it was because of the feelings Ilitch has toward his players, and also the appreciation the players feel toward the organization.

That's a foreign trait in pro sports these days.

NICE TOUCH

Here's another reason big-name free agents are attracted to the Red Wings organization.

During the summer of 2008, owner Mike Ilitch felt it was important to recognize the past Stanley Cup champions before 1997 who never received a Stanley Cup ring.

So the organization tracked down all living former Red Wings who had won a Cup in Detroit but never received a ring. They got them, special delivery, later that winter.

Alex Delvecchio said his Stanley Cup ring was the biggest piece of jewelry, by far, he now owns. Delvecchio said in his day the team received a dinner for its Stanley Cup victory.

"For the guys who've been here a long time, that have started here, it's like a big family here," said Marian Hossa, who admired that relationship from afar and signed a one-year contract for $7.4 million the summer after the Wings won the Stanley Cup in 2008. This after Hossa declined numerous multiyear offers worth over $70 million.

"Players want to come here because of the commitment of ownership," said Nicklas Lidstrom, who has stayed with the Wings throughout his illustrious career, accepting lesser contracts the past few years to remain with the Wings and give the organization flexibility to sign and retain big-name stars. "You're going to play with a good team, and there's just a good atmosphere from the front office down to the team. But it starts with the ownership, and Mr. and Mrs. [Marian] Ilitch."

If there's a place beyond rock bottom, past the worst professional organization possible, that's about where the Red Wings were when Mike Ilitch bought them in 1982.

Interest for this once-proud franchise in a hockey-mad market such as Detroit was never lower. The term "Dead Things" had pretty much replaced Red Wings, when referred to by fans. The negative vibes were never more evident.

Maybe the worst part about the entire situation was the rift between the Wings and team icon Gordie Howe, who left the organization amid salary disputes and angry words. That further painted the Red Wings as bad guys in the eyes of the Detroit sports public and sent the organization into oblivion in terms of interest, support, and loyalty.

But Ilitch, an avid sports fan but an even keener businessman, sensed an opportunity.

"A wonderful opportunity, and timing was on my side," Ilitch said.

Slowly, with a lot of hard work and passion, Ilitch got the Red Wings back on the sporting map in Detroit.

It took creativity—he would give away automobiles at games, cut ticket prices, acquire big-name stars on the downside of their careers—but gradually the Wings got back in the public consciousness.

"Mr. Ilitch is an entrepreneur. He's a guy that wants things done quickly. He was able to do that in his business," said Jimmy Devellano, whom Ilitch hired in 1982 as the team's general manager and was a huge factor in the rise of the organization. "And to be fair, I had to think a little bit like him, too, because [we only had] 2,100 season tickets on July 12, 1982. So there was some sense of urgency. We had to try to build for the future, but we also had to create some kind of buzz here."

Mainly because of Ilitch's aggressiveness and willingness to acquire players no matter how, even going to Eastern Europe

DOUBLE DUTY

Wings owner Mike Ilitch doesn't just own the Red Wings, but also baseball's Detroit Tigers.

Ilitch's Tigers reached the World Series in 2006, losing to the St. Louis Cardinals in five games.

Ilitch has a familiar face in his upper management team with the Tigers. Wings senior vice president Jimmy Devellano was named to a similar post, by Ilitch, with the Tigers in 2001.

when it wasn't done in the NHL, was another way of creating buzz while simultaneously making the Wings competitive.

The lengths Ilitch would go to are legendary, such as getting Petr Klima, a talented forward from then-Communist Czechoslovakia. "There were quite a few years I had to go to George Bush Sr. and go through distant political connections to get the embassies of all these other countries, trying to get players out. We're up 'til 3:30 AM talking to the embassies. We did a lot of work," Ilitch explained. "When we got [Petr] Klima out, we had a double trunk [to] get him into Austria. He wouldn't go unless his girlfriend came. So we squeezed the girlfriend in the trunk, too."

"The trunk of a car," said general manager Ken Holland, who was then a scout in the Wings organization. "He was going across the border. [Nick] Polano was over there. And he made some contacts and ultimately these people got Klima to defect. So they put Klima in a fake trunk and they drove across the border."

Then there was the time the Wings were intent on bringing over Russian defenseman Vladimir Konstantinov.

"I had a suitcase...full of money that we sent over to get [Vladimir Konstantinov]. I flew to Bulgaria to get the wife and the child, and then we got the money to him. We got him discharged out of the army," Ilitch said.

How much money was in the suitcase? "I can't say how much. It was a lot of pizza coupons, let's put it that way," Ilitch said.

Passionate is as good a word to describe Ilitch as any. Be it his baseball or hockey teams, defeat bothers him. "I appreciate the success. But you never get used to losing. It bothers you," Ilitch said. "You don't have a good day the next day. You talk yourself into it as much as possible. You say, 'Come on, let's go, be a man, you win some, you lose some, what the hell's the matter with you?'

"But I hate losing. I can't stand it. Baseball, the same way. Everybody competes and doesn't like to lose. But I've enjoyed it overall. I enjoy this relationship. I've enjoyed the success, and I remember all of it vividly, the glory of it all."

It was interesting watching the scene after the Wings defeated the Pittsburgh Penguins to win the 2008 Stanley Cup. Ilitch was near the Zamboni entrance soaking in the scene as players and

WISE INVESTMENT

When Mike Ilitch bought the Red Wings from Bruce Norris in 1982, the organization was like a stock that had hit rock bottom. The team was losing, fans weren't interested, and morale in the organization was near an all-time low.

Ilitch paid $8 million for the team, never knowing what a prudent investment it would become. Four Stanley Cups and a little more than 25 years later, the Wings have been valued at approximately $255 million, among the most lucrative franchises in the NHL.

families reveled in the victory. Every few moments, players would skate toward Ilitch and extend a hand, a hug. Ilitch's face beamed.

When he glanced at Nicklas Lidstrom raising the Stanley Cup, the first European captain to ever accomplish such a task, the moment touched Ilitch. The Wings had seven Swedes on the roster, all of whom made impacts during the regular season and playoffs.

Critics were quick to speculate the Wings couldn't win the Stanley Cup with such a heavy European influence. Playoff hockey was too physical, and players had to have heart.

"That was very special," Ilitch said. "There's been so much distinguishing of nationalities. I had a strong feeling when they [the Swedes] won the Olympics three years ago. They showed so much heart there."

So much for the Wings not being able to win the Stanley Cup in a salary cap era, too.

"Everyone anticipated with the salary cap we'd fall apart," Ilitch said. "That's the thing that really drove us. That's why I'm a little more excited about this one.

"We haven't done it [win the Stanley Cup] in six or seven years, and you get used to it."

JIMMY DEVELLANO

As job interviews go, this one was unusual.

Here was Jimmy Devellano, one of the up-and-coming executives in the National Hockey League, looking to land the

175

position of general manager of the Detroit Red Wings. Devellano was the assistant general manager for the New York Islanders, at the time the premier organization of the NHL, and had helped assemble a roster that would ultimately win four consecutive Stanley Cups.

But instead of conventional give and take with Red Wings owner Mike Ilitch, Devellano seemed to be getting a good education into Ilitch's pizza business.

"It was the funniest interview process I think anybody's ever been through," said Devellano, who began the reconstruction of the Wings from a dormant franchise into the powerhouse it is today. "Mike's son, Atanas, picked me up at the airport and he had a sign that said 'Devellano' and all that, because we'd never met," he said. "And he hustled me out to Little Caesars corporate headquarters. So I go into his office, and Mike and I chat a little bit, and then he takes me in to meet Marian [Ilitch's wife] and his daughter, Denise, and we all had a little chat.

"There was no formal interview, in that he asked me a lot of questions. He more or less wanted to hear what I had to say and what I thought needed to be done, how I thought we should build the team, and things like that. They sent me back to the hotel, and that night they came and got me and took me to dinner at Oakland Hills Country Club with Marian and Mike and Denise. And that was pretty much an informal conversation."

Devellano sensed he had an idea of why Ilitch was, to an extent, hemming and hawing with the entire matter.

"The way I read that was Mr. Ilitch wanted to get Mrs. Ilitch's and Denise's approval, or get a feel for what I was like, since I really was going to be the first employee that they hired," Devellano said. "So they were really kind of putting a lot of stock in the person they brought in. Then the next day was funny, because he drove me to Cranbrook High School where his kids went to school, and then he took me to a Wendy's franchise, and I thought, 'What am I doing going to a Wendy's?' I'm back in the kitchen, seeing how they're flipping the hamburgers. And then he takes me back over to Little Caesars and takes me into the room where all the cheese is and the dough and everything. And I thought, *Well, one thing about it is, if I don't get this job, at least I'm gonna know a little bit about the fast-food industry."*

Ilitch, for all his business acumen, in both the world of professional sports and various pursuits outside of hockey sticks and baseball gloves, likes to sense when a business relationship is right, that a person he hires has his same passion and determination.

Ilitch felt Devellano was that same type of person. But, there was still that one sliver of doubt. "I couldn't make up my mind. And I'd run out of places to go, I'd run out of conversation," Ilitch said. "So here I am driving around Cranbrook, saying, 'I want to show you where my kids go to school.' I was that hard-up for things to talk about. Because I kept thinking. I like to get that instinct, that feel, and I couldn't get it. I said [to myself], *It's not there.* I kept waiting and waiting, but something told me, *Don't say no. Just hang in there.* So I strung it out for a couple days. I know he [Devellano] got tired of driving."

At the end of the second day, July 2, Ilitch drove Devellano to the airport. Over coffee, totally unexpected as far as Devellano is concerned, Ilitch offered him the job of general manager of the Red Wings.

"He stuck out his hand, and I shook it, a little taken aback at the quickness of it, but I was delighted," Devellano said in his book *The Road to Hockeytown.*

And so it began, Devellano overseeing a franchise that had fallen into disrepair but was about to begin a long but successful road back.

As he settled into his new post, the depth of how far the Wings organization—which had been one of the league's best—had fallen began to sink in. Both on and off the ice. "The bad news was, the team was really in the Detroit River. I mean, really in the Detroit River," Devellano said. "In a 21-team league [where 16 teams made the playoffs], this team had missed the playoffs in 14 of the previous 16 years. Now I don't know how you do that. But somehow they did."

To get the Red Wings back to what they once were, Devellano would revert to his days with the Islanders and what he learned from Bill Torrey, the Islanders' esteemed general manager.

Scouting and drafting were going to be the bedrock of the Red Wings organization with Devellano in charge.

"I felt that with a good, solid owner, with one person to deal with, I thought we could go forth and build the team," Devellano said. "I kind of had the Islander blueprint, and that's kind of how we were going to do it. I guess the biggest thing I did at that time was I pledged to the Ilitches, the media, and the fans that we would not trade any draft choices. I would put a good scouting staff together, we would start to draft and get some good young players in the system. And of course we got real lucky."

Glib, always accessible with the media, and a man who has practically devoted his life to the game of hockey, Devellano went about rebuilding the Wings.

His first season with the organization, the team missed the playoffs. They would pick fourth overall and were quite interested in top prospects such as Sylvain Turgeon, Pat LaFontaine (who was from suburban Detroit), and a kid who played with a lot of heart and grit, Steve Yzerman.

Truth be known, Devellano, at the time, would have loved to have gotten LaFontaine. "Much has been written elsewhere about this draft day, but let me make the record clear," Devellano wrote in his book. "If Pat LaFontaine had fallen to fourth, the Detroit Red Wings would have selected him. Of that there is no doubt. We liked all three players, but LaFontaine was the same kind of junior hockey player that Yzerman was, and we needed to sell tickets. LaFontaine was a Detroit native, and a lot of people were hoping we'd somehow land him in the draft. We certainly would have taken him if he'd been available."

Thanks to a surprise pick atop the draft—Minnesota selected high school player Brian Lawton—the Wings would get one of the three players they wanted. It turned out to be Yzerman. "The rest was history," said Devellano. Yzerman would ultimately become one of the greatest captains in professional sports history.

That same draft, the Wings selected Joe Kocur and Petr Klima, two serviceable players for many years.

"The 1983 draft certainly started a foundation on which we could build our team," Devellano wrote in *The Road to Hockeytown.*

RING MAN

Jimmy Devellano, the Wings' senior vice president, won his 14th ring when the Wings defeated Pittsburgh in the Stanley Cup Finals in 2008.

Devellano has seven Stanley Cup rings, three as a member of the New York Islanders front office, and four with the Red Wings.

Three rings were won with the Adirondack Red Wings minor league team. Devellano won two Adams Cup rings, in 1977–1978 with the Fort Worth Texans and 1981–1982 with the Indianapolis Checkers. In 1993–1994 Devellano won a Riley Cup ring with the Toledo Storm.

Then, there was the 2006 American League championship ring as senior vice president of the Detroit Tigers baseball team.

Possibly no draft by any professional sports team was as successful and deep as the Wings' 1989 draft. In that draft alone, the Wings acquired Mike Sillinger (first round, 11th overall), Bob Boughner (second round, 32nd overall), Nicklas Lidstrom (third round, 53rd overall), Sergei Fedorov (forth round, 74th overall), Dallas Drake (sixth round, 116th overall), and Vladimir Konstantinov (11th round, 221st overall).

Lidstrom will be in the argument for being the best defenseman to ever play in the NHL. Fedorov was a Hart Trophy winner in 1994, and Konstantinov was on his way to a brilliant career before a tragic automobile accident ended it. Sillinger, Boughner, and Drake all went on to lengthy NHL careers.

Devellano believes that 1989 draft became the cornerstone for what the Wings would build into the future, largely due to adding Lidstrom and Fedorov to what was already there at the time.

"Without a doubt," Devellano said. "For this franchise, it was a draft for the ages. There's two drafts in the 26 years I've been here that really put us on the map. The first one was '83, and we got [Yzerman] by default by missing the playoffs. And then '89."

Drafting players such as Lidstrom, Fedorov, and Konstantinov ran somewhat contrary to the rest of the league. Bringing Eastern Europeans, especially, was a difficult, if not impossible chore.

Most teams felt it wasn't worth the time and effort invested. Not to mention, there was a feeling Europeans didn't understand the importance of winning the Stanley Cup. But Devellano felt the talent of these players equaled, or exceeded, what he and his scouts saw in North America.

"The one thing we always knew, and I learned this 40 years ago from Scotty [Bowman, when both were in the St. Louis Blues organization]: you have to have the best players. You've got to have good hockey players, or you're not going get anywhere," Devellano said. "And we had mucked around here for years, and we had to find a way to get above-average players. You couldn't get enough of them out of the draft with just North Americans. So we went into the European market and we were ahead of the curve."

In 1997, when the Wings swept the Philadelphia Flyers and won the Stanley Cup amid a celebration that cemented Detroit as Hockeytown, Devellano's rebuilding of the Wings became complete. "Perhaps having to wait so long made it so much sweeter," Devellano wrote.

Devellano would move up to the position of senior vice president after the 1997 title, and the man he groomed as his successor, Ken Holland, became general manager.

The Wings would go on to win the Stanley Cup again in 1998, 2002, and 2008. They won it when the NHL had no salary cap, and after the lockout, when a salary cap was instituted. They won the Stanley Cup spending more money than any team in the league, and in 2008 when they weren't even the highest-spending team in the salary-cap era.

That gives Devellano joy, especially given his desire to build the Wings through the draft.

"Kenny Holland and I have been in the company of at least two general managers—and I won't tell you who they are—[who said], 'We can hardly wait until we have a salary cap so we're on a level playing field with you. We can hardly wait.'" Devellano said. "[They were] intimating that once the salary cap is in place, they're going to come and pass us [neither have, according to Devellano]. But you know what? Isn't that how we feel about the

Yankees? Don't we get tired of them—we want to bring the Yankees down? Well, that has been the feeling [toward] our team, and I think that drives the whole organization to try to prove we can continue to keep this thing rolling."

SCOTTY BOWMAN

There was none of the endless speculation, stories every day about whether he would or wouldn't retire.

When Scotty Bowman decided to leave the Red Wings as the head coach, after the Wings won the 2002 Stanley Cup in five games over the Carolina Hurricanes, Bowman did it quickly, on the ice as the Wings were celebrating, and decidedly cut short any of the suspense.

Most members of the media felt Bowman would step down. Just, well, maybe not the way he did. In the end, though, it was typical Bowman. Catching everyone off-guard.

"I was shocked," said Brendan Shanahan, one of the veteran Wings at the time who had endured a delicate relationship with Bowman, and was as surprised as anyone by the announcement.

Then again, it wasn't really an announcement. Moments before the game officially ended, Bowman went down the hallway to his office to grab his skates. When the final seconds ticked down, and the Wings had won, Bowman skated onto the ice to join in the melee.

Bowman said he had always wanted to go on the ice and skate with the Stanley Cup, something he'd never done in eight previous

CO-COACHES

Associate coaches Dave Lewis and Barry Smith shared head coaching duties for the first five games of the 1998–1999 season while Scotty Bowman was recovering from surgery.

Lewis would eventually replace Bowman after Bowman retired following the Wings' 2002 Stanley Cup win.

Lewis was 96–41–21–6 in two seasons as head coach of the Wings.

Legendary Hall of Fame coach Scotty Bowman holds the record for most wins in NHL history, accumulating 410 of them on the Red Wings' bench.

times he'd coached a team to a championship [Bowman's nine Stanley Cup victories as a head coach is a record].

He soon found owner Mike Ilitch, for whom Bowman won three Stanley Cup victories. "It's time to go," Bowman would tell Ilitch. He then told general manager Ken Holland. On television replays, one could see the mild shock on the faces of Ilitch and Holland as Bowman was telling them of his decision.

But after the momentary shock subsided, everyone congratu-lated Bowman on a job well done. Including the players, who may not have always appreciated Bowman's less-than-perfect people skills but knew there absolutely wasn't a better hockey coach, ever.

"He doesn't get real close to the players," said Steve Yzerman, the Wings' captain, who grew into a complete player under the tutelage of Bowman. "He's not the kind of coach that opens his door and allows you to come in and chat. He's very businesslike: you show up when you're expected to, you do what you're expected to do, and let the coaches coach.

"With a bunch of older guys on our team [in 2002], we're kind of given a little extra room to do what we want—when we want—off the ice, but there's no question that it's his [Bowman's] team."

What was the secret to getting along with Bowman? "Show up, work hard, and keep your mouth shut," Yzerman said. "Simple as that."

Bowman told reporters afterward he'd decided 2002 would be his last season during the Olympic break that February.

The opportunity to get away from the sport and enjoy time with his family in Florida was simply too tempting to say no to for Bowman, 68 at the time. "It's just too much," said Bowman of the demands of coaching. "Other years, I never was sure, but after a couple of weeks, I wanted to come back. I know it's time now. I didn't know it was time then. I just felt it was time."

One of the things most everyone focuses on after a Stanley Cup is awarded is whom the captain passes the Cup to after he's done lifting it. On this evening in June, Yzerman simply handed it to Bowman, who raised the Cup high with a brilliant smile over his face.

"He taught us all the only thing that matters is getting to this point," Yzerman said.

The final numbers in terms of Bowman's coaching career were staggering: nine Stanley Cups (11 including his front office career), the NHL's all-time leader with 1,244 regular-season victo-ries, and 223 playoff victories. Bowman was also the only coach to win with the Stanley Cup with three different teams.

Mike Ilitch, the Red Wings' owner, is concise and to the point regarding Bowman's impact on the Red Wings organization. "We didn't win until we got this guy," Ilitch said.

When the Wings decided to terminate head coach Bryan Murray after the 1992–1993 season, Ilitch and Devellano set out to find the person capable of getting the Red Wings into the Stanley Cup Finals.

Under Murray, the Wings had a string of outstanding regular seasons but faltered in the playoffs. The Wings lost in the first round of the playoffs two of three years.

The organization and fan base were getting irritated.

"We were terribly, terribly frustrated with having teams sort of finish on top and then go out in the first round of the playoffs," senior vice president Jimmy Devellano said.

Many hockey analysts felt Mike Keenan was a good fit for the Wings, a successful coach who wanted to come to Detroit, confident he could help the Wings take the final step. But the Wings' front office didn't feel comfortable with Keenan, specifically his frequent clashes with management.

Devellano suggested another name to Ilitch, another coach fully capable of revitalizing the franchise—Scotty Bowman. After winning the Stanley Cup with the Penguins in 1992, Bowman guided Pittsburgh to the best regular-season record the next season, but the team was upset in the first round of the playoffs.

Mired in a contract dispute with the Penguins, Bowman fielded a call from Devellano. Bowman was intrigued with the

THE BOWMAN FACTOR

Scotty Bowman coached the Red Wings to a record 62 victories during the 1995–1996 season.

The 131 points the Wings earned that season was second only to the 132 points the Montreal Canadiens earned in 1976–1977. That team, arguably one of the greatest of all time, was also coached by Bowman.

Bowman was part of 11 Stanley Cup championship teams with the Red Wings, Canadiens, and Pittsburgh Penguins.

TOE'S BETTER

Former Wings coach Scotty Bowman is generally considered the greatest head coach in the sport, ever, but he respectfully disagrees, never mind the 11 Stanley Cups he's been part of.

Bowman said his mentor with the Montreal Canadiens was the best.

"He was far and away the best coach who ever coached in the league," Bowman said. "Toe Blake coached 13 years in the league and won eight Stanley Cups. I've had 30-some years at it. If you stay long enough in a job, you get yourself in that position."

Wings as it was, a team he felt was on the verge of championship contention. "I talked with Pittsburgh, and if they had come through [with a good contract offer], I might not have come [to Detroit]," Bowman said. "But then Jimmy said Mr. Ilitch wants to meet you, so they picked me up in Buffalo—Mike and Marian [Ilitch] were down in Florida—and they brought my family down. Actually, when I started to talk for about the first half an hour—we talked for about three hours—I knew right away. We hadn't even talked contract, but Mike said, 'I really want this team to win. And I think you can pull it off. We want you to come. And whatever it takes, I want you to know my door's always open. We'll do whatever it takes to win.' Then when he started to tell me what he was going to give me, I had a hard time not saying yes right away."

Bowman could tell right away what the Wings needed to improve upon to be legitimate contenders.

"They had a lot of good players, a lot of good young players, but just didn't play enough defense to win," Bowman said.

Young players such as Sergei Fedorov, Nicklas Lidstrom, Vladimir Konstantinov, Slava Kozlov, Keith Primeau, Martin Lapointe, Darren McCarty, and Chris Osgood were all on the roster and beginning to grow into impact NHL players. Yzerman was already there among the greats.

By Bowman's second year, the Wings reached the Finals. But New Jersey swept the Wings in four consecutive games, highlighting how far the Wings still were from being a championship team.

SCOTTY BOWMAN X 2

It's easy to get confused, but no, that wasn't Scotty Bowman, the coach, who played for the Red Wings from 1934–1935 to 1939–1940.

That was a different Scotty Bowman, who actually was a pretty fair player in that era and carved a niche of his own within the organization. Bowman, the legendary coach, never played in the NHL.

The growing process continued in 1996, when the Wings lost in the Western Conference Finals to Colorado.

But the Wings exhibited patience, kept their core together, made a key move acquiring Shanahan for Primeau, Paul Coffey, and a first-round draft pick, and it all paid off in 1997 with a Stanley Cup.

The first of three Bowman would win with the Wings.

"He took us from being a talented team to being a championship team," Holland said.

Bowman's Impact

After retiring as a coach, Bowman became a consultant for the Wings. He would scout the Southeast from his residence in Florida and supply input on trades and free-agent signings.

Many analysts felt Bowman would continue in that role into total retirement. But, then again, this is Scotty Bowman, and one should never expect the expected.

In the summer of 2008, Bowman left the Wings organization to join the Chicago Blackhawks. The move was largely lateral, with Bowman doing equal parts scouting, offering opinions on personnel, and largely doing consultant work. But there was one factor that Bowman was most excited about. With the Blackhawks, he would have the unique opportunity to work with his son.

About 18 months prior, Bowman's son Stan, the Blackhawks' assistant GM, was diagnosed with Hodgkin's lymphoma. Enabling him to be closer to Stan was a strong appeal.

"It's certainly an exciting day for me and for the family," Scotty Bowman said. "Being in Detroit for 15 years, I got to know

Gordie Howe. He often talked about how the most exciting time
of his career was when he got to play with his sons. I wanted to
work with my son Stan. This is a dream everyone has and it
doesn't happen very often."

Holland could sense talking with Bowman that working with
his son was something that intrigued Scotty.

And the Wings, after all that Bowman had accomplished and
done for the organization, weren't going to stand in Scotty's way.

"Talking to Scotty, working with his son was a chance that
Scotty couldn't pass up," Holland said. "That doesn't happen
often in professional sports. We're indebted to Scotty for what he
did."

There were rumors in the summer of 2007 of Bowman maybe
heading to Toronto and taking over a lead role in the Maple Leafs'
front office. But Bowman apparently wanted more power than the
Maple Leafs' hierarchy was ready to give, and Bowman chose to
remain with the Wings, and enjoy the Florida sunshine most of
the year.

"It's always a tough decision when you leave a place like
Detroit. It was a wonderful ride for 15 years," Bowman said. "I
spoke with all the people I worked with, and they understood the
situation." Bowman said his son Stan mentioned recently the
Blackhawks were looking to expand their front office. He was
intrigued by the possibility of working with Stan.

"It wasn't easy leaving Detroit, but I don't feel I would have
gone to any other team," Bowman said. "This came along at the
right time for myself and my family. Hopefully I can help them
get to the next level."

KEN HOLLAND

Growing up, Ken Holland loved numbers. He enjoyed looking at
the standings, especially in baseball and hockey—a couple of his
favorite sports—while living in British Columbia. With the standings, there was an orderly succession of who was best and worst.
Some teams stayed in the middle.

More often than not Holland's favorite baseball team, the
Yankees, would find their way toward the top of the standings.

Holland appreciated the fact the Yankees found ways to stay atop the standings while others couldn't maintain, or sustain, success.

The numbers always seemed to work in the Yankees' favor.

"At that time, growing up, you were either a Yankees fan or you hated them," said Holland, who sided with the fans proudly wearing Yankees gear. "They had so much success. I was a fan. They were always my team as a youngster. Those Yankees teams were always my favorites. Especially Thurman Munson and Don Mattingly."

Ironic, then, as life has fast-forwarded about 40 years, and Holland is the successful general manager of the Detroit Red Wings, generally considered the Yankees of the NHL.

No matter what the constraints, with or without a salary cap, being able to spend lavish amounts of money on unrestricted free agents, or not as much (or just as much as everyone else), Holland has been the point man of a front office that is the envy of the rest of the league.

No other organization has been able to draft as successfully, finding franchise-caliber players such as Pavel Datsyuk and Henrik Zetterberg in the late rounds, and meld those players with key free agents and veritable castoffs, building and creating a culture of winning that's the envy of the league.

PING-PONG EXPERT

Red Wings general manager Ken Holland was a minor league goalie in his playing days, but Holland also excelled in another sport. He is an elite Ping-Pong player and still likes to compete whenever he gets the chance.

"It really helped my hand-eye coordination," said Holland, who also is an accomplished golfer. "I don't play [Ping-Pong] as nearly as much as I used to, but every once in a while, I still like to play."

As for golf, Holland loves to watch as much as play. During the spring, he usually has a golf tournament on in the media dining lounge whenever one is televised.

He's gone to Scotland to play several links courses.

"That's a great team over there," said Barry Melrose, an ESPN hockey analyst who at the time was head coach of the Tampa Bay Lightning.

Melrose was talking down the hall from the Red Wings' locker room. His own team was struggling to find an identity, was losing consistently. Ironically, Melrose would be fired a day later, after the Wings had defeated the Lightning.

"Ken Holland and Jim Nill do a great job of finding young talent," Melrose said. "It's the organization everyone wants to be like. They're the best right now. Every organization in hockey right now wants to be like Detroit. Until Detroit proves it's not, it's the best team in the NHL."

Holland hears the talk and is proud of the accomplishments of the Wings organization. But he deflects the praise his way.

A former goalie who starred much more in the American League than the NHL, Holland began his post-playing career as a scout. He was credited with finding players such as Chris Osgood, Darren McCarty, Martin Lapointe, and Slava Kozlov, all important cogs in the Red Wings' machine.

Holland gradually assumed more responsibilities in the Wings organization. He worked closely with Devellano, a mentor of Holland's and a hockey man whose wisdom Holland leaned on considerably.

Working with the likes of assistant general manager Jim Nill, European scout Hakan Andersson, a talented group of pro scouts, and hockey minds such as Devellano and Scotty Bowman, Holland has excelled.

Drafting was the key for a successful organization, Devellano taught him. Nothing can beat a litany of solid, successful drafts, finding players better and more consistently than other teams.

"The challenge every year is to continue being an elite team, and that comes to drafting, developing, and then making the right decisions on who to keep and who to let go," Holland said.

Different Era

The true essence of how good a general manager Holland is occurred after the NHL ended its lockout in the summer of 2005.

The 2008–2009 season marked Ken Holland's 12th year as Detroit's general manager and his 26th year with the organization overall.

Before then, with no salary cap, the Red Wings really were the Yankees of the NHL, spending nearly $80 million to secure the 2002 Stanley Cup while signing free agents such as Brett Hull and Luc Robitaille, and acquiring high-priced goalie Dominik Hasek to a lineup that already boasted big-name talents such as Steve Yzerman, Brendan Shanahan, Nicklas Lidstrom, Sergei Fedorov, Chris Chelios, and Igor Larionov.

Still, Holland and his staff were finding players like Pavel Datsyuk and Henrik Zetterberg in the draft and working young talents into the lineup.

"You know, when we were in the old world [pre-lockout], when you had a $70 million payroll, we still had to put a team together," Holland said. "We had six or seven or eight guys that had the majority of the payroll, and we had to have some young kids. We tried to look for players that were looking for a home.

"I guess it's the same kind of philosophy in putting a team together now [post-lockout, with a salary cap] for us as it was before. The numbers change a little bit, but we kind of have the six or seven guys that command most of the salary, and we've tried to find some players that are looking for a home. Our scouts have done a good job to draft some players. We've got a philosophy, puck possession. We try to find players that fit our philosophy. We haven't changed our philosophy. All the drafting and the trading and all the moves that we make, there's a continuity going from year to year, and even when we lose in the first round, say to Edmonton in 2006, we've continued with the same philosophy, and that's been a real advantage. There hasn't been a change of philosophy here because there's been a change in our direction or there's a different manager in place."

It's a philosophy that's attracted players, many of the biggest names in the game, to come to Detroit in the dead of winter and not even get paid as much as they would in other trendier locales.

Consider the case of Marian Hossa, the biggest unrestricted free agent on the market in the summer of 2008. Hossa called Holland and said he'd sign a one-year contract for less than Lidstrom, the Wings' highest-paid player ($7.6 million to Hossa's $7.4 million) because he wanted to play for the Wings and have, what Hossa felt, was his best chance to win a Stanley Cup.

"Definitely," Hossa said. "Detroit being one of the best teams for so many years, nothing but winning acceptable. Just being here, it's another great experience for me, just being part of and learning something new. You're just going to play the game and everybody expecting to win. That's a great feeling."

A few months after Hossa signed, Henrik Zetterberg signed a 12-year extension for a total sum of $73 million, a $6.08 million average that was likely well below what he could have gotten on the open market.

"I've never seen any reason to go anywhere else," Zetterberg said. "I really like it on the ice and off. Great teammates. Great coaching staff. As a player, you know we'll have a good team every year. I love it here and I wanted to be here forever."

That's music to Holland's ears, who has wanted to cultivate that winning atmosphere and make it a destination for players.

Maybe players will take a little less money to stay in an organization that is committed to winning. That's the hope anyway.

Unquestionably, the Wings have won under Holland.

Since taking over in July of 1997, in the next 10 seasons with Holland in control, the Wings had won three Stanley Cups, won their division eight times, and were second the other two. Success, with or without a salary cap.

"I do think it's possible to be a good team, a legitimate Cup contender year in and year out. You've got to really start at the draft table in developing players and then from there you've got to find your nucleus, your foundation, your key players to build around and then keep adding to it," Holland said.

"Again, our scouts are guys who deserve a real large portion of the credit for us being able to continually be competitive. We've had the best defenseman in the world [Lidstrom] for a decade. Again, being a former minor league goaltender, I put a lot of importance on defense. When you've got a guy that can play 30 minutes like Nick Lidstrom and be one of the leading scorers in the league as a defenseman and lead the league in plus-minus, he's a tremendous advantage.

"We got lucky that two players, Zetterberg and Datsyuk, who we got with later round picks, have developed into superstars. We've had real good fortune that we've had good teams. We haven't had to rush these players. We haven't had to put too much responsibility on them. Datsyuk and Zetterberg were allowed to kind of watch the Yzermans and Larionovs and the Shanahans, and coming out of the work stoppage, the team was slowly turned over to them, and they've been able to kind of grow into superstar status.

"I don't know what constitutes a dynasty, but we're proud of what we've accomplished here. It's hard to win."

But with an owner like Mike Ilitch, and the passion and competitiveness that Ilitch exhibits passes down to others in the Wings organization, the business of winning becomes somewhat easier.

"Our success goes back to the fact the Ilitches are going to do everything they can [to help the Wings win]," Holland said.

JIM NILL

Being somewhat quiet and humble, anyway, it's easy on occasion to forget Jim Nill, the Red Wings' assistant general manager. Which is what owner Mike Ilitch did in a press conference announcing the signing of star forward Henrik Zetterberg to a long-term contract.

Ilitch credited many people in his introduction and simply forgot to read off Nill's name from written notes. After a few more front-office types had spoken, Ilitch grabbed the microphone and made sure everyone knew he had forgotten to name Jim Nill.

Nill's contributions to the organization's success over the last decade aren't easy to overlook. It's the diligent work that Nill and his scouting staff have put in—finding such talents as Zetterberg and Pavel Datsyuk in the late rounds of the draft, finding players such as Johan Franzen, Jiri Fischer, Niklas Kronwall, and undrafted Brett Lebda—that have bolstered and fortified the Wings' roster.

"It's amazing what that organization has done," said hockey analyst Bill Clement of the Wings' ability to continually restock its system with talented young players. "The job Kenny Holland, Jim Nill, and all those scouts have done is amazing, finding these players in the late rounds, when any other team could have taken, and much higher in the draft. They know the type of player they want, they know who'll fit into the style they play. They put in a lot of work, a lot of hours, finding those players."

It is tougher, said Nill, to find those players who used to fall through unsuspected by other NHL teams. It used to be few teams would venture into Europe very aggressively. Now, all 30 teams are stalking Sweden, Russia, the Czech Republic, everywhere hockey is played.

"I don't know if we're doing it differently than any other teams. Everybody's in Europe now," said Nill, who added skill is something the Wings organization looks at, no matter the size of the player. "But we had to change our philosophy a little bit because we started trading away first-round picks and that. So you're focusing on different players, which probably helped us in that."

The Good, the Bad, and the Ugly: Detroit Red Wings

Every time an opening in an NHL front office appears, Nill's name invariably comes up as a potential successor. From openings with the Toronto Maple Leafs, to the Boston Bruins, to the Calgary Flames, to the New York Islanders, Nill's name has been in the mix. But, inevitably, Nill always remains in Detroit and part of the Red Wings' front office.

"He's had everybody wanting him, same thing with Kenny," Ilitch said. But Nill is comfortable with where he's at. Being part of a fabled organization like the Wings, which is committed to winning and gives him a level of authority and decision-making that Nill appreciates, is just fine with him. Being part of a winning organization is what matters most, and few organizations have had the winning tradition the current Red Wings have had.

Nill runs the Wings' draft table and oversees the development of the prospects in Grand Rapids (the Wings' minor league affiliate), in the Canadian and European leagues, and in the U.S. colleges.

It's not an easy job. The travel is extensive and beyond comprehension. There's an immeasurable amount of time away from home, on the road, in cold rinks as far away as Siberia.

Nill often talks about the numerous times he's called home, only to have his wife talk about an appliance not working, and Nill was thousands of miles of away, unable to help. Or, equally painfully, unable to watch his son play a game back in Detroit while Nill is watching someone else's sons play in Europe. Or Canada. Or Minnesota. Anywhere but in Detroit.

"That's the drawback," Nill said. "You try to make it up to them [the family] as much as you can."

But, that's the price to pay for winning. And Nill has contributed incredibly to the Wings' winning ways.

"It's all about winning. We just want to win," Nill said. "People don't realize how hard it is to win, and how lucky you have to be. And this team always has a chance, and that's what we take pride in. You're always there."

MIKE BABCOCK

The number of bodies keeled over, sticks on knees, and just panting, out of breath. That will always be the most vivid memory

194

THE ONLY ONE

Coach Mike Babcock has already secured a place in the coaching annals, specifically in Canada.

Babcock is the only Canadian coach to serve as a gold medal–winning head coach for both the World Championship men's team and junior teams.

Babcock also coached the Lethbridge Pronghorns of Canadian Interuniversity Sport to the University Cup in 1993–1994.

Oh, and Babcock coached the Red Wings to a Stanley Cup in 2008, defeating the Pittsburgh Penguins in six games.

of the first day, or actually, days of Mike Babcock coaching the Red Wings.

This was the training camp in Traverse City, Michigan, a tiny resort town in northwestern Michigan, in September 2005, just weeks after the NHL lockout had officially ended.

Babcock was hired to replace Dave Lewis, axed after twice not getting past the second round of the playoffs before the lockout. He had coached the Anaheim Ducks to the Stanley Cup Finals in 2003 (sweeping the Wings and Lewis in the first round) and was known to the Wings' front office as someone who was doing a good job with Detroit's minor league affiliate at the time, Cincinnati.

General manager Ken Holland felt the Wings needed a new voice moving forward with a much younger team, and Babcock was the right choice. Still, there were quite a few veterans who didn't know Babcock as well. They got to know him pretty quickly, though, at that training camp.

"Some of the toughest practices I've been through," said Chris Chelios, in his mid-forties at that time but still generally regarded as one of the Wings in the best physical shape. But even Chelios, in all of his years in hockey, was beat and spent after practice.

"Very physically demanding. But he did it for a reason. That's the way he wanted us to play," Chelios said.

"That first year, it was more like culture shock, the practices and everything," Tomas Holmstrom said.

Intense, fast-paced, an attention to details. Babcock would drill that the entire first season, a season in which the Wings earned a staggering 124 points and won the President's Cup (given for having the league's best regular-season record), only to get upset in the first round by the Edmonton Oilers.

That defeat stung Babcock and the organization, who felt they had a team capable of going much further. But, looking back, it was a learning experience of epic proportion.

"He came in here and he's a hard driver," said owner Mike Ilitch of Babcock. "It took him a little while to find a happy medium as to how hard to push these guys, and that's been a key. But the guys know he knows his stuff, and he has a real positive attitude."

The Wings gradually became a hard-nosed team that worked excessively at both ends of the ice, stars and role players, and relentlessly skated into the tough areas of the ice to score goals and control pucks.

A team that used to be pushed around—the Wings weren't that team anymore.

"It's been a process," said Babcock, who took the Wings to the Western Conference Finals in 2007, losing to Anaheim in six hard-fought games. The Wings would win the Stanley Cup in 2008, Babcock's third season with the team.

"My first year here in Detroit was a real learning experience at playoff time," Babcock said. "The fact that I've been in the playoffs and been to the Stanley Cup Finals and lost, so I've been through that. But I had no idea what it was going to be like the first year when the playoffs started, because the expectation, not

50 IS A GOOD NUMBER

By winning 50 games in each of his first four seasons with the Wings, Mike Babcock became the first coach in NHL history to win 50 or more games in each of his first four seasons with a franchise.

Babcock's thoughts on the record?

"It means you coach good players," Babcock said.

just because of the expectations, but because of previous defeats and the tightness of our team. But we've come through that."

"He gets the most out of his players," said goalie Chris Osgood, who resurrected his career under Babcock. "We're a harder and tougher team to play against. Not fighting, or a goon squad, but we realize we have to get the puck deep and grind out teams. We're more capable of winning tough, grinding-it-out games than we've been in the past."

Babcock often talks about walking down the hall to the Wings' locker room and seeing the plaques and pictures of all-time greats that have played and coached in the organization. It's an impressive list, to be sure. But it was never intimidating to him.

"Not one bit," Babcock said. "And you know why it wasn't? Because over time, you build a foundation of success and your belief in that, and of your belief in yourself. That's the most important attribute for a head coach, especially in the NHL: it's confidence. If you don't have it, they can smell it a million miles away."

Ilitch likes the positive attitude Babcock instills in the players. The fact Babcock is confident doesn't bother the owner, either. "He's a little on the cocky side, but he does have a real good, positive attitude," Ilitch said.

Bowman Clone
Babcock often draws comparisons to Scotty Bowman, the legendary Wings/Montreal Canadiens coach, for his passionate approach to hockey.

Both could talk for hours nonstop on every aspect of the sport, enjoyed its rich history. But the real similarity is in the fiery focus both bring to the rink, the desire to win, and doing whatever is necessary to win.

Even if bruising some feelings is necessary along the way.

"They're similar in the way Scotty could be real intense, too, behind the bench and really stay on us," said Nicklas Lidstrom, the all-world defenseman who has played for both. "Other times he would kind of leave the team alone. And I see the same things with Babs, too. I think Babs is more hands-on, where he's involved in a lot more decisions than maybe Scotty was. Scotty used [assistant coaches] Barry Smith and Dave Lewis a little more because they had some experience, too."

Lidstrom saw other common threads.

"They don't let the group be too loose at times, and at other times, you have to get on them a little bit. Knowing who to push and who to leave alone a little bit," Lidstrom said. "So I think they both have that, how to react to different people, where some you have to stay on and push a little bit. Others you're going to have to encourage a little bit. I see a lot of similarities in that."

Babcock and Bowman spoke regularly when Bowman was a consultant with the Wings (Bowman's now in a similar role with the Chicago Blackhawks).

"I knew he was the best coach in the world," Babcock said of Bowman. "But I didn't know the kind of man he is, and I never, ever knew we'd be friends. I'm not Scotty Bowman, and I don't pretend to be. But it's incredible to have that [opportunity to talk to Bowman]."

Said Bowman about Babcock, "He's got a lot of things going for him, but the thing that stands out to me is he's ultra-competitive. His train of thought was like mine: he's thinking about what he can do to get better all the time. He's intense, you know?"

So what has Babcock learned from his mentor?

"Sometimes talking too much doesn't do you any good. 'When you don't talk,' Scotty always tells me, 'they don't know what you're thinking,'" Babcock said.

Wings general manager Ken Holland knew Babcock back when Holland was a scout in the Canadian junior leagues out west, and Babcock was a young, up-and-coming coach.

Holland appreciated the work ethic Babcock had, but also Babcock's ability to get everything out of his players. Holland also appreciated the fact Babcock made the players accountable. That, too, became a major catch-phrase with the Wings right after Babcock arrived in town.

"He's really challenged our team," Holland said.

"It was a lot different when he [Babcock] first came here three years ago," Osgood said. "He brought some new things to our

Mike Babcock has won more than 200 games as head coach of the Wings and won the Stanley Cup in 2008.

team that helped us get to where we are today. Everybody said we weren't physical enough and we weren't tough enough to play against just after the lockout, and we've really improved on that over the years. Our guys realize what it takes to win.

"He's instilled in us we had to be a harder team to play against and we had to be more physical. And that's just not the big guys, it's the guys, smaller players need to finish checks and be tough around the goal and be tough in the offensive zone. We've done a good job of doing that where we've gotten to the point now where we can win ugly games 2–1 and grind it out and be able to put pucks behind the defense, and go after it, and grind down a team rather than just being a flashy team like maybe we were a bit too much before."

Passion for the Game

Just how much the history of the game means to Babcock was clearly evident during a 2008 pre-Finals series press conference when a reporter asked Babcock what it would mean to see his name on the Stanley Cup.

Babcock said he purposely never got close enough to see all the different names on the storied trophy until a visit to the Hockey Hall of Fame in Toronto the previous summer. That day, Babcock spent a lengthy amount of time reading some of the names on the Stanley Cup.

"I'm not thinking about that. I'm not thinking about my name," said Babcock, who suddenly stopped and was visibly moved. Then, he took a swig of water and composed himself. "That'd be nice," Babcock said.

What happened after he won the Cup?

"The more you hear from people, the more it sinks in," Babcock said. "I got up this morning [after winning the Cup], and there was a huge [banner] over the play structure in our backyard saying, 'Congratulations on winning the Cup.' And when I went for break-fast after dropping the kids off [at school], people are running over to you with the newspaper wanting you to sign it. I mean, it's real."

Just like any coach in the league these days, Babcock is working lengthy days during the regular season.

With more video available than ever before, the resources on the Internet, and detailed advance scouting, coaching has become a 24-hour job. "There's way more work because you have access to more information," said Babcock, who loves the fact his assistant coaches and the members of the Wings' front office are equally in tune to what's going on around the league at all hours of the day. "It's never done. [But] our staff here has the same passion that I do. They care about hockey."

The practices are still intense around Joe Louis Arena, but there seems to be a little more loosening of the reins compared to several years ago. Babcock is the first to admit that both sides have become more comfortable with each other.

"Mike has developed into one of the best coaches in the league," Holland said. "He's found the line between pushing our players and having that relationship where he can talk to our players."

JACQUES DEMERS

Occasionally a head coach will walk into a situation that seems absolutely ideal for him. That doesn't happen often, at any level or in any sport. So many variables come into play. But, sometimes, the coach seems like he's been made to order for a particular situation.

When analyzing the four seasons Jacques Demers coached the Wings, that's exactly what happened. At a time when the Wings were near their lowest point, when there was little reason to care about the team, Demers gave fans (and players) hope and enthusiasm.

Fans wanted to care and love hockey again in Detroit, but just didn't have a reason to do so after a miserable 17–57–6 season in 1985–1986 (which cost then–head coach Brad Park his job).

Demers, with his infectious personality, brought the fans back to the organization.

As for the players, they were mostly young, still searching for guidance and finding their way in the NHL. There was certainly talent, albeit young talent. A nucleus of Steve Yzerman (who Demers quickly named captain despite Yzerman being only 21), Petr Klima, Bob Probert, Gerard Gallant, Adam Oates, Shawn Burr, and Steve Chaisson would be the envy of a lot of general managers at the time. Add to the fact general manager Jimmy Devellano acquired goalie Glen Hanlon, forward Tim Higgins, and defensemen Lee Norwood and Dave Lewis, and there was potential for improvement in the standings.

Demers walked in and pretty much began the Hockeytown craze and movement in Detroit. With an ideal blend of veterans and young players on the rise, Demers, who would ultimately have a restaurant named after him in suburban Detroit (such was his eventual popularity in suddenly hockey-mad Detroit), used his motivational skills to get the most possible out of those teams.

"When Jacques came into Detroit, he was a perfect fit," Lewis, who played and later would become an assistant coach under

Demers, told Paul Harris in Harris' book *Heroes of Hockeytown*. "There couldn't have been a better man to take over the organization, coaching it at that time. He was energetic; he was upbeat. He was very emotional. He respected older players. He wanted to put the people on the ice that would perform hard every night for him and play the way that he wanted them to play, yet had the character in the locker room that brought it out on the ice every night."

The Wings' team that couldn't find its way out of the dregs of the league suddenly became Final Four participants. They reached the Campbell Conference Finals the first two seasons under Demers, losing both times to the Edmonton Oilers (who would go on to win the Stanley Cup each time).

Demers, deservedly so, won the Jack Adams Trophy in 1987 and 1988, given to the league's Coach of the Year.

"He was a great motivator, he really was," said Joe Kocur, another of the young Wings on their way up during the Demers years. "He'd always be up, keep you going. He had the ability to get you excited, and you couldn't wait to get on the ice for the next shift. He deserves a lot of credit for the success we had."

Demers' personality worked well with the veterans on those particular Wings teams, said Lewis, veterans who had been forgotten by other teams and wanted to prove those organizations wrong.

"A group of guys that wanted a lot of respect," Lewis said in Harris' book. "Guys who thought it was their third or fourth chance or maybe their last chance. Jacques grabbed everybody and molded them into a team."

But just as unexpectedly as the Wings going deep into the playoffs, so to, was the quick and somewhat surprising fall under Demers. It all began with that second appearance in the conference finals, in Edmonton, during the 1988 series. The night before Game 5 in that series, a group of Wings, including forwards Probert and Klima, who had starred during the playoffs, spent most of the evening drinking at a bar called Goose Loonies. The story broke the day of the game, and the chaos around the team likely contributed to an awful 8–4 loss to the Oilers. That certainly didn't put an end to the story, either. Talk radio and the newspapers went on endlessly with the Goose Loonies story and suggested Demers was losing control of the team.

True or not, the perception continued into the next season. The Wings won the Norris Division, but did so while only playing .500 hockey (34–34–12, 80 points, 13 worse than the season before).

What hurt more, though, was the playoffs. Still optimistic about having a successful playoff run, the Wings instead were upset by the Chicago Blackhawks in six games in the first round.

The slide downhill was beginning to accelerate. The Wings earned only 70 points the next season, cementing a last-place finish. They missed the playoffs, and Demers was fired days later.

"Mr. Ilitch felt the players weren't responding to me, but there were never any specific names mentioned," Demers told the *Detroit News* after being fired. "What else can I say?"

The final two seasons were filled with speculation, and the continuing escapades of Probert and Klima seemed to undermine any authority Demers had. Comments from Yzerman and Burr seemed to indicate Demers had lost some control, as well. Demers said the quotes hurt, initially, but over time, feelings have soothed.

The impact Demers had on the organization will not be forgotten. "Jacques deserved a lot of the credit for the turnaround," Devellano said in his book *The Road to Hockeytown*. "He was a very different guy than Harry Neale or Brad Park, and his biggest strength was his ability to motivate. He was such an enthusiastic guy, very passionate, and he made each and every player feel important on that club. He made a big impact."

"There was a time we put four flags [for various titles] up at the arena [Joe Louis Arena]," Demers told the *Detroit News*. "I had players who believed in me and I believed in them. I'm glad I know I had that."

Years later, Demers admitted in his book he was basically illiterate during his days as an NHL coach. He didn't read or write and purposely gave any of those kind of responsibilities to assistant coaches or administrative staff.

"I was stunned," Devellano wrote. "Jacques wasn't afraid to talk to a hockey team, wasn't afraid to talk to the media, and wasn't afraid to talk to me about ways to improve the hockey team. I have nothing but the highest regard for Jacques, both as hockey coach and as a human being. Hiring him was one of the best moves I made in my time as general manager."

FAN FAVORITES

WINTER CLASSIC

This was special, something the Red Wings players and those of the Chicago Blackhawks were going to remember for a long time: all the people on the rooftops, in the Wrigley Field stands, just everywhere you turned and looked. There were fans in Wings and Blackhawks jerseys everywhere.

Yes, it was cold. But it was January 1 in Chicago. And they were playing hockey outdoors. Sure, it was going to be cold. And windy. And the ice, though not bad, wasn't exceptional. Overall, it wasn't as comfortable as playing in a plush, new arena.

But this was different. Playing hockey at Wrigley Field. A once-in-a-lifetime experience.

Red Wings forward Jiri Hudler, who had just scored two goals in the 6–4 victory over the Blackhawks on New Year's Day 2009, was reliving the past two to three hours. What an enormous amount of fun this had been. "I still can't believe it," said Hudler, after a throng of media had left. "You just shake your head. It wasn't cold. I just needed this [a long-sleeve underarmor] because I was always moving. I couldn't believe all the people."

A crowd of 40,818 was announced, but certainly in the years ahead, 2 million will swear they were at Wrigley Field that day. Certainly they could have been outside the legendary ballpark that morning, milling around, drinking, eating, cussing each other's favorite teams.

Talk about your unique experiences.

"I just kind of looked around with my mouth open in the beginning," Hudler said. "We're standing there during the national anthem and we're looking at each other and saying, 'Wow, this is awesome.'"

The NHL gets knocked religiously for its myriad bad decisions. The terrible national television contracts are ridiculed all the time. Fans who prefer a more physical game say the league has gone too much toward the playmakers and taken fighting out of the game. The fans who love the Original Six say the league has entered into too many Sun Belt markets who couldn't care less about the game.

But the NHL and commissioner Gary Bettman have gotten it right with the Winter Classic. Playing outdoors on January 1, amidst all the bowl games going on, has turned out to be a great idea.

And you know the Red Wings would get the call to play in the affair soon. Much to their delight, too.

"I walk away from this experience with nothing but positive feelings," said Kris Draper, whose comment echoed what many others in the Wings' locker room were saying that day.

Funny, too, but it seemed that wintry afternoon it was the veterans on the Wings' roster who enjoyed the entire experience even more than the younger, fuzzy-cheeked Wings.

"I would do it again in a heartbeat," said Tomas Holmstrom, of the opportunity to play in another such game.

"The favorite part was coming out of the dugout and seeing the crowd and seeing the excitement and the faces of the people and hearing the crowd noise, too," Nicklas Lidstrom said. "Just sucking everything in once you stepped onto the field."

Coach Mike Babcock had a theory as to why the Wings "were like they were 12 years old out there" for the 48 hours the team was in Chicago practicing, and playing, in the Winter Classic. "Over the two days, having your kids [and families] and being on the ice with them, that's what makes it so good," Babcock said. "It's energizing. It's not Groundhog Day again. In the National League, lots of times it's Groundhog Day. A fair part of the day for me, just coming out and the excitement of the people, and the

The Wings beat the Blackhawks 6–4 in the second annual Winter Classic on January 1, 2009, at Chicago's Wrigley Field.

weather, and the facility, all that and just being part of it was special. We talked a lot about that, taking it all in as a group. You've got to enjoy the moment."

Chicago Boys

Probably no Red Wings enjoyed the Winter Classic more than native Chicagoans Chris Chelios and Brett Lebda.

Particularly Chelios, obviously in the latter stages of his career, and having a miserable season to that point. Blocking a shot in the preseason, Chelios broke a bone in his left leg. When he returned, already expecting to play sparingly, Chelios found himself a regular healthy scratch.

The Winter Classic was only the fourth game Chelios had played (in 37 Wings games) that season. Getting an opportunity to play in this event, in his beloved Chicago, seemed to touch him. "Just standing on the ice and looking at the surrounding rooftops and bleachers and being on an ice surface in the middle of Wrigley Field, that's not the normal everyday thing," Chelios said. "I've skated on outdoor rinks, but you're never going to get a better setting than this."

Chelios is a passionate South Sider, but he's a sports fan. And every sports fan loves Wrigley Field, no matter if it's on the North Side of Chicago.

Chelios felt Wrigley was a perfect setting for an outdoor hockey game with two Original Six rivals. "There's only a few [stadiums] you could have picked—Fenway, old Yankee Stadium, old Tiger Stadium would have been a great setting, too—but Wrigley Field's got the most history," Chelios said. "Other than the people in Chicago, there's tons of Cubs fans because they're on WGN and there's such a big fan base for the Cubs and this building. People come from all over the country to see this park. We got the greatest opportunity to play.

"They should do Wrigley every year. That's just my own opinion. Anyplace, but why not do Wrigley every year? They could sell out here and a few other places."

Chelios said winning the Stanley Cups with Montreal and the Wings bettered playing in the Winter Classic. Participating in an All-Star Game at the old Chicago Stadium was great. "But this is right up there. You don't get a chance like this too often. This was a great thing to be a part of," he said.

OUTDOOR GAME?

Before being selected to play in the Winter Classic against the Chicago Blackhawks, there was much speculation the Wings were going to host the outdoor game themselves.

Comerica Park and University of Michigan's football stadium were two places where the game could have been held. Comerica Park's sightlines aren't particularly good for hockey, but could be passable for one game.

The Wings are expected to host the Winter Classic in the years ahead.

As for Lebda, he was a North Sider who loved the Cubs growing up. He liked the Blackhawks, too, and was especially excited when it was announced early on the two teams would play in the Winter Classic. "I couldn't wait," Lebda said.

What better way to cap the memory than scoring a goal in the game. Although the celebration was somewhat muted.

Lebda's goal had to go to video replay before finally getting the okay.

"I wish I would have known it went in right away. I would have changed my celebration a little bit," said Lebda, smiling. "But you can't be picky, and I'm glad we got the two points."

Lebda had the requisite family and friends at the game. He'd usually be joining them for Cubs games, though, but in this instance, he was on the field playing.

Hockey, that is.

"You're usually on the other side of the fence sitting in the stands," Lebda said. "Just to be out there playing a hockey game in Wrigley Field was a pretty neat experience."

"Take Me Out to the Hockey Game"

This was the capper to the entire experience at Wrigley Field. On a day with so many memories—with fighter jets roaring overhead in the pregame ceremonies, legends from both teams being paraded, and 40,000 fans roaring for the singing of the national anthem (old Chicago Stadium–style)—several Blackhawks and Cubs legends, including Blackhawks Bobby Hull and Stan Mikita and the Cubs' Billy Williams, sang "Take Me Out to the Ballgame" when the two teams switched sides in the middle of the third period (because of wind conditions).

Perfect. The crowd at Wrigley roared and were in fine voice, never mind it being January. Just one more set of goose bumps on a day filled with many.

"It was kind of funny because we were wondering if that was going to happen," Kris Draper said. "I must admit I heard Bobby Hull's voice more than anybody else's from where we were.

"I've said it once and I'm going to continue to say it: every-thing about this game and this day was a great feeling. We were wondering if they were going to sing that. We knew that at the first whistle after the 10 minutes we were going to switch ends, and so we kind of figured they were going to sing that.

"How can you be at Wrigley Field and have an event going on and not sing that song?"

SWEDEN'S FAVORITE TEAM

Somewhere around Joe Louis Arena in the near future there ought to be a sign that designates that little part of Detroit as a sister city to the country of Sweden.

Ever seen those signs along the freeway or just as you're entering a city? Somehow they're associated with an outpost somewhere in Europe or China, or somewhere in this big world. Usually there's a link that associates the two communities, be it in natural resources, products produced, or something that's grown.

With the Red Wings and Sweden, it's hockey. More specifically, over the last 10 to 15 years, it's the hockey players that Sweden has produced for the Wings organization.

No team has mined Europe for players—specifically in Sweden, in the Wings' case—like the Wings.

And when the Wings were playing the Pittsburgh Penguins in the 2008 Stanley Cup Finals, there was just as much excitement in Swedish cities such as Stockholm, Vetlanda, Vasteras, and Njurunda as there was in Detroit suburbs like Dearborn, Northville, Royal Oak, and Wyandotte.

Everywhere in Sweden, hockey fans were bypassing sleep in favor of watching the Wings. For good reason, too. When you looked at the Wings' roster in the series against Pittsburgh, the lineup pretty much resembled the Swedish national team, or could be mistaken for one of the Swedish Elite League teams.

Almost a Team Sweden, as it were.

"There is interest over there, maybe a little more than usual," said winger Mikael Samuelsson, one of seven Swedes on the Wings' roster against Pittsburgh. "With so many of us on this team, it's just natural."

Further, the Wings promoted several of their minor league players for the 2008 NHL playoffs, kind of a taxi squad, and there were two Swedes—Mattias Ritola and big-time prospect Jonathan Ericsson—from that group. That made, actually, nine Swedish Wings walking around Joe Louis Arena during the playoffs.

And hot-shot goalie prospect Daniel Larsson was on his way the following season.

"It doesn't end," said Holmstrom of the Wings' Swedish explosion. Which has made the Wings extremely popular, maybe even more so than usual, back in Sweden.

"That is a big reason for it," said Lidstrom, who ultimately became the first European-born captain to be a Stanley Cup champion. "We have quite a few [Swedes] on the team, and the fans back home are excited. People are definitely following the games."

A little unnatural? Sure. But it wasn't a grand master plan by general manager Ken Holland and his scouting staff. Really, it was just a coincidence. The Wings have always been on the lookout for talent, and they have happened to find a lot of it in Sweden. "There's no master plan," Holland said. "Our scouts have done a great job, there's good chemistry among our scouts, and we've had success [drafting] in Sweden."

Because of the Red Wings' continued success, they've historically drafted very low and rarely (if ever) have had opportunities at can't-miss draft picks. With that in mind, the Wings have gambled in the draft. They drafted players from Europe with the hopes the players will mature both physically and mentally and

OPENING IN SWEDEN

The Red Wings will open the 2009–2010 season in Stockholm, Sweden, against the St. Louis Blues.

The large contingent of Swedes on the Wings' roster make the pairing a natural. The Wings could have as many as eight Swedes on the roster by the time the game rolls around.

"It'll be a wonderful experience," Andreas Lilja said. "To be able to play in front of family and friends, in your home country, it's something that doesn't get to happen very often, obviously."

Few NHL teams have found more talent in Sweden than the Wings, including players such as Niklas Kronwall, Johan Franzen, and Mikael Samuelsson.

help the organization once they arrive in North America. That's where Holland gives ample credit to assistant GM Jim Nill and director of European scouting Hakan Andersson, who have drafted vast amounts of talent in the deep stages of the draft. Much of it from Sweden, a consistent hockey talent–producing factory.

Nicklas Lidstrom, the six-time Norris Trophy winner was picked in the third round (53rd overall) in 1989. The 2008 Conn Smythe winner Henrik Zetterberg was selected in the seventh round in 1999, 210th overall. Rapidly developing star Johan Franzen was a third-round pick (97th overall) in 2004.

And maybe the largest heist of all was the Wings getting Tomas Holmstrom, arguably the NHL's best net-front player for close to 10 years now, in the 10th round (257th overall) in 1994.

"These guys have cornered the market in Sweden," defenseman Chris Chelios said. "Those are outstanding players. It's amazing no one else found those guys. It just shows how smart the scouts are [in Detroit]."

Add Samuelsson and defenseman Andreas Lilja, both of whom were free-agent pickups off the scrap heap, basically, and defenseman Niklas Kronwall, a rare first-round pick in 2000 (29th overall), who fell into the Wings' laps when he fell like a stone on draft day (the head-hunting defenseman was deemed too small to be a physical defenseman by most teams), and the Wings have taken to Sweden like Metro Detroit shoppers have migrated to the new IKEA in the suburbs.

"We probably wouldn't be in the playoffs [without the Swedes]," Holland said.

Back in the pre-lockout NHL, when there were no salary caps, the Wings were able to take chances on players like Zetterberg and Russian Pavel Datsyuk (a sixth-rounder in 1998) and afford to make mistakes by simply signing big-money free agents.

"You would let them stay there and develop at their own pace," said Nill of the European selections. "We didn't have to rush them over here."

The Wings have become who they are because of the keen eye of Nill, Andersson, and director of amateur scouting Joe McDonnell for unearthing gems that no other team felt were going to develop into NHL players.

"Hakan has a real ability to kind of say to us heading into the draft, 'I like Johan Franzen and I think we can get him in the third, fourth round,'" Holland said. "So the chemistry of being together, working together for so long is a real advantage for our staff, and obviously Hakan has been an MVP behind the scenes. He's really a guy that's really responsible for Johan Franzen, Pavel Datsyuk [okay, he's Russian], and Tomas Holmstrom.

"It's funny how it works. You've got to be lucky. Jimmy Nill and Hakan Anderson were going on a scouting mission to watch a player by the name of [Mattias] Weinhandl, who was going to be—he went from a second- to a fourth-round pick—and they went to northern Sweden, and there happened to be this little guy Zetterberg. When the game was over, they left really having some good feelings about Henrik Zetterberg. Weinhandl went in the third or fourth round to somebody else [third to the New York Islanders], and we get in the mid-rounds and we end up taking Henrik Zetterberg, and the rest is history.

"You've got to be lucky, but at the same time, again, there's real good chemistry between our scouts because of how long they've worked together."

Obviously the Wings' locker room is rather unique because of its Swedish domination. "Sometimes they'll start talking [in Swedish] without realizing it, but not as much as you'd think," said Chicago-born defenseman Brett Lebda.

There's a reason for that, said Lilja. The defensive-minded Lilja was once one of the lone Swedish players on a team populated with players mainly from Finland. That was a rude awakening and a cold slap in the face. Lilja felt awkward in the environment and always filed it away for future reference. "You remember things like that and don't want to do that in this locker room," Lilja said.

Still, it's a huge luxury for the Swedes on and off the ice to have so many of their fellow countrymen around. They can talk their native language and keep track of what's going on back home, whether it be politics or entertainment or style.

Maybe even more so, there's a big level of comfort for the players' families. That can easily be forgotten sometimes. Six of the seven Swedish Wings live in the suburb of Novi (Zetterberg lives in posh Bloomfield Hills, a short drive away).

"When you go on the road trips, you can relax knowing they can hang out with the other families," said Samuelsson, who lives a short screen-shot away from Lilja (and is even two locker stalls away in the locker room). "That's one of the reasons we live there [Novi]. My wife wanted to live by other countrymen."

SUNSHINE, PLEASE

Tomas Holmstrom is from Pitea, Sweden, where during the winter, sunshine is at a premium. Pitea is as north as you can get when looking at the map.

There are days when sunshine lasts for about an hour or two before darkness descends again. But it gets better in the summer. There is several hours of darkness, at the most, during the summer.

"So it evens out," Holmstrom said. "But, yeah, it can be tough in the winter. It can get depressing. You want to see the sun."

Kronwall, Zetterberg, and Franzen were still relatively young players three seasons ago when the Wings essentially became Team Sweden. For those three players, they've been able to get acclimated to life in North America and the NHL with so many other fellow Swedes around.

"There's a comfort level, it's real nice," Zetterberg said. "You can talk about what's going on back home."

During the Red Wings' 2008 playoff series against Colorado, the Wings were one of several teams at the time who were recruiting unsigned and undrafted Swedish player Fabian Brunnstrom. A late-bloomer, Brunnstrom didn't attract the attention of scouts until that winter, and the Wings liked the potential that Brunnstrom exhibited. Wings coach Mike Babcock was asked about Brunnstrom possibly signing with Detroit. Babcock was aghast. He couldn't believe Brunnstrom was even thinking about other teams, although Brunnstrom evidently was.

"It's so obvious it isn't even funny," Babcock said. "Just move into Novi, Little Sweden, and hang out. I can't even understand how anybody else is in the running. Makes no sense to me whatsoever. All they [Swedish players] do is they come here, they're comfortable, they play better than they ever have in their life."

Alas, Brunnstrom wound up signing with the Dallas Stars, believing he'd get more of an opportunity at the NHL level quicker with the Stars than he would with the Wings.

No matter. The Wings still had Sweden cornered.

"It's pretty crazy how it's worked out," Samuelsson said. "We've become Sweden's favorite team."

FLYING OCTOPUS

Every playoff season it starts anew. Excitement in Detroit, the Red Wings usually on their way to another long playoff run, and an octopus lands on the Joe Louis Arena ice in celebration, much to the joy of Wings fans who proceed to go crazy as building manager Al Sobotka picks up the octopus off the ice and twirls it over his head.

Obviously, this is a unique tradition in Detroit. But it's one Wings fans adore and cherish. Opposing teams don't, though. They've made that perfectly clear over the years.

Most recently, it was the Nashville Predators during the 2008 playoffs that voiced their displeasure over the entire matter. The Predators told the league they would remove any octopi thrown onto the ice before Game 5 of their first-round playoff series against Wings. Sobotka's services as octopus cleaner-upper and waver weren't needed.

The NHL informed the Wings a $10,000 fine would be issued if any Zamboni driver were to clean up the octopus mess left on the ice. Nashville's Jordin Tootoo picked up the octopus and threw it down the tunnel near the Predators bench.

The sellout crowd at Joe Louis Arena booed loudly.

Now, if Sobotka (who doubles as the Zamboni driver) wanted to twirl the octopi in the Zamboni entrance, he was welcome to do that. But Sobotka never got the chance, although he would for succeeding games that playoff season at JLA.

Fans were angry, and players couldn't believe the league didn't have larger issues to tackle. "It's a shame," Wings goalie Chris Osgood said. "Certain traditions, they should just be left alone. It's great for the atmosphere, and the fans love it. The league should ask fans before they do anything. It's the fans who pay to get into the rink and watch the game."

Opposing teams don't like the custom for a variety of reasons. Never mind the fact it ignites Wings fans into a frenzy. But the fact that sticky substances fly off the octopi and stick to the ice could become a game-impacting matter.

Al Sobotka is the man responsible for removing an octopus that's been thrown on the ice, a longstanding tradition at Joe Louis Arena during Wings playoff games.

So how did this playoff tradition begin?

Legend has it beginning during the 1952 playoffs. Peter Cusimano, an owner of a local fish market (Superior Fish Company of Royal Oak, Michigan), threw an octopus onto the ice for good luck at the conclusion of the national anthem. In years since, fans have taken to throwing octopi after the Wings score goals. On the road, Wings fans will throw octopi after victories have been securely won.

Fans customarily boil the octopi to curtail the odor. That helps fans getting the octopi through security, usually wrapping it in a plastic bag and tucking it under a sweatshirt. Since arena regulations forbid throwing any objects onto the ice, etiquette usually holds for fans sitting around an octopi thrower to stand close so as to make it difficult to identify the actual hurler.

During the early days, it took eight wins for a team to win the Stanley Cup. An octopus has, you guessed it, eight legs. The Wings eventually swept both opponents during that spring's playoffs, spawning a rush to the fish stores throughout Metro Detroit every spring.

"Scotty [Bowman] always tells me that he hated it, because it got the other team all fired up," Wings coach Mike Babcock said. "I don't know why, but I kind of like it."

NEWFOUNDLAND'S HERO

One of the nicer stories of the Red Wings winning the 2008 Stanley Cup involved Dan Cleary.

After the Wings defeated Pittsburgh, the province of Newfoundland rejoiced about as much as the state of Michigan.

Cleary is from the sparsely populated, easternmost province that had never before been home to a Stanley Cup winner. From Harbour Grace, to be specific, an area that became highly popular as the Wings advanced through the playoffs, Cleary excelled, and the possibility of bringing the Stanley Cup became realistic.

When Cleary raised the Cup high above his head after the Wings disposed of the Pittsburgh Penguins, the hopes and dreams of Newfoundland, as hockey-mad an area as any in Canada, rejoiced with him.

"I won it for Newfoundland," said Cleary on the ice amid the celebration at Mellon Arena. "I can't wait to bring it home. I watched all the Stanley Cup celebrations as a kid growing up. To be part of this, to be able to do it, it's all still so unbelievable."

Newfoundland premier Danny Williams was at Joe Louis Arena for Game 5 of the series (which turned out to be a 4–3 Penguins triple-overtime win).

Cleary took the Cup to Newfoundland in early July 2008 amid a media frenzy usually reserved for a movie star or political candidate. There was a parade, a trip to a children's hospital, and numerous opportunities for local residents to see the Stanley Cup and take pictures with it.

"It was an experience I'll never forget," Cleary said.

Interestingly, the only Newfoundlander to ever reach the Stanley Cup Finals was former Red Wing Alex Faulkner. In 1964 his Wings reached the Finals only to lose to the Toronto Maple Leafs, dashing Faulkner's hopes.

"I know his history, and he was a great player," said Cleary, who credits Faulkner for paving the way for other young players out of Newfoundland. "The fact we both played for the Red Wings is quite a coincidence."

Cleary's story somewhat typifies the tough-minded people in Newfoundland, a barren area dependent mostly on the fishing industry.

After the lockout, Cleary was without a team. He had played with the Phoenix Coyotes, but the Coyotes didn't offer a contract

THE HANDOFF

When Nicklas Lidstrom handed off the Stanley Cup in 2008, there was one person he was specifically looking for.

Dallas Drake, the veteran who'd never won the Stanley Cup in a long career in the NHL.

"It was heavier than I thought it would be," Drake said.

Drake then handed it to Dan Cleary, the first player from Newfoundland to ever win the Stanley Cup.

when the NHL resumed operations. Cleary was invited to the Red Wings' training camp on a professional tryout. There were no guarantees of a contract, roster spot, even minor league invitation. "Just a chance," Cleary said.

Which it turned out was all Cleary needed. He clinched a spot on the roster after a heated battle with several other forwards who also had NHL experience. After a good first season with the Wings highlighted by his checking and defensive play, Cleary flourished the next two seasons, scoring 20 goals each season.

That third season, the Wings' Stanley Cup season, Cleary also signed a five-year contract worth $14 million. He could have tested unrestricted free agency and possibly earned an even larger contract somewhere else. But he felt loyalty to the Wings, an organization that gave him a chance when no one else did.

"This has all been so incredible," said Cleary, who was invited to Team Canada's Olympic training camp in the summer of 2009. "Maybe this can inspire other kids in Newfoundland."

JOE LOUIS ARENA

Most Red Wings fans, if speaking truthfully, really don't care much for the place. Joe Louis Arena either is too cramped, smelly, lacks atmosphere, has too many stairs and too few elevators, lacks creature comforts, and isn't close enough to the bars and restaurants of downtown Detroit.

If fans had their way, the old Olympia probably wouldn't have ever been torn down. And a new arena (likely by Comerica Park) would be built pronto.

But the sudden collapse of the economy will likely delay the construction of a new arena in the city of Detroit for some time. Like it or not, fans and the Wings will have to live with JLA for the foreseeable future.

Which, if you listen to some players, isn't as disliked by the team as much as by the fans. "Teams talk about a home-ice advantage but you don't always notice it," defenseman Niklas Kronwall said. "We feel we have one with our rink."

The main reason: built in 1979, JLA has simply a lower and upper bowl, with suites way above the upper bowl, a long way from the ice surface. But for those sitting in the seats, they're closer to the action on the ice than in a vast majority of new arenas in the league.

At its loudest, the din at Joe Louis Arena rivals that of any arena in the league. Opponents know it. The Wings do, too. "It can get real loud," Nicklas Lidstrom said. "The fans are right on top of you. It's a fun place to play for us. Maybe not as much if you're the road team."

For all the talk about its blandness, lack of character, or history, there sure has been plenty of memorable games at Joe Louis Arena. Consider it's hosted six Stanley Cup series—and the Wings have won four of them (1997, 1998, 2002, 2008), only losing to New Jersey in 1995 and Pittsburgh in 2009.

The NHL All-Star Game was held there in 1979–1980, the arena's first season, which was noteworthy for the appearance of Gordie Howe, the former Wings legend who was then with the Hartford Whalers. Howe was 51 at the time, and received a lengthy and heartfelt ovation.

Steve Yzerman and Lidstrom spent (or will spend) an entire playing career at Joe Louis Arena, creating lasting memories. Yzerman's double-overtime Game 7 goal against St. Louis in 1996 was as loud as JLA has ever become, in the estimation of many longtimers around the rink.

The fact the Wings don't share the facility with any other team—the NBA Pistons have their own arena in suburban Auburn Hills, The Palace—gives them much flexibility and aids in making the ice surface among the best in the league. Add the fact building manager Al Sobotka is known throughout the league as one of the better ice specialists in the NHL, and Detroit's normally cold weather outside, and that makes the ice good and fast.

"There aren't many places in the league with better ice," Kronwall said.

The Wings don't have a practice facility. They practice daily at JLA, which makes them that much more comfortable with their surroundings and all the nooks and dead spots on the ice or the boards.

Even as early as 2002, when the Wings won the Stanley Cup with a roster full of Hall of Fame players, their locker room was among the worst in the league because of its cramped nature. But ownership blew out some walls, expanded a few rooms, and the Wings' area now, arguably, rivals the home locker rooms of many of the newer arenas. There's a players' lounge with cherry wood finishing, a large plasma television, an expanded training room, a shower/sauna area, and a weight room that has been doubled in size. The actual locker room area is centered by another huge plasma screen, and is surrounded on the walls on top by black and white photos of great Wings players from the past.

There have been numerous unsubstantiated rumors of Cobo Hall (next door to Joe Louis Arena) being expanded so as to create more room for its big event, the North American Auto Show. That would mean Joe Louis Arena would need to be torn down.

But nothing ever becomes of those rumors. And the arena continues to stand, all gray on the outside, hard by the Detroit River, for a while longer.

NEW YEAR'S EVE GAME

Is it the most important game on the regular-season schedule? No, of course not. Championships aren't decided on December 31, and the playoffs are still half a season away.

Does it trigger a flood of memories, spectacular highlights, and instantly makes you remember what you were doing that particular evening? Probably not. Usually because you were nursing a hangover the next day.

But the New Year's Eve game at Joe Louis Arena is a special tradition that Red Wings fans have grown to love and appreciate over the years. The game is moved up to 7:00 PM, allowing for fans to watch a little hockey before ringing in the New Year.

Hockey fans at Joe Louis Arena are usually enthusiastic. But on New Year's Eve, they're a bit more festive. "It's always a fun atmosphere in the rink that night," said Kirk Maltby, who has seen his share of December 31 games at Joe Louis Arena. "For sure, it's a lot better dressed crowd than usual."

Ah, the matter of clothing.

You won't see a hockey game with better dressed people. The women arrive in their elegant gowns and jewelry that's likely been put away the entire year. High heels are in, sneakers are out.

For the guys, gone are the Wings sweaters while tuxedos suddenly appear in the upper bowl.

"The fans seem to come in early, some of them are dressed up real good, the atmosphere is just a little different than usual," Nicklas Lidstrom said. "It's always a lot of fun."

Except for twice during the 1990s, when arena management tried something different and staged concerts instead (the idea, to put it mildly, didn't work), the Wings have played home games in Detroit on New Year's Eve going to back to the 1950s.

And it's a tradition the Wings won't think of changing.

"Our fans have told us they like the New Year's Eve game," said Jimmy Devellano, senior vice president of the Wings. "They make an evening of it. The fans have spoken."

There have been some memorable individual games on New Year's Eve. Gordie Howe notched a hat trick against Montreal in 1951—a 5–3 Wings loss—and against Toronto exactly 10 years later—a 4–2 Wings victory. Frank Mahovlich scored three goals against Minnesota in 1968, a 6–3 Wings victory. And Bob Probert scored three times against St. Louis in 1987 during a 7–2 Wings victory.

The Red Wings turned away from the New Year's Eve game for 2008 when they were chosen to participate in the Winter Classic, the outdoor game against the Chicago Blackhawks.

Wings management was skittish about the fans' reaction, having to play on January 1 and foregoing the New Year's Eve tradition. But the fact there was a game against the Blackhawks on December 30 at Joe Louis Arena, and the fact the Winter Classic was such a unique event, seemed to soothe the feelings of Wings fans.

Especially with the promise of the New Year's Eve game returning to Joe Louis Arena the following season.

FATHER-SON TIME

The scene takes place outside an ice rink near Scottsdale, on the edge of an Arizona desert, during a Red Wings practice. A handful of men, with accents from Sweden, the Czech Republic, and Canada—yes, they have their own accent, too—were gathering near a cactus.

Right, a cactus. None had ever seen one up close. The cactus was near the entrance to the rink where the Wings were practicing, the practice facility for the Phoenix Coyotes.

These were the Wings' dads, on the annual Father-Son trip the Wings began organizing during the 2005–2006 season. Eventually, the group of dads got a passer-by to take a picture of them crowded around one single, solitary cactus. A bit touristy? Sure. But can you really blame the dads for being excited?

"It's more of a family-like atmosphere, and I like that a lot," Wings coach Mike Babcock said. "It's pretty nice to get your dad to be in the league for a few days."

More than a few Red Wings now say one of the most important days of the calendar year is when the NHL schedule is released. Dads will call and see if their sons have heard when the next trip—taken once a season—will be.

"I mean, my dad asks me every time we talk," Andreas Lilja said. "Every time."

The idea of a dads' trip was one general manager Ken Holland swiped from a few other teams that began the practice before the lockout. Opposing general managers told Holland the trips were enjoyable, and broke up the monotony of a long regular-season schedule.

That's all Babcock needed to hear. He often talks about how the endless regular-season schedule can become like Groundhog Day. All the days and games are alike. The games and practice run together, sometimes endlessly. At times, there isn't much to look forward to.

But when the dads come along on a long trip to the Southeast, or through California and Phoenix, it's different. It's something to circle on the calendar. Something to look forward to. Also a heckuva lot of fun for everyone involved in the traveling party.

A few days after that scene near the practice rink, the Wings defeated the Phoenix Coyotes and closed the locker room after the game for a few moments longer than usual. Reporters could hear as much noise and commotion inside the locker room as the Wings would make after winning a playoff round. But, no, this was just the Wings' players, coaches, and their dads taking a group picture inside the spacious Glendale Arena visiting locker room.

"They had a lot of fun, and we did, too," Henrik Zetterberg said.

"We have great people on this team, so it's no wonder their fathers are phenomenal people," Babcock said. "They're good to have around, and their kids are proud of them. That's what I like. It's great to be proud of your dad."

It's not always the dads that come along on the trip, either. Chris Chelios and Dominik Hasek have taken their sons on the trips. One year, Chelios took his sons, Jake and Dean, while having his dad, Gus, meet up with them in Phoenix. "That [made] it pretty special, the three of them all there," said Chelios of his father and sons. "I thought they'd have a lot of fun on it [this trip] together."

Hasek relished the opportunity, too. "This is the first time I've ever had him [his son, Michael] on a road trip with the team. It's a great experience," Hasek said.

Every year, though, there are questions about a certain other family member.

How about a moms' trip?

"My mom wants a mom trip," Henrik Zetterberg said of his mother. "She asks me when we're going to take the mothers. I tell her I don't know."

A few other Wings' moms apparently feel the same way. When the first dads' trip was announced, then–Wings goalie Manny Legace said he had to talk his mom out of calling Holland and inquiring about a trip for the mothers. "She was pretty upset," Legace said.

There were minor discussions about taking the moms on a shopping spree to New York, or maybe do something on a short trip to Chicago, or the like, but nothing came of it.

Simply put, it's just easier with the dads along. "It's easier for the dads because they can do a little more," Brett Lebda said. "They get to come into the locker room and stuff like that. With the dads, it's a little easier. I don't know if the boys can take their moms on a trip for a couple of days."

WHITE HOUSE VISITS

A championship team receives perks. Along with the adulation of the home crowd, there's a special trip it gets to make that's become standard for most professional or collegiate teams. The championship team gets to travel to the White House and meet the president, something the present-day Red Wings did for the fourth time in 11 years with a 2008 visit to George Bush.

And their second time with President Bush.

"In 2002, the Red Wings were the first NHL team I hosted for a Stanley Cup ceremony," Bush said at the ceremony. "Turns out they are the last team I'll be hosting. You guys may be back next year—but not me."

The Red Wings have visited the White House as Stanley Cup champions four times since 1997.

No matter the political preference, it's always been a special honor for Wings teams to visit the White House. Both Presidents Bush, father and son, and Bill Clinton, who famously mispronounced Steve Yzerman's name, have welcomed the Wings for a brief ceremony that leaves the players, and head coach, a little awed.

"You get to meet the president of the United States," coach Mike Babcock said. "That's a fantastic thing, a great honor for our team. You want to relish [an experience such as that one]."

"You're there with one of the most powerful men in the world, if not the most powerful," said Niklas Kronwall said. "To go to the White House, with all the history, it's humbling, it really is."

Funny, but while all the players talk about what a unique experience it is to see a sliver of the White House inside, it's the actual drive from the airport to the White House that's exciting and memorable for many. Because of time restrictions, it's usually a sprint to the White House so as to keep the president's schedule on time. So the team gets a police escort on the way to the White House.

"The whole process of getting from the airport to the White House," said Kirk Maltby, when asked what his favorite part of the drill is. "The whole mystique of it. Whether you like the president or don't, the whole atmosphere is pretty cool. Especially the bus ride with the police escort. It's almost like the president's in the bus with us."

"You get to meet the president of the United States, that's a fantastic thing and a great honor for our team," Babcock said. "You want to relish all the things you've done. But as a coach, it is [about] this year."

Chris Chelios has met different politicians, movie celebrities, famous athletes. But even Chelios admitted being awestruck when meeting Bush in 2008. "You think you won't be nervous at something like this, but when he comes and shakes your hand, you think about it," said Chelios, who was mentioned by Bush during his Wings introduction in the 2008 visit. "It's a great day and I know a lot of players in the league would like to have this kind of experience."

Bush also used Darren McCarty as an example of perseverance and dedication after McCarty's battle with alcoholism forced McCarty to return to the minor leagues before rejoining the Wings late in the 2007–2008 season. "Darren played 11 seasons with the Red Wings between 1994 and 2004," Bush said. "Then he had a problem—he drank too much—and it brought his career to an early end. But Darren McCarty did not give up. Darren McCarty decided to do something about it."

"I got choked up," said McCarty of being mentioned by the president. "To be a part of this day, to be at the White House and to be called out by the president, it sort of reiterates that the path I am on is the right one."

CHILDREN'S HOSPITAL VISITS

The visit always occurs near the Christmas holidays. The Red Wings annually head to Detroit Children's Hospital near that special time of year when everyone seems to be a little more excited and joyful—or could use a smile, or two, which the children and their parents at Children's Hospital certainly can use.

The holiday tradition of visiting these kids—going over 20 years now—doesn't have anything to do with on-ice matters. But those few hours spent with kids who need a reason for hope and a chance to meet a favorite player can mean just as much as anything done on the ice the night before.

The players get as much, or more, out of the experience every year as the kids do.

A few reporters remember seeing former goalie Manny Legace wiping away tears after just exiting a room of a cancer-stricken girl, not even in her teens.

"Our problems, like having a bad game, losing a game, or giving up a goal, none of that matters compared to what these kids are going through," Legace said.

One year, many Wings met up with Jack Zaidel, a 14-year-old hockey player who was diagnosed with lymphoma only two months before visiting the Wings. Zaidel, a defenseman, always patterned his game after Lidstrom. "That's the position I play," said Zaidel as he looked around the greeting room and saw many of his favorite hockey players, including Lidstrom, come to life in front of him. "It was nice getting a chance to meet and talk to him."

As much as a thrill it was for Zaidel, the annual visit also touches the Wings.

"If you can just make him smile for a few minutes and take him away from his troubles, it's a good feeling for us, too," Chris Chelios said.

Coach Mike Babcock is a spokesman for a cancer foundation and regularly hosts kids and their families at every home game at Joe Louis Arena. For Babcock, the visits to Children's Hospital puts things in perspective for himself and his players.

"What an inspiration they are to all of us," said Babcock of the kids and their families. "One of the gifts of our profession is you're allowed to help other people. These kids are motivators."

Just like Alicia Alwood, 12, who suffered from hydrocephalus, a condition where water rests on the brain. Alwood has had over 50 surgeries according to her mother, Cindy. The particular morning Alicia was to meet the Wings, her favorite team, her mother said Alicia was as excited as she's been in a long time.

"She loves the Red Wings, it's her favorite team," Cindy said.

Alicia trembled but smiled as Chelios, one her favorite players, approached. This was going to be something Alicia would remember and talk about for a long time, said Cindy.

"It's kind of neat for the kids when they see them on television, they can say they know them," Cindy said. "Everyone seems so at ease. It's nice to see her smile."

BUDD LYNCH

You would have thought Nicklas Lidstrom or one of the highly popular Red Wings players suddenly was forced out of the lineup and there was no announcement. But, no, it was public address announcer Budd Lynch whose voice wasn't heard after a goal during an early season Red Wings game in 2008.

The very next day, the emails to the local newspaper came in by the hour.

"Where was Budd?"

That didn't surprise John Hahn, the Red Wings' vice president of communications. "He's as much a part of this team as the ice on the floor," Hahn said.

Lynch, 91 at the time and as witty and modest as he ever was, couldn't believe the attention. "Don't they know there's a game going on?" Lynch said.

But, like Hahn said, Lynch is part of the Wings experience going to the arena. As of the start of the 2009–2010 season, he's been part of the organization for 60 years and has watched everyone from Howe to Yzerman to Datsyuk and Zetterberg.s

Special memory? "Watching eight Stanley Cup being won," said Lynch, who was also the television voice of the Wings for 25 years.

He's approaching a similar length of time as the public address announcer, as well. "I've retired twice, but they won't let me follow through on it," Lynch said. "They keep asking me back."

Lynch returned from World War II in 1944, having lost his right arm. He was hired by Channel 4 in Detroit in 1950 and began broadcasting games the station televised that season. WXYZ radio hired Lynch to do play-by-play, and all 70 games, the following season.

"It was different back then in that we'd ride the trains, and you got to know the players in a different way," Lynch said.

He stayed in the broadcast booth until after the 1974–1975 season, forming one of the most popular duos in Detroit sports history with Bruce Martyn. "A dear friend," Lynch said.

Lynch won the Foster Hewitt Memorial Award, whose winners are recognized in the Hockey Hall of Fame, in 1985. Martyn was likewise honored in 1991. "For me, that was a special honor because I knew Foster well, he was a good friend," Lynch said. "That was something I didn't expect."

Lynch has seen quite a few players, teams, and memorable hockey moments over the years. Here are some of his favorites in his own words:

Best hockey player he ever saw: There have been a lot of great ones, Jean Beliveau, Rocket Richard, [Wayne] Gretzky. But for my money, it was Gordie Howe.

I believe it was King Clancy [the former Toronto Maple Leafs executive] who said Gordie "had the best elbows he's ever seen in hockey." Gordie could play whatever style you'd like. But he was so darn big and tough, along with all that skill he had. There won't be another one like him.

People tend to forget he didn't always wear No. 9 from the start. When he began with the Wings, he was issued No. 17, but when the player [wearing No. 9] got cut, Howe grabbed it. The lower the number, the further up the train you could move.

Most unusual moment in the booth: The night the Montreal Forum was cleared out, fans began rioting after Rocket Richard was suspended [and commissioner Clarence Campbell attended the very next game in Montreal, against the Wings]. Being a former army man, I knew what I was smelling [tear gas]. They whisked us out of there [after the first period]. We made it to the airport, but we heard reports of what was going on. It was pretty bad.

Fond memories from the 1997 Stanley Cup championship, the first in 42 years: You know, that was a team that had pecked away, pecked away, gotten so close, kept getting better and then finally did it. It was fabulous to see Steve Yzerman finally win the Cup. The goal by [Darren] McCarty, [to clinch Game 4]. It was an exciting evening.

But, then, to see that team win again the very next year, after the terrible tragedy involving [Vladimir] Konstantinov. You just didn't see, and don't see to this day, teams winning back-to-back like that anymore. To have done that just showed how talented of a team that was.

The excitement of March 26, 1997: You could sense something was going to happen that evening. [Colorado's Claude] Lemieux had rammed Draper into the open door [of the dasherboards, the year before in the playoffs], and poor Draper came out looking like a mess. As soon as McCarty had an opportunity, he took on Lemieux, and Lemieux turtled. Never even did anything. Then eventually the goalies got into it, players were flying around. I don't know if anybody quite expected all of what occurred to happen, but there was a feeling something was going to happen.

On Steve Yzerman: I remember early in his career [Yzerman's rookie season] I took Stevie up to a banquet, I think it was, in Chatham, Ontario, and he was just such a nice kid. Polite, well-mannered, just a great kid. We got to the function, and the people there were saying things like, "This kid is so skinny, frail, this kid doesn't look like a hockey player. How is he ever going to be a professional hockey player?"

He turned out okay, though, didn't he? What a captain, what a leader.

On the Olympia: It was a wonderful place to watch a hockey game. I loved every part of it. Many of those arenas during that era, Maple Leaf Gardens, the [Montreal] Forum, those were special places with a lot of memories. But the Olympia, it just felt like hockey.

On Scotty Bowman: There probably has never been a better coach. He was always trying to stay a step ahead of the other guy. Even when he did some broadcasting for *Hockey Night in Canada.* He'd come over to me before the game started and wanted to know who was playing. He'd ask me every time, before anyone was even on the ice. I wouldn't tell him until the lineups were announced. But I think he already knew.

SOURCES

Detroit News
Detroit Free Press
Booth Newspapers
detroitredwings.com
Red Wings Essential by Nicholas J. Cotsonika
The Road to Hockeytown, by Jimmy Devellano and Roger Lajoie
Gordie Howe: My Hockey Memories by Gordie Howe with Frank
    Condron
Heroes of Hockeytown by Paul Harris
The Gods of Olympia Stadium by Rich Kincaide.

ABOUT THE AUTHOR

Ted Kulfan is a sportswriter for the *Detroit News*. He has covered the Detroit Red Wings and the NHL for the last 10 years and has been part of several national award-winning projects by the newspaper. He's been featured in publications ranging from the *Sporting News* to *Basketball Weekly*, and contributed essays for the book *Wayne Gretzky: The Making of the Great One*. A native of Dearborn, Michigan, Kulfan resides in Dearborn with his wife, Angela, and son, T.J.